WARS WITHIN

JANET STEELE

WARS WITHIN

The Story of *Tempo*,
an Independent Magazine
in Soeharto's Indonesia

EQUINOX
PUBLISHING
JAKARTA SINGAPORE

INSTITUTE OF
SOUTHEAST ASIAN STUDIES
Singapore

First published in Jakarta and Singapore in 2005 by

PT Equinox Publishing Indonesia
Menara Gracia 6/F
Jl. HR Rasuna Said Kav. C-17
Jakarta 12940, Indonesia
www.equinoxpublishing.com

and

Institute of Southeast Asian Studies
30 Heng Mui Keng Terrace
Pasir Panjang
Singapore 119614
www.bookshop.iseas.edu.sg
for worldwide distribution

Text © 2005 Janet Steele
All photos courtesy of *Tempo*
10 9 8 7 6 5 4 3 2 1

ISEAS Library Cataloguing-in-Publication Data

Steele, Janet E.
Wars within : the story of Tempo, an independent magazine in Soeharto's Indonesia.
1.   Tempo (Jakarta, Indonesia)
2.   Journalism-Indonesia.
3.   Freedom of the press-Indonesia-20th century.
4.   Indonesia-Politics and government-1966-1998.
I.   Title.
II.   Title: Story of Tempo, an independent magazine in Soeharto's Indonesia
PN5449 I5S81   2005

Equinox Publishing ISBN 979-3780-08-8
ISEAS ISBN 981-230- 327-8
Printed in Indonesia.

The Institute of Southeast Asian Studies (ISEAS) was established as an autonomous organization in 1968. It is
a regional centre dedicated to the study of socio-political, security and economic trends and developments in
Southeast Asia and its wider geostrategic and economic environment.
The Institute's research programmes are the Regional Economic Studies (RES, including ASEAN and APEC),
Regional Strategic and Political Studies (RSPS), and Regional Social and Cultural Studies (RSCS).
ISEAS Publications, an established academic press, has issued more than 1,000 books and journals. It is the
largest scholarly publisher of research about Southeast Asia from within the region. ISEAS Publications works
with many other academic and trade publishers and distributors to disseminate important research and
analyses from and about Southeast Asia to the rest of the world.

For Jerry Macdonald,
who gave me Indonesia

CONTENTS

introduction: wars within

"Why should the army fear us when they are the ones with the guns?"

For a long time I kept the paper napkin on which I had scribbled Goenawan Mohamad's words. Like many Americans, I had first heard of *Tempo* magazine when it was banned along with *Detik* and *Editor* in June 1994, presumably because of a cover story on a dispute within the Soeharto regime over a plan to buy thirty-nine used war ships from the former East Germany. During the summer of 1997, just a few weeks before leaving the U.S. to begin a year as a Fulbright professor at the University of Indonesia, I heard Goenawan speak at an awards luncheon at the Freedom Forum in Arlington, Virginia. After receiving the Louis M. Lyons award for conscience and integrity in journalism, Goenawan described the demonstrations that had greeted the banning of his magazine, and the violent response from the police. He spoke of *Tempo Interaktif*, the website that was read and downloaded and photocopied and sold to those who didn't have access to the internet. When someone in the audience asked whether *Tempo* was concerned about copyright violations, Goenawan just laughed. *Tempo* wanted the website to be read. "We don't care," he said. "They can have it for free."

Back at George Washington University, I put the napkin in my desk drawer, a reminder of the sacrifices that journalists in Indonesia were willing to make for something that most Americans take for granted.

The days flew by, and before I knew it, I was in Jakarta. As a Fulbright professor, I was responsible for teaching about American mass media in the American Studies program at the University of Indonesia. To my surprise, it seemed that nearly everyone I met during those first few weeks had some connection with *Tempo*. Journalists, scholars, poets, historians – they all wore their affiliation like a badge of honor. Soon something else became clear. The government might have banned *Tempo* three years earlier, but the magazine had hardly disappeared. In fact, for a magazine that didn't exist, *Tempo* still had a remarkable grip on Indonesian intellectual life.

Within a month of my arrival in Jakarta, I was introduced to Bambang Harymurti, *Tempo*'s Washington bureau chief and a former Fulbrighter, who was then the executive editor of the newspaper *Media Indonesia*. With characteristic energy, Bambang was always willing to talk about *Tempo*. He told me the story of the banning. He explained the origin of the relationship between

Detektif dan Romantika, March 7, 1998

Tempo and the newspaper *Media Indonesia*. He invited me to the Utan Kayu Community to meet Goenawan Mohamad. And then one night he took me to a dark office on a quiet street in Cikini. "If you would like to see the real spirit of *Tempo*," he said, "you will need to talk to Bambang Bujono." At the office of a news magazine with the improbable name of *Detektif dan Romantika* (Detective and Romance), I met Bambang Bujono, the "Editorial Consultant" of a publication that was staffed largely by ex-*Tempo* writers. In just a few months, Bambang Bujono and chief editor Margiono would be questioned by the police for over nine hours because of a cover story that had the audacity to imply that General Soeharto was more like a king than a president. The meaning of the magazine's striking cover art, which depicted President Soeharto as the King of Spades, was perfectly clear even to those who, like me, couldn't read the words.[1]

At *Media Indonesia* newspaper I met other *Tempo* alumni, and learned that there were many informal networks of ex-*Tempo* employees: there were study groups, the "Tebet group", the "*Kontan* group", and the "drinking group".[2] One meeting led to another, and before long I had interviewed dozens of writers and editors, all of whom had played key roles in *Tempo*'s history. I visited *Gatra*, the pro-government magazine owned by Soeharto crony Bob Hasan that had supposedly "replaced" *Tempo* after the banning. The more *Tempo* alumni I met, the more intrigued I became. Was the point simply that despite its best efforts, an authoritarian government

---

[1] *Detektif dan Romantika,* March 7, 1998. Although Bambang Bujono was the true chief editor of *D&R*, as it was known, it was Margiono whose name was registered with the Department of Information. Margiono actually had nothing to do with the magazine, and had been "borrowed" from the *Jawa Pos* newspaper, which was also owned by Grafiti Pers, the company that owned *Tempo*. The infamous cover was designed by *Tempo*'s Malela Mahargasarie.

[2] The Tebet group referred to those former *Tempo* employees who joined with Bambang Harymurti in a cooperative firm called P.T. Reksa Mitra Berjaya. Tebet was the name of the neighborhood in East Jakarta where *Tempo*'s management paid for a small office. *Kontan* was an economy and business tabloid that also employed a number of ex-*Tempo* journalists.

couldn't kill an idea? That the spirit of *Tempo* had refused to die? I wasn't sure, but I knew that I had found a great story.

Tempo was founded in 1971, at the beginning of the New Order – the term given to the autocratic regime that General Soeharto brought to power in 1966, after a failed coup attempt ended President Soekarno's experiment with Guided Democracy. The magazine's founders were all members of the "Generation of '66," meaning that they had been among the students and activists who, together with the military, brought an end to Soekarno's rule.[3] In the beginning, *Tempo* had supported certain aspects of the New Order. It aligned itself with the "technocratic" policies of the Berkeley-trained economists who emphasized the rational planning and economic development that would become the hallmarks of the new administration.[4] *Tempo* always had friends in the government. There were economists in the State Planning Board (Bappenas) who leaked evidence of corruption and mismanagement in the state-owned Pertamina oil company to Fikri Jufri, their former student at the University of Indonesia. There were friends in the military who remembered their debt to the young activists who had helped to bring them to power. And there were friends in Golkar, Soeharto's organization of "functional groups" that was the political engine of the New Order. *Tempo*'s publisher, Eric Samola, was Golkar's treasurer. Even Harmoko, the Minister of Information who signed the letter that banned *Tempo* on June 21, 1994, was a former comrade, if not a friend. The former cartoonist had known Goenawan Mohamad and Fikri Jufri since the 1960s, when as young journalists they had played dominos together at the anti-Soekarnoist newspaper *Harian Kami*.

---

[3] The term "Generation of '66" has both literary and political nuances. See A. Teeuw, *Modern Indonesian Literature*, vol. II (The Hague: Martinus Nijhoff, 1979), pp. 41-46.

[4] For the relationship between the Indonesian press and the political economy of the New Order, see Daniel Dhakidae, "The State, The Rise of Capital, and the Fall of Political Journalism" (Ph.D. thesis, Cornell University, May 1991).

Tempo grew strong and wealthy while Soeharto's economic development plan, bolstered by the rise in oil prices of the mid-1970s, transformed Indonesia into one of the new "Asian Tigers". Yet Goenawan Mohamad's often-quoted statement that editing *Tempo* was like trying to pilot a hijacked plane with the journalists as his passengers, was a grim reminder of the perils of editing a magazine during the Soeharto years. "If I don't pay attention to the censors," he said, "my passengers will be the first victims."[5]

By the time the New Order had calcified in the mid-1980s, other more outspoken papers had long been shut down. The multiple bans of 1974 and 1978 left a press that was either too cowed or too docile to report the truth.[6] But despite a few close calls and one temporary banning in 1982, *Tempo* had always managed to evade such overt acts of power. Perhaps this good fortune was because of *Tempo*'s shimmering language, or the result of what Benedict Anderson called the magazine's style of "mannered knowingness".[7] Others said that *Tempo* was a kind of "structural collaborator" with the government, permitted to exist because its very presence allowed the regime to boast of its openness.[8] Yet despite the ambiguous nature of *Tempo*'s relationship with the New Order, *Tempo* was an independent institution, a truly "non-government" organization. Although necessity forced the editors of *Tempo* to conform to the rules of the New Order state, they were nevertheless able to offer independent perspectives on the nation and society of Indonesia in ways that were subtle but unmistakable. Indeed, it may have been this independence that rankled most with *Tempo*'s enemies in the Soeharto regime.

---

[5] Quoted in Adam Schwarz, *A Nation in Waiting: Indonesia in the 1990's* (Boulder: Westview Press, 1994), p. 240.

[6] David Hill, *The Press in New Order Indonesia* (Jakarta: PT Pustaka Sinar Harapan, 1994), pp. 37-39.

[7] Quoted in David Hill, *The Press in New Order Indonesia*, p. 89.

[8] Interview with Arief Budiman, December 6, 1999.

The banning of *Tempo* marked the beginning of the end of the New Order. The popular reaction was unprecedented. For over a year demonstrations protesting the banning occurred throughout Indonesia. As Atmakusumah Astraatmadja of the Dr. Soetomo Press Institute said, "something was happening, something different was happening in the country. Many of the demonstrations were started by students; there were lawyers, there were artists, there were intellectuals…as well as journalists."[9] Perhaps the biggest surprise was the outburst of support from ordinary people, middle class Indonesians who had kept silent throughout the nearly thirty years of Soeharto's rule. Although *Tempo*'s readership had been relatively small – weekly circulation was never higher than about 190,000 – its influence was far greater than these numbers would suggest. For Jakarta's intellectual elite, *Tempo* was what sociologist Arief Budiman referred to as a kind of "space", a place in which writers could exchange ideas with relative freedom.[10] For ordinary people, *Tempo* was a sign of middle class status, an indicator of achievement and of belonging to the select readership of Indonesia's only world-class magazine. The fact that such a magazine could be closed down was simply unthinkable.

I thought I already understood the sadness, frustration, and anger that accompanies the death of a newspaper. My brother Bayard was working as a reporter for the *Tampa Times* when it died in 1982, a victim of market forces and the expansion of local television news that was slowly strangling the afternoon newspaper. But the death of *Tempo* was not a natural death, it was a murder. And the *Tempo* alumni were not about to let the crime be forgotten. They met and rallied. They organized discussion groups, published books and white papers, and initiated a lawsuit. Each June 21 they

---

[9] Interview with Atmakusumah Astraatmadja, June 30, 1998.
[10] Interview with Arief Budiman, December 6, 1999.

commemorated the magazine's banning. And they set up an unconventional version of the traditional neighborhood mutual help society, in which over one hundred *Tempo* alumni pooled and shared the wages of those who had found jobs. Under the leadership of Bambang Harymurti, this "Tebet group" provided a livelihood for dozens of ex-*Tempo* journalists as they fought to keep their struggle in the public eye.

If *Tempo*'s enemies had expected the magazine to crash and burn as the result of the 1994 banning, they were mistaken. Indeed, the banning of *Tempo* had the unintended effect of freeing editor Goenawan Mohamad from his government "hijackers". With *Tempo* gone, Goenawan had nothing to save. Suddenly in enormous demand as a spokesman for freedom of expression, Goenawan dedicated his formidable talents to the arena of political struggle. As the editor of a magazine that didn't exist, Goenawan Mohamad was now completely free.

Kebetulan, or "coincidence" is one way that Indonesians think about fate, and fate played a big part in the writing of this book. It was *kebetulan* that I was living in Jakarta during 1997-1998, a tumultuous time in which the Indonesian economy collapsed and President Soeharto was forced to step down after thirty-two years of authoritarian rule. In his masterful work *Java in a Time of Revolution*, Benedict Anderson wrote of the experience of living through one major historical crisis while writing about another.[11] I was lucky to have a similar experience – and perhaps by witnessing the end of the New Order, to see things about its beginning that would not have otherwise been apparent.

I was especially lucky to have an opportunity to meet and interview *Tempo* journalists while *Tempo* was still a ghost. In 1997 there was little reason to believe that *Tempo* would ever be published again. *Tempo* people were eager to talk, and to tell me their stories.

---

[11] Benedict R. O'G. Anderson, *Java in a Time of Revolution: Occupation and Resistance, 1944-1946* (Ithaca: Cornell University Press, 1972), pp. xi-xv.

Many of the people I interviewed still felt so emotional about the magazine and the events of the banning that they wept during our conversations. Ex-*Tempo* journalists who had joined with *Gatra* would ask "what do *Tempo* people say about me now?" Later I told Bambang Harymurti that sometimes I felt as if I were doing a kind of "group therapy" with ex-*Tempo* writers.

I was also lucky that my friend and colleague Lars Willnat from George Washington University was visiting Jakarta during the last week of the Soeharto regime, because without Lars' absolute conviction that I should stay in Indonesia, I might have evacuated with the other Americans. But most of all I was lucky to be in Jakarta on May 21, 1998, when Soeharto was forced to step down from the presidency. As the televised images of Soeharto's resignation flashed around the world and the New Order regime appeared to be crumbling for good, everything seemed to be happening at breakneck speed. On June 6, the new Minister of Information announced that he was abolishing the regulations that had allowed his predecessor to cancel newspaper licenses. Within a few weeks *Tempo* would have its license back. As my Fulbright year drew to an end, I watched in amazement as the *Tempo* alumni resigned from other jobs *en masse* and prepared to re-start the magazine.

Before leaving Indonesia, I met with Atmakusumah, the former managing editor of Mochtar Lubis's newspaper *Indonesia Raya*. When I told him of my astonishment at *Tempo* journalists' willingness to drop everything and return to the magazine, he just laughed and said that he and Mochtar Lubis had also discussed the possibility of bringing back *Indonesia Raya* – twenty-four years after the newspaper had been banned. Atma told me that he had said, "But it's been twenty-four years! We're old men now. Instead, let's ask the government to build a monument to *Indonesia Raya* – a big one! – and put it in the Department of Information's yard."

On October 6, 1998 *Tempo* magazine resumed publication.

Back in the United States, I tried to make sense of what I had witnessed. I had initially planned to write about *Tempo* as "the magazine that doesn't exist," but obviously that was no longer possible. Moreover, I had come to realize that *Tempo* was much more than a very potent symbol of freedom of expression. For the twenty-three years prior to the banning, *Tempo* was Indonesia's most important news magazine. For many of these years it was Indonesia's only weekly news magazine.[12] Many scholars have described the political culture of the New Order, but as I soon came to learn, surprisingly few had analyzed it from the perspective of news.[13] It seemed to me that it was worth examining *Tempo* as an institution that had helped to shape and define modern Indonesia. So I studied Indonesian, and read widely in Indonesian politics and culture. My plan was to do the research for a book-length study that would examine *Tempo* as a window into the history of the New Order.

I went back to Indonesia in May, 1999 during a sabbatical leave from George Washington University. This time I was an "honorary Fulbrighter"and a visiting fellow at the Institute for the Study of the Free Flow of Information (ISAI), a think tank established by Goenawan Mohamad and other ex-*Tempo* journalists after *Tempo* was banned. Atmakusumah agreed to be my official sponsor.

---

[12] There were other weekly news magazines in Indonesia, including *Editor*, which began in 1987 with an "exodus" of journalists from *Tempo*. But none were able to challenge successfully *Tempo*'s position as market leader.

[13] An important exception is Krishna Sen and David T. Hill, *Media, Culture, and Politics in Indonesia* (New York: Oxford University Press, 2000). See also Benedict R. O'G. Anderson, *Language and Power, Exploring Political Cultures in Indonesia* (Ithaca: Cornell University Press, 1990); and the still valuable Karl D. Jackson and Lucian W. Pye, eds., *Political Power and Communications in Indonesia* (Berkeley: University of California Press, 1978), esp. Nono Anwar Makarim, "The Indonesian Press: An Editor's Perspective", pp. 259-281.

I don't remember exactly when I first started taking chocolate chip cookies to *Tempo*, but it must have been at some point early in my sabbatical year. Food and performance are both essential to Indonesian culture, and a gift of cookies made with "imported" ingredients was a good way of overcoming my feelings of awkwardness at speaking the Indonesian language and becoming part of the group. And for a shy person, it was certainly easier than dancing to the sinuous beat of *dangdut*, or belting out American pop tunes from the 1970s, the other two ways of fitting in at *Tempo*. Although I eventually learned to dance to *dangdut* (rather badly, I've been told), I never did agree to sing *karaoke*.

I spent a total of fifteen months doing research at *Tempo*. For most of that time I simply observed. I attended planning meetings, editorial meetings, and checking meetings. I participated in *Tempo's* training for new journalists, stayed late on deadline nights, and spent numerous hours just watching and listening. I attended all of *Tempo's* formal social gatherings, and a lot of informal ones as well. Many of my days were spent in *Tempo's* library – where, like everyone else, I spent more time talking than reading. *Tempo* people were curious about me, but always friendly and interested in what I was doing.

I wanted to understand the culture of *Tempo*, and how it influenced what became news. As a scholar with a background in American cultural history, I had already written a book on the 19th century American newspaper the *New York Sun*. But chief editor Charles A. Dana had been dead for nearly one hundred years by the time I finished that book, and for me it was a new experience to write a study of the living. So I drew up my own rules about what constituted research and what constituted friendship and where to draw the line between the two. Journalists understand reporting, and they also understand that everything that happens is on the record unless someone says it isn't. From George Washington University anthropologist Joel Kuipers I learned always to carry a notebook, and to make sure that it was out when I was talking with someone. From the *Tempo* journalists, I learned that the best way to understand something that doesn't make sense is simply to ask. I felt that I had attained the right balance between research and friendship when one of the writers introduced me to a visitor by saying, "This is Janet. She is writing about us, but we think of her as our sister."

In 1988, six years before *Tempo* was banned, Goenawan Mohamad wrote a *Catatan Pinggir* ("Sidelines") essay that described an accidental meeting with an old friend in San Francisco, a man he called "W". The two had been friends at the University of Indonesia, although they had chosen different sides in the events leading up to 1965-66. Goenawan had worked for the anti-Communist newspaper *Harian Kami*; W had attacked it as his enemy.

When they met twenty years later on Geary Street, W had been transformed. Married to an Argentinian woman, he had become an American citizen. "This was an amazing transformation," Goenawan wrote. "W, a leftist student, [was now] completely transformed into a middle-class capitalist American!"

The two old friends met again for dinner, and talked of the idealism that had attended the early days of the New Order. W told of his disillusionment with "Marxism, Leninism, Maoism, and the cult of the worship of individuals," and the cynical snuffing out of the revolutionary spirit by the Communist victors in China. Finally W said, "I have changed – really changed. But you haven't. You are just as you used to be. You are still a New Order man."

"I laughed," Goenawan wrote. "That evening we parted again. He returned to his home and family in the prestigious area near Golden Gate. I returned to [the] David Hotel…That night I was suddenly aware that I was already forty-seven years old."[14]

---

[14] *Tempo*, October 29, 1988. Quoted from the translation by Jennifer Lindsay, in Goenawan Mohamad, *Sidelines: Thought Pieces From Tempo Magazine*, (Jakarta: Lontar, 1994), pp. 205-6.

It is little wonder that reflections upon the birth of the New Order evoked such melancholy and ambivalence from Goenawan. By 1988, *Tempo* magazine occupied an ambiguous position in Indonesian society. Clearly a product of the New Order, *Tempo* nevertheless presented independent points of view, often at considerable risk. Like the epic battles depicted in the Hindu-Javanese version of the *Mahabharata*, *Tempo*'s struggles marked a war within the New Order. It was fratricide, or *perang saudara*, the Indonesian term for civil war that literally means a war of brothers. *Tempo*'s founders had helped to bring the New Order to power in 1966, and they played a crucial role in the wave of social protest and upheaval that brought it down thirty-two years later. But as the Indonesians who came of age before television learned from the tales of *wayang kulit* or shadow puppetry, nothing is ever black and white. Although *Tempo* was not unambiguously part of the "opposition" until after it was banned in 1994, it nevertheless challenged the Soeharto regime in ways that were subtle but clear. In this endeavor the magazine had many friends, some within the regime itself.

As Goenawan Mohamad is fond of saying, the New Order was never monolithic. When I once suggested to Goenawan that the four years in which *Tempo* didn't exist may have been the most significant period in the magazine's history, he didn't disagree. And like the Bharatayudha, the battle that ended the civil war between the Pandawa and Kurawa, the banning period was a fight to the death.

prologue

"Soeharto went too soon."

Goenawan Mohamad's words were barely audible against the drumbeat of the rain on the corrugated roof. The iron legs of my chair rasped against the rough concrete floor as I pulled closer. A heavy curtain of rain enveloped the open-air café. Inside, the air was damp and unexpectedly cool.

"If he had stayed longer, we could have got a better infrastructure of democracy on the ground," Goenawan said. "But he went too easily, and too soon, and we were left with this chaotic opposition force. And disillusion. I always think that disillusion will follow after every revolution."

It was June 20, 1998, one day short of the fourth anniversary of the banning of *Tempo* magazine. One month earlier, Soeharto had resigned as the second president of the Republic of Indonesia. After thirty-two years of authoritarian rule, his regime had suddenly collapsed in failure and disgrace. An economic crisis of epic proportions had unleashed political forces beyond the control even of the "Father of Development", while a loose coalition of student activists and democratic opposition groups demanded nothing less than *reformasi total*. Indonesians had greeted the victory of Soeharto's resignation with a mixture of euphoria and disbelief.

Two weeks after the President's resignation, the new Minister of Information, Mohammad Yunus Yosfiah, had announced that he would revoke the ministerial declarations of his predecessor, Harmoko. With one stroke, Yunus had cut through the thicket of regulations that choked the press under Soeharto. He had also swept the way clear for *Tempo* to return to publication.

From the street, all that could be seen of the Utan Kayu Community was a small blue sign reading No. 68H. Goenawan Mohamad, the former editor of *Tempo*, had built the office, theater, and gallery complex known as Komunitas Utan Kayu, or KUK. KUK was a bustling safe haven for journalists, artists, and writers. It was also the epicenter of other, more secret, activities. A Honda service center in a two-storey cement storefront hid the complex from the view of casual passers-by on the busy street outside.

Goenawan Mohamad had agreed to meet me at Utan Kayu at 2 PM on a Saturday. On Saturdays the café was empty, the kitchen closed. None of the young writers or activists who usually frequented the place were anywhere to be found. Aside from the security guards, alert for unfriendly outsiders or crewcut "Intel", the complex was deserted. I arrived early – having hired a car and driver to bring me from the annual Fulbright conference being held 70km away at "Safari Park" in West Java – and waited alone in the café. A few minutes after two o'clock, a Toyota Kijang pulled into the driveway, and Goenawan stepped down from the driver's side. He greeted me warmly, and we moved to a small table in the back, somewhat sheltered from the rain. Goenawan selected the chair that faced out from the rear cinder block wall. I had noticed that he usually sat where he could keep an eye on the entrance to the café. I pulled out the chair next to his.

Setting his hand phone onto the green wood slats of the table, Goenawan asked politely about my trip into Jakarta. A handsome man in his late fifties, Goenawan has fine features and a quick smile, and looks much younger than his years. His manner is reserved, almost courtly. He dresses casually, and the cuffs of his sleeves are folded back, revealing muscular forearms strong from tennis. His voice is soft and melodious, and he speaks almost perfect English.

Goenawan and I had met several times previously during the past year. He knew that I had been planning to write about *Tempo* magazine. I was interested in how *Tempo* had lived on after the 1994 banning as a symbol of freedom of expression. I had already interviewed him about the spirit of a magazine that would not die, and its enduring influence on Indonesian journalism and cultural life. But this was the first time I had seen him since the fall of Soeharto.

Goenawan said that he had watched Soeharto resign on television. "It didn't move me at all," he said, "because I knew that he was going to resign. At 2:00 in the morning somebody called me, and another friend called me as well. And then I sent messages through email to all over the world that Soeharto was going to resign tomorrow and there was still a lot of uncertainty."

"I watched television with my children," he added. "To me it was not dramatic. Which is good. Because you can see that power is nothing special."

A lone office boy passed by the entrance to the café, and Goenawan called out, asking him to get coffee. Nodding, he disappeared into the pelting rain.

A few nights earlier, the *Tempo* "alumni" had met in this same place to debate whether the magazine Goenawan Mohamad had founded at the very beginning of the New Order should be brought back from the dead. For Goenawan, who had spent four years in the wilderness fighting for democratic reform, the results of the vote were painful to accept.

"My selfish interest is not to publish again," he said.

The discussion had been emotional. Some people, Goenawan recalled, thought "we should leave *Tempo* embalmed as it is now, dead. A kind of memorial. A kind of legend."

"But the majority voted to publish it again," he said. "The

rest of them said you will tarnish the legend. But then other people said why should we bother about being a legend? And somebody in the meeting asked, what do I, how do I feel about it. I could not be honest. I was not honest."

Rainwater dripped through the cracks in the clear plastic roof, darkened with mildew and dead leaves. The office boy returned with a small tray, and we stirred clumps of coarse sugar crystals into the thick black coffee. Oblique light from outside bathed the café in pale green.

"When I walked out from the meeting," Goenawan continued, "one of the office boys told me that he had made a promise to himself and to the neighbors next door in his *kampung* [inner-city village] that he would make a party, that he would slaughter a goat or two to celebrate if *Tempo* would be published again. And he asked me to come when the party was on. And I realized that many people are like him, who have been deprived of a kind of self-respect."

I leaned in, straining to hear Goenawan's words beneath the din of the rain on the roof. "And then I decided okay, I'll take it," he said. "I'll come to his party. I said to myself, okay, I'll take it."

What Goenawan had agreed to take was the job of chief editor of *Tempo*, a position he had held for the first twenty-three years of *Tempo*'s existence. It was a job that had brought him international renown. It was also a job that he no longer wanted.

"For me it is a sacrifice," he said. "Maybe I am more acceptable than other people. But then I heard already, the bickering has started, and I was angry. I was real angry. And I told them, look, I made a lot of sacrifices. I don't have to prove myself to be the editor of *Tempo*."

One of the things that Goenawan would have to sacrifice was the opportunity to be a resident scholar at Columbia University, a time which was to have been both a respite from his activities as an underground essayist and pamphleteer and an opportunity to finish the libretto for the opera that he was writing with composer Tony Prabowo.

Goenawan Mohamad speaking in front of *Tempo* employees
after the banning, Tebet, South Jakarta, 1994 [*Tempo*]

"And the other thing I have to sacrifice is this," he said, gesturing around the place that he had built, the place he often described as his habitat. "And my writing. So I was angry. And so I said, would you please sacrifice something for me? Control this – the other people, old grudges, trying to settle old scores. I said look, if you continue this I am not going to be the editor, I am not going to be as involved as I was with personnel problems. I don't want to spend my emotions there, because that was the hardest part when I was the editor. All the bickering, rivalry, jealousy, things like that were too much. And now it's getting tougher, because of the four years of separation."

During the four years of the *Tempo* "diaspora", much had changed. Indonesia's most highly-respected journalists had become warriors, taking to the streets as demonstrations protesting the banning drew hundreds of supporters and a brutal response from the police. Later, with elegant displays of verbal skill and legal finesse, *Tempo*'s allies had fought in open court to have the Department of Information's decision banning *Tempo* overturned. Press conferences, interviews, and prizes from international organizations had kept the struggle in the public eye.

Yet not all of the battles had taken place in the open. There was an underground press, still clandestine, and moving frequently from one location to another. Computer technicians and information specialists posted many of these stories on the internet, beyond the reach of the Department of Information. Writers published "instant books" documenting the struggle. Many of these activities had been secretly coordinated out of the community that Goenawan had built at Utan Kayu.

"You see, from the beginning after *Tempo* was banned I was involved in more political activity. We still have this underground network," he said. "Because we are not quite sure whether the army or the forces of reaction will stay outside the gate or not."

Goenawan picked up his phone, absent-mindedly turning it over in his hands. His hands are smooth, his skin a light golden-brown.

"And to tell you the truth, I am more at home now with these things," he said. "When you are in the underground, you meet selfless people, really selfless people, wonderful people who dare to sacrifice their own life. And it becomes a habit."

The thought of leaving this life and going back to the routine of editing a weekly magazine was almost unbearable.

When I asked Goenawan when it had first occurred to him that *Tempo* could return to publication, he said that he hadn't really thought about it until after the demonstration at the Department of Information on May 28. The demonstration had been organized by AJI, the Alliance of Independent Journalists. They were demanding that independent journalists' associations be recognized, and also that the ministerial regulations shackling the press be revoked. It was after the demonstration was over that a foreign journalist asked Goenawan if he was going to publish *Tempo* again. Goenawan recalled saying "I'm not going to do it before they revoke the law and they revoke the ministerial declarations. And then I met the Minister, and he said it will take time to revoke the law, which has to go to the Parliament. But it takes only a matter of days to revoke ministerial decrees. So I settled for the second option. That I would agree to publish *Tempo* if the second condition were met. Then my friends called me. Shall we do it? What do you think? And then we said yeah, before somebody else grabs it."

I asked about how he had felt during these conversations. "Nothing," he said. "Because my mental state was not to publish *Tempo* and to be an editor again. I was not expecting that I would be involved again. I was kind of screening my mind from the worries of the thing."

"I'm not, well, I'm not very happy," he added.

Goenawan said that before agreeing to take on the editorship again he had told his friends that he had certain conditions. That he would only stay for one year. And that the ownership of the new *Tempo* would have to be different from what it had been in the past. The old *Tempo* had been owned by Grafiti Pers, a limited company owned in part by the founders and employees of *Tempo*, and in part by the Jaya Raya Foundation. The Jaya Raya Foundation (or Yayasan Jaya Raya) was controlled by the developer Ciputra.

The new company should no longer include Grafiti, Goenawan said, and no single individual should have a share. "Institutions can have shares, like employees, cooperatives, the alumni, foundations, and then the partners. But then not a single one of us can have individual shares. Because I don't want anybody to own *Tempo*." In the past, *Tempo* had been scarred by too many disagreements and hurt feelings related to ownership of the shares.

Goenawan told me that during the negotiation process, he had learned that it would be very difficult to get rid of Grafiti Pers. One reason was that the board members of Grafiti – which included many of the magazine's founders – would then not be able to join the new magazine.

"Then I said okay, but stay in the minority. And they agreed to have only 20%. Now I'm going to have to negotiate further, because we also have Yayasan Jaya Raya."

The problem with Yayasan Jaya Raya was that after *Tempo* was banned, the foundation had become an investor in *Gatra* – the news magazine that Bob Hasan, one of Soeharto's cronies, had created to "replace" *Tempo*. *Tempo* loyalists believed that *Gatra* was a puppet of the regime – and that the *Tempo* writers who had joined the magazine were traitors.

"That is why we should get rid of Yayasan Jaya Raya," Goenawan continued. "Yayasan Jaya Raya should withdraw from *Gatra* as a shareholder if they want to own us. That is going to hurt the feelings of some people, but okay, I don't mind."

There were other equally complicated issues involving the ownership of the new *Tempo*. One of the most painful for Goenawan was the fate of the feisty news magazine *Detektif dan Romantika*, or *Detective and Romance*. "*D&R*," as it was known, was edited by former *Tempo* managing editor Bambang Bujono – although his name didn't appear anywhere in the magazine. As Bambang Bujono had explained to me a few months earlier, "this is just a trick to survive." Many people believed that *D&R* was a kind of reincarnation of *Tempo*. Goenawan himself was a regular contributor.

It was an open secret that Grafiti Pers owned *D&R*. According to Bambang Bujono, Grafiti Pers had not bought the magazine, but had instead "bought" the owner. "But there is not a piece of paper that says that," he told me. If there had been evidence of the real ownership of *D&R*, the government would have banned the magazine. Now the problem was that if *Tempo* were to return to publication, Grafiti Pers would own two competing magazines.

At first the directors of Grafiti Pers thought that they could publish both magazines, Goenawan said. "But then we discovered that there's not enough money to publish both."

"There are going to be problems if we publish both in the same room," he said. "Jealousies. Because the *Tempo* salaries will be higher. And also, how would I divide my time because I used to write for *D&R* too. And there's going to be the feeling of being a second class magazine. Also, market-wise, maybe it's not wise to have two. But if we merge *D&R* staff with *Tempo* staff, we are going to be bloated."

I asked Goenawan if he had discussed this problem with Bambang Bujono.

"No," he said, "I haven't talked to him. But he's not – he's not very enthusiastic about *Tempo*."

Although neither of us mentioned it, several months earlier Goenawan had given me a copy of a poem he had written in 1995 about the banning of *Tempo*. Goenawan had read the poem at a commemoration held at Taman Ismail Marzuki cultural center. It was called "If We Were At Sarejevo,"and Goenawan had dedicated it to Bambang Bujono and comrades.

"It is very hard," he said. "That is why I started to defend myself by not being too emotional about it. By not being involved emotionally, because it's too hard."

Later, Goenawan again brought up the topic of Bambang Bujono. "I was thinking," he said, "I was planning to write him an email because there is no time to meet and talk. And maybe by writing, I'll tell him that we should be honest. I think he will understand. I think he is also the kind of person who thinks that he does not very much have the privilege to choose."

Perhaps Goenawan was also the kind of person who did not think he had the privilege to choose. Four years earlier, on June 27, 1994, two groups protesting the banning of *Tempo* had been attacked by riot police and soldiers armed with rattan canes.[1] Shaken by the brutality, Goenawan felt he had to sacrifice something for those who had supported *Tempo*. He told a reporter from *Forum Keadilan*, "I cannot ignore the sacrifice of friends

---

[1] These and other details of the banning can be found in Alumni Majalah Tempo, *Buku Putih Tempo: Pembredelan Itu* (Jakarta: Yayasan Alumni Tempo, 1994), and Alumni Majalah Tempo, *Mengapa Kami Menggugat* (Jakarta: Yayasan Alumni Tempo, 1995).

who are protesting against the cancellation of our SIUPP [permit to run a press business]. I am indebted to them. I have to repay them by giving up the possibility of holding office in any future magazine."[2]

Goenawan's sacrifice in 1994 had been public. Laudable. He had offered up his own career as an editor to pay a debt to those who had suffered. But the great irony was that the banning of *Tempo* had actually given Goenawan an unexpected opportunity for personal development. It was a period of remarkable growth for him, as he was finally freed from the burden of editing a magazine under the unspecified and often capricious restrictions of the Soeharto regime. Now he was being asked to take up the responsibility for *Tempo* once again. But this time the sacrifice was personal. And it was a sacrifice that only his closest friends would recognize.

"It was my happiest moment, right here," Goenawan said.

He was silent for a moment. "There was a meeting in *Tempo*'s old office," he said. "and one of the secretaries said 'Well, we won it. We won.' They have a right, those people. They also sacrificed something. They want to get the proof of it."

The rain had stopped. The air was fresh, and smelled of wet leaves and earth.

I looked at Goenawan. "You don't have a choice, do you." I said.

"Not much," he answered sadly. "I do, but then I have to disappoint many people who were here with me also. There were two kinds of people who were here with me. The *Tempo* alumni and the underground."

When Goenawan and his friends established *Tempo* in 1971, the magazine had in many ways embodied the aspirations of the founders of the New Order. *Tempo* had flourished under Soeharto's

---

[2] *Forum Keadilan*, "Goenawan Mohammad: Saya Tidak Percaya Revolusi", July 21, 1994, quoted in David Hill, *The Press in New Order Indonesia* (Jakarta: Pustaka Sinar Harapan, 1994), p. ii.

rule, only to be killed by the same regime that it had helped to legitimize.

"There is a novel written in Indonesia called *The Post-Revolution and Pain*," Goenawan said, "and after you give birth to a child there is pain also. And that is going to happen. I have a lot of sympathy for the students. I was thinking of writing an open letter to the students. You have to be prepared for the pain, because the revolution requires, even induces purity in people's hearts. And every revolution should be followed by the normal political pressures, and normal political pressure has to be tainted with compromises. And that is the reality, and that's going to happen in this country. From the underground to the dissidents."

Moreover, as Goenawan pointed out, the break with the old regime was not yet complete. Look at the army, he suggested, with its record of brutality. "And that's not settled," he said. "The dust is not yet settled."

"And that puts me also in a difficult position," he added. "I am afraid that if I am back in *Tempo*, of course *Tempo* will not be like it was. In the old days you had to compromise, now you don't have to compromise. But you know, you become part of the system – you can be easily be co-opted by them."

I asked Goenawan if he meant that by becoming the editor of *Tempo* he would once again become part of the establishment.

Goenawan looked irritated. "The problem is not that I am part of the establishment," he said, "but that the institution itself will have to cooperate with the government."

Embarrassed, I explained that what I meant was that Goenawan had not always belonged to "the opposition".

"I've always been part of the establishment anyway," he conceded. "I've always been. No matter how involved I am with the people here, the guerrillas."

"I'm fortunate in a way," he added, "because I have been through this before in 1965. And after the political change there is some bickering and some problems with cooperation, and people who you don't really like become leaders, and things you don't really like to do. So I'm rather prepared to deal with it."

What Goenawan was not prepared to deal with, he said, was his own lack of enthusiasm. "Because it is dangerous if you have a leader who is disinterested, and that is what I am afraid of myself. That I will discourage people to give their best to this new magazine. I may not be the right person, because I have mixed feelings. That worries me. That worries me more than anything."

"I keep telling myself if you decide to take it, you have to take it 100%," he said. "Because everything is at stake. The reputation of *Tempo*, your own reputation, and the people who work with you. The people – all those who want to be back in the promised land."

Goenawan's solution to the problem of leadership was that he would become chief editor, but that after one year the job would go to Bambang Harymurti. Bambang had been *Tempo*'s Washington bureau chief when *Tempo* was banned. After the banning, he had become the *de facto* leader of the *Tempo* "diaspora". Nearly all of the *Tempo* alumni I met had credited Bambang Harymurti with keeping the *Tempo* loyalists together under very difficult circumstances.

"Bambang is very generous," Goenawan said. "Maybe he's not the person that we should go for during the fighting time, because he is like, in the *Mahabharata*, he is like Yudhistira, who doesn't want to fight. Very generous, very noble, and Bambang Harymurti is like that. Except you need people who really fight and are mean. And Bambang is never mean."

Left unspoken was Goenawan's hope that this would not have to be a fighting time, but rather a time of consolidation, a time of creating new institutions to safeguard the fruits of victory.

Bambang Harymurti had told Goenawan that he wanted *Tempo* to become a "clearinghouse of information" – accurate, fair, balanced, non-partisan. Goenawan liked this idea, but he also wanted the magazine to have a strong editorial side. "You can be very open about it," he said. "You can be very tough. Sober, but tough. And don't mince the words. It's about time to do that. Twenty-three years – I'm tired of negotiating with it. But you also have to have the very good support of sober people to bring credibility to the magazine, and Bambang is the right person."

The shadows had begun to lengthen. Outside the café, slanting afternoon light reflected off the puddles in the driveway. There were more sounds from the street now, and the smell of diesel.

The next day would be June 21, the fourth anniversary of the banning. For each of the past three years, *Tempo* had commemorated the banning with some kind of solemn event. But how would they commemorate the banning this year, I asked, when everything was so different? "That's a good point," Goenawan said, looking surprised. "That reminds me that maybe I have to make a speech tomorrow."

There was going to be an event at Utan Kayu. It had already been planned. "Please come," he said politely.

Then, slowly, he said, "maybe I have to tell the people, to tell the guerrillas and everybody that I will do it but only for one year. In public. So it's kind of a commitment to them. Maybe it's a kind of cowardice. Maybe I have to tell them honestly that it's not an easy choice."

"My heart is really not into it," he said. "That's why I am afraid."

"When I was in *Tempo*," he added, "one thing I never said was that I was tired. You cannot say you are tired in front of any of your friends. I can say it now. But when I am back in *Tempo* I cannot say it."

Goenawan was quiet for a moment. "It's difficult," he said. "You know I've realized that with every single step you make in your life, you have more moral problems than you are aware of. More moral entanglements. And how can you walk in this fearsome battle, this fearsome government…without trying to be pure? But purity is also vanity, and that's wrong too."

"But I don't want to be an activist for the rest of my life, either. I want to be a writer. I hope the dust will settle down soon, and institutions established to contain the democracy, the freedom we have gained. It would be the most peaceful moment of my life."

Goenawan looked thoughtful, and a little bit sad. "Bambang can pour his ideas into *Tempo*, change it," he said. "He can do whatever he wants."

"But this is your moment too," I suggested. "You have had a victory, a moral victory."

Goenawan picked up a stray pen lying on the table. He looked at it deliberately for a moment, and then he looked at me.

"That's what is curious," he said. "I don't feel as if it's a victory. I have to convince, to tell myself, 'This is a glorious revolution.' No bloodshed, no army used to topple Soeharto, and something which is quite – extraordinary. That somebody who has been in his job, held power, for thirty-two years is gone. A major historical event. I have to tell myself that."

"Maybe it's difficult for me to change from one space to another. And after I've gotten used to this, it's going to take me a while. For me, it has become a kind of habit, like being careful, like using different names for your phone or your beeper. And I've tried to change that habit, but it's not been very easy."

"People who expect me to be active in politics will be disappointed," he said. "I know I will disappoint some people."

It is hard, perhaps, to coax guerillas out of the underground. But nothing is eternal, and even the most fearsome warriors must eventually lay down their arms and plant rice in their fields. As a soft dusk settled and I began to pack up to leave, Goenawan said, "I'm not one of those Japanese officers that will stay in the jungle."

He was laughing when he said it.

WARS WITHIN

the community

It is Friday evening at *Tempo*, and *magrib*, or evening prayer, has passed.[1] As prayer rugs are folded and writers settle back into their cubicles, the office boys carry big insulated containers of rice to an empty table near the stairs. An old dot-matrix printer spits out articles downloaded from the international press. A few reporters and writers hover nearby, like students at a university cafeteria, early arrivals for the evening meal.

The food is simple at *Tempo*, but there is plenty of it and on deadline nights it's free. Tonight it's fried chicken, with shrimp crackers and *sayur asam*, a pungent vegetable soup. There are bananas, too, and people crowd around filling their bowls. Some take their plates back to their desks, others move to an empty table near the television, which is tuned to the evening news report on SCTV. The reporters tend to eat together in their own part of the newsroom. Much of their work is done, their reports already submitted to the writers who will use their interviews and "reportage" in writing their stories. The reporters, especially those who are still in their nine-month probationary period, like to stick together with a kind of informal *esprit de corps*.

While the dress code at *Tempo* is always relaxed, on Friday

---

[1]   This account is based on notes taken August 6-7, 1999.

nights it is even more so. Rubber sandals replace shoes, and flannel shirts and sweatshirts are brought out for the chill of the Jakarta night. Dirty dishes are left on the desks. The office boys are busier than usual, as they collect the bowls and wash the glasses for the long night ahead. In their gray uniforms they add an element of uncharacteristic drabness to the bustling office.

On Fridays the "aquarium" is busier than usual. In a nod to the sensibilities of the predominantly women writers who objected to the smoke, *Tempo* has built a smoking room at one end of the third-floor newsroom. With glassed-in walls, a huge exhaust fan, and sliding doors, the smoking room resembles a large fish tank, with space for about twelve desks. On deadline nights the all-male denizens of the room have extra company, as many of the occasional smokers from outside join them during breaks. As they lean against the cubbies, laughing and telling jokes, the aquarium is hazy with smoke.

The atmosphere is relaxed but purposeful. *Tempo* writers pride themselves on their professionalism and their ability to get the job done. Each has his or her own rituals. For some, it's cups of sweet hot tea or thick Indonesian coffee. For others it's special mixes of ginseng, milk and honey. The office boys are busy, boiling water for the thermoses and keeping the cups and glasses washed.

As the night wears on, there are plenty of interruptions. The quiet clicking of keyboards is broken by laughter, as writers huddle with their editors or with one another. A young reporter plucks out a plaintive tune on his guitar, and another bursts out with a line of an American song. There are plenty of comedians at *Tempo*, story tellers who can gather a crowd with a funny rendition of something that happened earlier in the day. And there is always food, either ordered through the office boys, who supplement their wages with the tips from appreciative writers and reporters, or supplied by the editors, who stop to buy fried cassava or stuffed tofu on the way back to the office from the almost nightly receptions they are expected to attend.

Tempo's deadlines are legendary, and it's a matter of pride to work all night. As the evening wears on, some writers stretch out on the sofas, or the floor of the *musholla* or prayer room. Others curl up at their desks, or rest on tables beneath a blaring TV, a kerchief or magazine shielding their eyes from the flourescent lights. The toilets are busy, the floors wet from water splashed on tired faces and arms.

Not many writers actually stay at the office all night. Some who are responsible for departments with early deadlines leave the office as early as 9 or 10 PM. Others go home at 2 or 3 in the morning, hoping to sleep a few hours before finishing up on Saturday. But for the reporters, especially the unmarried men, there is a tradition of sleeping at *Tempo*.

Early Saturday morning, the office is still. The office boys sleep on the sofas at the stair landings, and the sound of a lone radio floats up the staircase from the reception desk near the door. An old woman selling noodles sits at the stoop of the building. She begins to find a few customers, as the rumpled writers come downstairs in search of breakfast. It will be several more hours before those who have gone home drift back into the office.

By late Saturday afternoon, all but a few writers have left. There are fewer jokes now, and the writers who are still there are sunk down deep into their computers. When they finish, they leave quietly, without fanfare. Everyone knows what it's like to be on deadline.

Later in the day the editors take over. The atmosphere is still relaxed, but more determined, as the Saturday night deadline approaches. The office boys set out another meal. There are last-minute meetings to discuss breaking news, as well as the cover art and the total number of advertisements. It won't be over until Sunday morning, when the last files are sent to the printer and the magazine is closed down.

The weekly deadline is probably the most important ritual at *Tempo*. Beginning at dusk and ending at dawn, the deadline is the engine that drives the magazine. As relentless as the ticking of a metronome, its approach regulates the week's activities. New reporters speak of it in hushed terms. Stick as well as carrot, the deadline propels the week along, a fixed mark in a culture that generally places little importance on punctuality. Everyone, from librarians, photographers, artists and designers to the senior editors must observe the deadline. No one wants to face the opprobrium aimed at those who hold up the magazine by being late with a story or a piece of reportage.

Although many things have changed at *Tempo* since the magazine was founded in 1971, by 1999 the ritual of the deadline had changed very little.[2] Computers had replaced manual typewriters and smokers worked in the thick haze of their own special room, but deadline nights remained essentially the same. The office boys still boiled endless pots of water for tea, the long hours were still interrupted by singing and jokes, and tired reporters and writers still snatched a few hours of sleep underneath their desks or wherever they could find a quiet place.

Although it is seldom discussed openly, one of the most important aspects of the deadline is the sense of community, the feeling of being together and working toward a common goal. Since the very beginning, everyone – from founding editor Goenawan Mohamad to the greenest reporter in the office – has shared an equal footing. Whether it was in the colonial-era storefront at Jl. Senen Raya 83 in the 1970s, with its shaky floors and antique glass windows, or the modern office proudly situated amidst the corporate high rises on busy Jl. Rasuna Said in the early 1990s, *Tempo* writers have always been part of a community.

Tempo's current chief editor, Bambang Harymurti, who joined

---

2   At the beginning of my fieldwork in June 1999, Goenawan Mohamad was still chief editor of the magazine. Bambang Harymurti replaced Goenawan in July, but most people agree that the culture of the magazine changed very little during his first year as editor.

Bambang Harymurti in *Tempo*'s office on
Jl. Senen Raya, 1985 [Nanang Baso/*Tempo*]

Tempo in the early 1980s, remembers how in the mornings after deadline nights everyone – "including Goenawan" – would breakfast together, sharing a simple meal of rice porridge and talking "about all sorts of things."[3] Bambang is in his mid-forties now, with a disarming friendliness, a nimble mind, and an eager smile. He likes a challenge, and friends tell of how he very nearly fulfilled his boyhood dream of becoming Indonesia's first astronaut – while on assignment for *Tempo* – by becoming one of four finalists in a competitive training program sponsored by NASA. When Bambang and others remember the early days of *Tempo*, they talk about the shared meals, the sense of accomplishment, the feeling of togetherness, and the opportunity to talk freely with the senior editors. But of all these elements, the most important was the closeness with Goenawan.

If it is possible to imagine a *pesantren* or Muslim boarding school in a secular context, then *Tempo* under Goenawan Mohamad resembled a *pesantren*.[4] A *pesantren* is a "24-hour learning

---

[3]   Interview with Bambang Harymurti, July 2, 1999.

[4]   In his classic description of a *pesantren*, Clifford Geertz writes: "A *pondok* [or *pesantren*] consists of a teacher-leader, commonly a pilgrim (*haji*), who is called a *kyai*, and a group of male pupils, anywhere from three or four to a thousand,

Goenawan Mohamad [left] and Syu'bah Asa in *Tempo*'s office
on Jl. Senen Raya, 1973 [*Tempo*/Budiman S. Hartoyo]

environment."[5] The *santri*, or students, are like brothers. They
live together, eat together, study together. They will drink coffee
out of the same glass, take drags off the same cigarette, and share
their worldly possessions.

Young men join a *pesantren* because of the reputation of the
kyai, or spiritual leader. A *kyai* is a scholar and teacher, one who is
concerned with interpreting and teaching the *Qur'an* to a
community of believers. He is knowledgeable and charismatic,
and people are drawn to him. A *kyai* is not "holy" in the sense that
a priest is holy; indeed both he and the community he serves exist
outside of any formal religious organization. One does not need
permission or special training to become a *kyai*; one only needs a

---

called *santris*. Traditionally, and still to an extent today, the *santris* live at the *pondok*
in cloister-like dormitories, cook their own food, and wash their own clothes…The
kyai may hold…classes anywhere from one to five hours a day, but there is no
required attendance by anyone. (Advanced students may lead the others if the
kyai is not present.) One goes if he wishes to, stays away if he does not want to
attend.…People go at their own speed, learning as much or as little as seems
necessary to them." Clifford Geertz, *The Religion of Java* (Illinois: The Free Press
of Glencoe, 1960), pp. 177-178.

[5]   I am grateful for the insights of Ahmad Fuadi, a *Tempo* reporter who attended the
modernist *pesantren* Gontor between 1988 and 1992.

reputation among a community of believers. A *kyai*'s obligations are to the teachings of God and to the social organization he serves. Although a *kyai* is located firmly within a physical community, his influence usually spreads far beyond the borders of that particular place. The *kyai* may be the leader, but he is "not separate…he touches everybody." People want to be close to the *kyai*, and to touch him as well.

Since its very early days, *Tempo* has been a magnet for young writers. Some came because they wanted to learn to be journalists. And others came because they wanted to work with Goenawan.[6] In the old days, nearly all of these writers were men, and most of them were unmarried. Many of them came close to "living" at *Tempo*, sharing meals together, bathing in the washroom, sleeping in the *musholla*. "In the beginning, even during the Muslim holidays, the most important holiday, we were working, because almost all of us at the time were bachelors. So it was really our house. We slept there," said Salim Said, who joined *Tempo* in 1971.[7] When Susanto Pudjomartono, long-time managing editor of *Tempo*'s National section, left the magazine in 1991 to become chief editor of the English-language newspaper *The Jakarta Post*, he commented that since joining the magazine in 1977 he had probably stayed all night at the office about seven hundred times.[8]

Since he was a young man, Goenawan Mohamad has had the kind of charisma that draws people to him. A "star" at a very young age, he had already developed a reputation as a poet and intellectual by the time he reached his early twenties. Sociologist Arief

---

6   According to Muslim scholar Ulil Abshar-Abdalla, the Utan Kayu community, which was established by Goenawan Mohamad after the banning of *Tempo*, is also just like a *pesantren*. Ulil said that as a young man, he read Goenawan's poetry and "wanted to come to this place [Utan Kayu] and to know him." According to Ulil, Goenawan always wanted to create a place like Utan Kayu, in which literature and intellectual life could be mixed with politics and journalism. Interview, June 30, 1999.

7   Interview with Salim Said, April 1, 1998.

8   "Surat dari Redaksi," *Tempo*, August 24, 1991.

Budiman, who is one of Goenawan's oldest friends, first met him in 1961. "Goenawan was in his second year when I started at the University of Indonesia," he said. "He was studying to begin his career as a poet. His essays were published in *Sastra* [the literary magazine edited by H. B. Jassin]. He became the star of the young artists at the time."[9]

Goenawan Mohamad was born in 1941 in Batang, a village on the north coast of Central Java, where he grew up as the youngest of eight children. Batang is only a few kilometers from Pekalongan, a small town on the Arab, Indian, and Chinese trading routes that has long been renowned for the innovative designs of its jewel-colored batiks. Goenawan's mother was from one of the wealthiest families in Batang, and he remembers his grandmother's house as being cool and dark and full of antiques. His father was from East Java, a mysterious figure about whom Goenawan knows very little. In reconstructing his father's life, Goenawan remembers that he spoke fine Javanese, and must have been an educated man. He knows that his father was arrested in the Communist rebellion of 1926, and exiled to the notorious Dutch prison of Boven Digoel in West Papua. After he was freed he ended up in Batang, where he started a business with capital that came, oddly enough, from an American.

Goenawan assumes that his father must have continued his political activity when he returned to Batang, because in 1946 he was arrested by the Dutch. Three or four days later he was executed. Goenawan was five years old at the time:

> Before my father was killed, my mother told me that he knew he was going to die. He had a dream. He was kind of mystic too, then. He told my mother, 'I had a dream. I was eating three pieces of jackfruit, very sweet, and I think I'm going to die. And you had better prepare. And keep some of your gold

---

[9]   Interview with Arief Budiman, December 4, 1999.

buried to make it possible for the children to go to school.'
That was always the obsession. The children should go to school.
And then, soon, he was killed with three bullets in his head.
And I didn't see the body. I was prevented from seeing it.[10]

Although Goenawan grew up without a father, his father's memory has had profound effects on him. Never possessing anything tangible of his father other than an old photo, a 1939 Webster's dictionary (both of which he has since lost), and his *keris*, he still meets his father in his dreams. One of the most powerful of these dreams occurred in 1994, on the eve of the banning of *Tempo*.

Perhaps, like his father, Goenawan is intensely Javanese. A soft-spoken man, he exudes a powerful force. His slim athletic build reflects the same iron discipline that drives his writing. Somewhat shy, he is most comfortable with close friends and associates. No one feels neutral about Goenawan Mohamad. People are drawn to him, and even former colleagues and friends with whom he has had a falling out continue to describe him with a kind of awe. During the course of an interview, these former friends will ask, "what does Goenawan say about me now?"

When Goenawan enters a discussion or joins a meeting, the atmosphere in the room changes. People defer to what he says, and look to him for approval when they speak. Goenawan doesn't usually say much, but what he does say will frequently shift the course of the conversation in a new direction. Goenawan Mohamad fills up a room.

Young journalists are drawn to Goenawan like moths to light, and a word of praise from him warms the hearts of even the most experienced writers. His gifts, like his praise, are talismans. A hat brought back from a trip to America becomes a prized possession. A belt left behind while visiting a *Tempo* writer overseas becomes a treasure, a sign of friendship and time spent together. People,

---

[10]   Interview with Goenawan Mohamad, April 17, 1998.

especially women, want to do things for Goenawan. Although Goenawan is friendly and accessible, there is nonetheless a reserve about him. When he is displeased with someone, that person knows it. As warm as it is within the circle of his smile, it can be equally chilly outside.

To *Tempo* journalists, Goenawan is "GM", or "Mas Goen". *Mas* means older brother, and its usage is particularly Javanese. It is respectful, but it also signals a degree of closeness. It is obvious to the most casual of visitors that the model of journalism that is practiced at *Tempo* today is one that originated with Goenawan Mohamad.

Many people have described *Tempo* as a kind of school for journalists. As Bambang Bujono, who joined *Tempo* in 1978, said, "*Tempo* is my *alma mater*....We had what we called in-house training in *Tempo*. We learned how to interview, how to report, and how to write an article. Mr. Goenawan is our *guru*. He critiqued every story, so we learned."[11]

The in-house training that Bambang Bujono and others have described is one of the most significant aspects of what makes a *Tempo* journalist. Beginning in the mid-1970s, training was developed for both reporters and writers. Senior editor Leila Chudori says that for many years the training was led by Goenawan himself. "The training lasted about three months, and met once a week," she explained. "Goenawan ran it. The participants had assignments, and then critiqued their own stories as well as others'." Leila recalled that Goenawan took such an interest in the development of each writer that it "drove some people nuts." In the old days, she said, "Goenawan was always looking over our shoulders, sometimes even working on our leads. His concern for each writer was part of the experience of being a *Tempo* journalist. As everyone knew, "Goenawan's heart and soul were with *Tempo*."[12]

---

[11]   Interview with Bambang Bujono, February 23, 1998.
[12]   Interview with Leila Chudori, July 8, 1999.

Tempo nearly always trains groups of reporters together. The group of ten prospective reporters that I trained with in January 2000 was culled from eight hundred applicants.[13] The application process took about three months, and included five tests: a general "administrative" test in which candidates had to write about their university experience and backgrounds, a psychological test, an interview, a research presentation, and a health test. The psychological test is a standard one, and one of its most important objectives is to determine which of the candidates will be good "team players". About two hundred people made the first cut and took the psychological test, and about thirty people made it to the final stage of the seminar and presentation. One unfortunate applicant made it through the entire process and then failed the health test.

The testing process has been the same for many years. In fact the competition for placement may have been even sharper in the 1980s, when *Tempo* had few real competitors in magazine journalism. Gabriel Sugrahetty, who joined *Tempo* in 1988, said that when she applied to *Tempo* there were several thousand applicants. One hundred and fifty candidates were invited to take the psychological test, and from those fifteen were chosen to participate in the research and writing competition. She was one of the seven who were ultimately hired, and the only woman among them.[14]

Tempo prefers to hire very young people right out of school as reporters, and in fact the ideal candidate will have had no experience in journalism whatsoever. In some ways this is not surprising, as Indonesian universities have traditionally not offered degrees in journalism. In the Indonesian model, young people who wish to become journalists generally pursue courses of university study other than journalism. If they are lucky, they then

---

[13] The following discussion of training at *Tempo* is based on my field notes. The training for new reporters began on Friday, January 14, 2000, and ended two weeks later on Saturday, January 29.

[14] Conversation with Gabriel Sugrahetty, August 2, 1999.

learn the basics of reporting and writing either at exemplary newspapers and magazines such as *Kompas* and *Tempo*, or at post-graduate institutes such as the Dr. Soetomo Press Institute. The educational backgrounds of Indonesian journalists are thus astonishingly rich and diverse. Prior to joining *Tempo*, for example, chief editor Bambang Harymurti studied engineering, assistant chief editor Toriq Hadad studied agriculture, and executive editor Malela Mahargasarie studied art and design.

One of *Tempo*'s objectives is to ensure that the young recruits will have had no bad history with "envelope" journalism (the acceptance of bribes that is still the scourge of the Indonesian press), and that *Tempo* will be able to train them into the "culture of *Tempo*." A 1999 notice advertising openings for reporters stated a "maximal" age of thirty-two years. *Tempo* never recruits – or raids – established writers from other publications. It is a point of pride at *Tempo* that the magazine would rather train its own.

As a result of *Tempo*'s hiring practices, people's ages are closely related to their positions and status – with very young people working as reporters, and their elders functioning as writers, editors, and *defacto* instructors. This stratification by age adds to the school-like atmosphere. Bambang Harymurti explained that "*Tempo*, like many other 'modern' organizations born under the New Order era, is following the military management style in its 'career planning system.'"[15] "In earlier times," he added, "many bright people in Indonesia thought very highly of the military's personnel management system."[16]

During the first day of training in January, 2000, Goenawan said

---

[15] Email correspondence, August 13, 1999.

[16] Bambang's point is supported by Harold Crouch's study of the army and politics in Indonesia. The Indonesian military was admired for its modern, rational system of recruitment, training, and promotion, especially after the opening of the Indonesian Armed Forces Academy at Magelang, Central Java in 1957. Harold Crouch, *The Army and Politics in Indonesia*, revised edition (Ithaca: Cornell University Press, 1993), p. 305-6.

how happy he was to see the variation in backgrounds among the young reporters, and then explicitly compared *Tempo*'s meritocracy and system of recruitment with that of the military. "Since the beginning," he said, "*Tempo* has been proud of its diversity. Maybe it wasn't intentional at first. But later, when I met with a former Siliwangi Regional Military commander, I compared the performance of Siliwangi [in West Java] with that of Diponegoro [in Central Java], and asked him why Siliwangi was better. He said that it was because Siliwangi never relied only on Sundanese commanders. The first Siliwangi commander was Batak, than Menadonese, another was Javanese, and then again Sundanese. In Diponegoro, the majority were Javanese, finally Soeharto. This variation strengthened the command, not because of the variation itself, but rather because the criteria for promotion was based on performance instead of special connections."

The training for new reporters that I attended lasted for two weeks, including Saturdays. It was organized in two-hour blocks running from 10 AM to 6 PM, with a mid-day break for rest and prayers. Because delays and distractions are inevitable in a news organization, the day's schedule usually ran overtime. Moreover, the new reporters were encouraged to stay around the office until late at night, just like everyone else. During the first Friday night of training, the reporters were at *Tempo* until well after midnight, working on an assignment that their leader Setiyardi (who was himself still a reporter) had handed out earlier. As the week went on, each of the senior editors and managing editors was responsible for teaching a session, and most of the instructors gave out assignments. Goenawan Mohamad delayed an overseas trip in order to meet with the new reporters and talk about the philosophy of *Tempo*. Lunch and dinner were served every day, and the class was expected to eat together.

There were eight men and two women in this group of candidate reporters. Five members of the class (including the two women) were to become regular *Tempo* reporters, four would be assigned to the website *Tempo Interaktif*, and one would work with *Tempo*'s research department. All were in their mid-twenties, only one was married. There were plenty of jokes about how if you had a *pacar* or "special friend" you might as well forget about him or her right now. The group reflected the ethnic and regional diversity admired by Goenawan: one of the new reporters was from Flores, one was from Ambon, one was from West Sumatra. The rest were from Jakarta or Java. Most went to the prestigious University of Indonesia or University of Gadjah Mada, with two having graduated from the Catholic University of Atma Jaya in Yogyakarta. None of the class had studied journalism, and fewer than one-half had any prior journalistic experience at all.

In some ways *Tempo* modeled its orientation for new reporters on *Ospek*, the "boot camp" initiation experience inherited from the Dutch that is still practiced at Indonesian universities today. During the opening ceremony, which was held outdoors in the *Tempo* parking lot, the new reporters were each given name tags, which they were told to wear at all times. (Most stopped wearing them after the first day.) Each reporter was also given a *Tempo* reporting notebook and told to get the autograph of everyone who worked at the magazine. Their assignment was to interview each person in the company from the directors to the office boys, finding out about what it is that they do, whether or not they are married, and how many children they have. The group was expected to work together, eat together, and – for several nights – even to sleep together at Wisma Tempo Sirnagalih, *Tempo*'s "villa" in the nearby mountain town of Puncak. There were lots of pranks, with the apparent goal of building a sense of community among the group.

During the first week of training the program was interrupted by a special event introducing the new reporters to the rest of the *Tempo* "family" at Wisma Tempo Sirnagalih. The ostensible reason for the gathering was the Halal Bihalal ceremony that occurs during Lebaran, a period of celebration the marks the end of the holy month of Ramadhan. The company paid for four air-conditioned buses, which left the office at 9 AM. The program included speeches from the senior editors, a prayer led by one of the new reporters, and the Halal Bihalal ceremony of greeting one another and asking for forgiveness. After an elaborate lunch of spit-grilled goat and other local foods served from stands set up around a large common room, the reporters were asked to introduce themselves to the rest of the group. Questions from the current *Tempo* journalists focused primarily on the marital status of the new women employees. Later there was a *dangdut* band, with singing and dancing.

At about mid-afternoon, the new reporters were lined up for a group portrait behind a rope at the edge of the pool. Bambang Harymurti gave each reporter an ear of steamed corn, with instructions to hold it high. Then somebody pulled on the rope, and like a row of dominos the unsuspecting reporters all tumbled backwards into the cloudy green water. The quiet afternoon exploded into wet chaos, as the now-dripping reporters and office boys charged after bosses Bambang Harymurti and Toriq Hadad. Soon nearly everyone else had been thrown into the pool as well. I was thrown in too – after a polite pause to make sure I had removed my watch and hand phone. The day ended with a wet ride home in the sub-zero temperatures of the air-conditioned bus. Being *dicemplungin* or "thrown in" is a *Tempo* tradition of long-standing, and for days afterwards I was greeted with shy smiles and declarations that I had now become a "real" *Tempo* journalist.

Once training began in earnest, many of the speakers emphasized the democratic quality of *Tempo*, pointing out that even though the reporters were the newest recruits, their views were just as important as those of anyone else. The reporters addressed each speaker as *Mas* and *Mbak*, or "brother" and "sister", and many of the speakers referred to the group as *teman-teman*, or "friends". Yet despite the friendliness, there was a formal quality to the training. Reporters were asked to sign the roll during each session, just as they would in an Indonesian university course, and although occasionally someone would walk in late, there was considerable pressure to be on time. Once, during a late evening session in which no one had yet had dinner, Toriq Hadad noticed a reporter nodding off, and asked "are you sick?" It was assumed that all participants would pay strict attention to what was going on.

The content of the training for the new reporters resembled a crash undergraduate course in the basics of journalism. There were practical sessions on story ideas, and discussions of *Tempo*'s criteria for story appropriateness. Reporters learned to develop sources, and how to write "reportage", or descriptive reports. Toriq Hadad explained interview techniques, and other managing editors discussed investigative reporting and accuracy. There were sessions on *Tempo*'s style book and spelling, as well as more theoretical discussions of *Tempo*'s history, philosophy, and code of ethics.

New reporters were also introduced to the various divisions of *Tempo*'s business organization. By the end of the week participants had been deluged with flow charts that illustrated everything from the magazine's overall system of organization and management to the way in which stories are assigned and how story ideas move through various levels of reporting, writing, and editing. They learned about the financial structure of the organization and the relationship between the divisions of the library and *Tempo*'s research wing PDAT. In a development that can perhaps be traced to the influence of Bambang Harymurti's years as Washington bureau chief, the new reporters also watched the American films *All the Presidents' Men* and *Absence of Malice*, and discussed some of the more idealistic aspects of what it means to be a journalist.

What do the new reporters learn about being a *Tempo* journalist? They learn that they will be held to a higher standard than virtually any of their peers in the Indonesian media. *Tempo* reporters are expected to get a variety of views and seek out material from many sources. As Goenawan Mohamad told the group of new reporters, "A *Tempo* journalist's job is to search for truth. We can't assume that we're right. Looking for truth is our inheritance. Always be skeptical."

"In a diverse society such as Indonesia," he added, "anger comes when there is too little information, opinion, debate, and data. We don't just occupy one room."

Toriq Hadad emphasized that it is a matter of pride that covering press conferences isn't good enough for *Tempo* reporters. Other journalists might be proud if they attend a press conference and their question gets published, he said. "Hey, look at this, there's my question!" he joked, waving an imaginary newspaper. But not *Tempo* journalists. "You don't want to see your question in the paper," he admonished.

"If you don't have ideas you should pick a different job," said senior editor Yusril Djalinus. Yusril has been with *Tempo* since its founding, and it was he who designed the position of "coordinator of reporters" to organize and manage the reporters in the Jakarta bureau. Magazines are different from daily journalism, he said. "We must look for an angle that the newspapers don't see. Even if you go to a press conference you have to think about it in a different way."

At *Tempo*, the reporter's job is to collect data. Each story's angle has already been decided upon by the writer who drew up the assignment and who will write the story. A reporter's job is to "go to the field," interview the sources, and give the resulting transcript along with background "reportage" to the writer. Many of the speakers in the training session emphasized the importance of the reporter's job in gathering background material. As Jakarta bureau chief Ahmad Taufik said, "This is *Tempo*'s model and others don't have it." Reporters are rotated from department to department so that they will master each of the sections of the magazine.

The *Tempo* writer "borrows the eyes" (*pinjam mata*) of the reporter. Managing editor Gabriel Sugrahetty told the new class of reporters that it was their job to "describe the situation" for the writer. Is there fear? Anger? She gave an example of a report describing the conditions in a hospital during the monetary crisis. The water wasn't running and the trash hadn't been collected. This is the kind of reportage that is important, she said. "It's better to include too much description than not enough, but don't include boring details. Don't be stingy with details."

In another session on writing reportage, economy and business editor Dwi Setyo Irawanto, or Siba, asked the group to complete an exercise in which each participant had to describe one of the previous speakers. Several chose to write about Bambang Harymurti. One described "BHM" as wearing blue pants and a white shirt. "Is this interesting?" demanded Siba. "Is this unusual? BHM's clothes would be interesting if he were wearing a polka-dot shirt and clown nose. But blue pants and a white shirt are not interesting."

In addition to writing reportage, the reporters will also be responsible for interviewing, which Toriq Hadad described as the most important thing they do. "If the process of interviewing isn't complete, then the story isn't complete," he said. "It shames *Tempo* if journalists aren't prepared." Toriq instructed the reporters to do research, read magazines and clippings in the library. "A portion of your wages is to buy *Kompas* [newspaper]," Toriq said, "but it's a place for reference, not for story ideas. Look for a different angle. Call the source. What hasn't been written? Read the paper."

Interrupting a source can be difficult in a culture in which young people have been trained to be polite to their elders, and Toriq pointed approvingly to a televised interview aired some months earlier in which Bambang Harymurti had interviewed – and several times interrupted – the loquacious Indonesian President B. J. Habibie. Toriq also described how generals will sometimes invite senior editors to come for an "interview" and then read a prepared statement. If this happens "jump in," he said. "Ask questions. Try not to let them do this. Remember that the information is not to please us, but rather to please the reader. Enter the interview looking for information for the public, not for yourself."

Something that the young reporters heard over and over again was *Tempo*'s policy against *amplop*, or envelopes containing bribes. As Toriq explained, "there are two *Tempo* rules that are never broken: stories that are lies (*berita bohong*), and envelope stories (*berita amplop*). *Tempo* has a war against envelopes. It is a kind of ideology. Our regulations are very harsh. We know that 50% of Indonesian journalists still receive envelopes. If you're in a group and can't refuse an envelope, bring it back to the office and let us return it. Or return it to an official at one level above the official who gave it to you." Yusril Djalinus also warned the young reporters that there would be no second chance for anyone who accepted a bribe. "Since the very beginning we were against envelopes," he said. "We were considered arrogant as a result. We were independent, we used a different language, we had a different mentality."[17]

As Yusril's words suggest, much of *Tempo*'s training focused on what distinguishes the magazine from other Indonesian media. "We write in a very different way from a daily," he said. "We don't do hard news; there is no inverted pyramid here. Sometimes the introduction is the most interesting part. We want writing that's good: good reporting, good writing, that's the ideal. Even though you're not yet writers, you must begin now."

One of the most interesting aspects of training for new journalists at *Tempo* is something that is not mentioned at all: objectivity. *Tempo* has never really tried to be "objective" in the

---

[17] *Tempo* journalists are allowed to accept hotel accommodation and plane tickets if it is to attend a seminar. Wicaksono, who in 1999 was responsible for "Information Technology" and "Monitor" (*Tempo*'s popular survey article) used the example of a Microsoft conference in Seattle, in which the company invited journalists from around the world. Microsoft paid for airfare and hotel accommodation. *Tempo*'s rules allow for this kind of subsidy, along with acceptance of souvenirs worth less than Rp. 100,000 (about $12) like pens, tee-shirts, and baseball caps.

Western sense of separating facts from values. Although *Tempo* journalists are instructed to "cover both sides," and the magazine generally adheres to what sociologist Gaye Tuchman has called the "strategic ritual" of objectivity, there is nonetheless a tone in *Tempo* that is strikingly different from American news magazines.[18] The *Tempo* writer is present in the story, and he or she frequently has a distinctive voice and point of view. As Goenawan Mohamad told the young reporters, "In the United States facts are sacred, opinion is in the background only. In the U.S., for example in the *New York Times*, it is bad to insert opinion. In France it is different. In Indonesia there are differences too. The new *Tempo* has more opinion. Freedom is wider but the pressures are different."

For much of *Tempo*'s history, the pressures to which Goenawan referred were related to the political context of the New Order. The injustice of a political system in which there were virtually no limits to the government's authority led *Tempo* writers to lend subtle support to ordinary people in their struggle against the overwhelming power of the state. As Bernard Lewis has argued, in classic Islamic political thought, rulers and subjects alike are bound by certain obligations towards one another. In the case of the ruled, these obligations include obedience to those in authority. Yet the authority of rulers is not unlimited. If those in authority violate the law, or if their rule is "illegitimate or unjust", they may forfeit their claim to obedience.[19] This concept of justice, and its relationship to the legitimacy of those in authority, was central not only to *Tempo* journalists' understanding of their role in society, but also to the way in which the magazine covered the news. As

---

[18]   Tuchman defines this strategic ritual as presenting conflicting possibilities, using quotations strategically, supporting assertions with verifiable evidence, and structuring information in an appropriate sequence. Gaye Tuchman, "Objectivity as Strategic Ritual: An Examination of Newsmen's Notions of Objectivity", *American Journal of Sociology* 77 (January 1972): 660-679.

[19]   Bernard Lewis, *The Political Language of Islam* (Chicago and London: The University of Chicago Press, 1988) pp. 91-92.

Goenawan Mohamad once said, "it is very difficult in Indonesia if you don't speak about justice. Indonesian history is the history of searching for justice, more than searching for freedom."[20]

If the search for justice can be seen as *Tempo*'s "paraideology", in practical terms this meant that for *Tempo* journalists, being "balanced" in a system that was inherently unbalanced was not enough.[21] "There was one incident I remember from early on," Goenawan said, "it was when *Tempo* was in Senen. The law editor reported a story, something very evenhanded. But then the side of the weak was overshadowed, simply because he was weak. And I discovered that being even was not enough. And we had a debate about it, whether we should be so impartial, so even, when the victims are very weak. And we changed the story. We killed that story. And so I think from then on we decided that being even was not enough. Because before the philosophy had been to cover both sides. And we discovered it was not so easy."[22]

As executive editor, Toriq Hadad told the group of new reporters in January 2000, "the mission of *Tempo* is justice." Yet when Goenawan Mohamad and his friends established the magazine nearly thirty years earlier, it was not justice that was in the foreground. It was rather the quest for freedom.

[20] Interview with Goenawan Mohamad, June 20, 2000.
[21] Sociologist Herbert Gans has described progressive reform as the "paraideology" of American journalism. In Indonesia, the search for justice has different cultural roots, but serves a similar purpose. For a discussion of the "enduring values" of American journalism, see Herbert Gans, *Deciding What's News: A Study of CBS Evening News, NBC Nightly News, Newsweek and Time* (New York: Pantheon, 1979).
[22] Interview with Goenawan Mohamad, June 20, 2000.

the poet

Although *Tempo* magazine was founded in 1971, its roots extend deep into Indonesian intellectual and cultural life. As students, writers, and activists at the University of Indonesia in the early 1960s, Goenawan Mohamad and his friends rocketed to prominence at a very young age. Clustered first around H.B. Jassin's influential literary journal *Sastra* and then the newspaper *Harian Kami*, the founders of *Tempo* were leaders in the struggle against Communism and the tyranny of politics over art.

As the apparent winners in the cultural battles of the 1960s, Goenawan and his friends were hopeful that the "New Order" led by General Soeharto would bring about true freedom of expression. Yet by the time that *Tempo* was established in 1971, there were already signs that a new orthodoxy was emerging, one that would prove to be as insidious and difficult to stamp out as the left-wing hegemony it had replaced. *Tempo*, in fact, would be conceived in the aftermath of a power struggle within the PWI, or Indonesian Journalists' Association. The dispute would be papered over, but the fracture would remain. A child of the New Order, *Tempo* was born into a house that was dangerously divided.

When Goenawan Mohamad arrived in Jakarta in 1960 at the age of nineteen, he was already a published writer. His first piece, an essay on the poems of Emily Dickinson, had appeared in the journal *Sastra*, which was edited by H.B. Jassin, the "Pope" of Indonesian literature. Goenawan had translated Emily Dickinson's poems while still a high school student in Pekalongan, a ten-kilometer bike ride from his home in Batang. It was a public high school, and he was the first child from his village school to go there. "The rest didn't make it," he said. "Not because they were not as bright, some were much better than me. But because they didn't have the money. They had to stay with their families."[1]

Goenawan always wanted to be a writer. Once he was accepted into the University of Indonesia, he had to choose between studying French literature and psychology. "I was accepted into both," he said, "but I opted to choose psychology. Because I read somewhere in Jassin's book that to be a good writer you have to know a lot about philosophy and psychology and sociology, and the only department which linked all these three together was the department of psychology. The French department was just literature."[2] Because the psychology department had once been attached to the medical faculty, students were required to take statistics, as well as courses in human anatomy. "They treated you like a genius," Goenawan laughed.

As his influence over Goenawan's choice of a course of study suggests, Hans Bague Jassin shaped an entire generation of Indonesian writers. A literary historian, editor, and lecturer in literature at the University of Indonesia since 1953, Jassin was advisor and friend to young poets and writers, as well as the custodian of their letters and work.[3] Together with Dutch literary scholar Andries Teeuw, Jassin was responsible for establishing the dominant model of Indonesian literary criticism during the 1950s

---

[1]   Interview with Goenawan Mohamad, April 17, 1998.

[2]   Interview with Goenawan Mohamad, July 12, 1999. Goenawan also relates this incident in "Jassin", *Tempo*, August 8, 1987.

[3]   For an overview of Jassin's contribution to Indonesian letters, see David Hill, "Mochtar Lubis: Author, Editor, Political Actor", (Ph.D. thesis, Australian National University, 1988), pp. 1-10.

Arief Budiman, Jakarta, 1971 [*Tempo*/Lukman Setiawan}

and 60s.[4] David Hill characterized the Jassin-Teeuw tradition as one which sees literature as "a discrete category of writing which fulfills certain aesthetic standards in a way which can be evaluated objectively regardless of socio-political considerations. Literature may have political themes but is not, in itself, necessarily political."[5] This model differed sharply from the Marxist concept of "people's art" in which political goals were paramount.

Jassin's office was in the same building as the psychology department, one floor up. "Because I was published already," Goenawan said, "I was drawn naturally to Jassin's circle. But I was not very self confident. I didn't dare to introduce myself to him although I was published in his magazine." It would be a full year before the two actually met. The person who introduced Goenawan to Jassin was Soe Hok Djin (later known as Arief Budiman), a young Indonesian of Chinese descent who would become Goenawan's best friend.

---

[4] According to literary critic Keith Foulcher, the Teeuw-Jassin collaboration had the effect of creating what became the hegemonic view of "universal humanism" as the appropriate creative and critical aim of literature. Keith Foulcher, *Social Commitment in Literature and the Arts: The Indonesian 'Institute of People's Culture' 1950-1965* (Monash University: Centre of Southeast Asian Studies, 1986), pp. 2-3.

[5] David Hill, "Mochtar Lubis: Author, Editor, Political Actor", pp. 3-4.

Goenawan met Arief Budiman during initiation for new students. There was a bonfire, and new students had to make a speech. "Of course it should be for fun, everybody was joking," Goenawan said. "But Arief didn't take it lightly. He was speaking about Jean-Paul Sartre. And I was so embarrassed! Oh my God, what's this guy doing? He's that kind of a guy."

"After we met we became friends immediately because we had a lot of similarities," Goenawan added.

Goenawan made an equally strong impression on Arief Budiman. He recalled, "Goenawan was my senior when I started my study in psychology, so he was in his second year at that time. There was an initiation for new students. He got interested in me, so he was trying to torture me. He knew that I had already written short stories since I was in high school. Goenawan was writing poetry at the time, so he called me and we had a discussion on literature and many other things."[6]

"Goenawan was not a Jakarta person," Arief added. "He was kind of shy. He came as a person from a region, and tried to adjust himself. But I was born in Jakarta. Goenawan was very intelligent, he read many things. He was very innocent. We used to go to Jassin's, and we became very good friends."

Goenawan recalled that once he overcame his initial feeling of intimidation, Jassin turned out to be very nice. "So I came there very regularly," he said, "and became attached to the group. We met every week in *Sastra*'s office."

As a student at the University of Indonesia in the early 1960s, Goenawan was part of an explosion in tertiary education, a massive wave of young Indonesians who, as the beneficiaries of an improved educational system after Indonesia's independence, would for the first time have access to higher education.[7] Although it was very

---

6   Interview with Arief Budiman, December 4, 1999.
7   See Burhan D. Magenda, "Gerakan Mahasiswa dan Hubungannya dengan Sistem Politik: Suatu Tinjauan", in *Seri Prisma I: Analisa Kekuatan Politik Di Indonesia* (Jakarta: Lembaga Penelitian, Pendidikan dan Penerangan Ekonomi dan Social, 1985), esp. pp. 136-7.

difficult to get admitted to the University of Indonesia, if a young person was bright enough to be accepted, tuition was free. It was paying for room and board that was the barrier for many students, especially those from outside Jakarta. The life that Goenawan and his friends recall from that time had a vagabond-like quality, as they moved from house to house in search of books, conversation, and maybe even a place to eat and sleep.

One place where Goenawan sometimes stayed was the home of Wiratmo Soekito, an older friend who was the head of public affairs programming at Radio Republik Indonesia. Wiratmo was a well-known writer and intellectual who was associated with the anti-Communist Congress for Cultural Freedom.[8] According to Arief Budiman, Wiratmo was very "rightist" and conservative. "He was the richest," Arief said. "He had a collection of books. He was single. His house was just like a bachelor house. 80% was filled with books. Salim Said [who would later join *Tempo*] also joined this community. It's a friendly community especially for people who come from the regions."[9]

Wiratmo Soekito let his younger friends use his library, and even sleep in his small pavilion. "He was very generous," Goenawan said. "I slept in his place. It was a small room, a lot of books. The room was attached to a kindergarten. Sometimes I slept in the kindergarten. And the teacher in the morning would wake me up, and these young beautiful kindergarten schoolchildren came in finding me sleeping. I never told my family about it. Then one day, a friend who likes to romanticize this life wrote a small piece in a magazine about me sleeping on a ping-pong table, and my family read it and they were really unhappy."[10]

Although Goenawan Mohamad came from a relatively well-

8   Keith Foulcher, *Social Commitment in Literature and the Arts*, p. 115. See also "Wiratmo Soekito", *Apa & Siapa*, http://www.pdat.co.id/ads/html/W/ads,20030620-57,W.html
9   Interview with Arief Budiman, December 4, 1999.
10   Interview with Goenawan Mohamad, July 12, 1999.

off family in Batang, his friends remember him as being poor. Nono Makarim, a friend of Goenawan's who would become the editor of *Harian Kami* newspaper said, "His body ached, I could see him. We lived very close to each other, and when I see him walking down the street, ah, he must not have eaten for a day or two." Would Goenawan ever acknowledge this? "Oh no! He never said he was hungry. Goenawan, never. He's a very proud person."[11]

Today Goenawan dismisses these memories. "Yes, then I was poor but then I would just go back to my sister's house and have good food. And I could, I was always sure that I had something to fall back on," he said.

"In Indonesia nobody gets really hungry because suddenly you have friends and they will help you," he added. "It's true, once I was very hungry, and I was broke. And several houses from the office was a friend's house, and I came there. 'Are you hungry?' And he knew it. And then he brought food. So I was never terrified by the possibilities of starvation or being really broke."[12]

Another place where Goenawan sometimes stayed was student housing owned by the Indonesian Socialist Party, or PSI. "It was sort of an informal house," Arief Budiman explained. "Goenawan comes from a poor family. He doesn't have enough money to rent a good apartment. So he lived as a kind of student 'hobo.' His friends were very limited. He doesn't aggressively make friends. Goenawan lived from place to place. Basically his house, his belongings were in that house with the PSI students. He lived with them."

The PSI was widely considered to be a party of "salon socialists" or "liberals" living in the wealthy Jakarta suburb of Menteng. Closely resembling the European democratic-socialist parties that had influenced PSI founder Sutan Sjahir, the PSI was notable for its "concern for individual freedom…openness to world intellectual currents, and…rejection of obscurantism,

---

[11]   Interview with Nono Makarim, June 23, 2000.
[12]   Interview with Goenawan Mohamad, July 28, 1999.

chauvinism, and the 'personality cult'."[13] In 1960, President
Soekarno banned the PSI, along with the Islamic party Masyumi,
as a result of its role in the PRRI/Permesta rebellions of 1958.
Harold Crouch asserts that many Javanese army officers disliked
the PSI, viewing them as "westernized intellectuals [with a]
'superiority complex'."[14] Aristides Katoppo, who was friends with
Arief Budiman's brother Soe Hok Gie, recalled PSI sympathizers
tended to be "anti-Communist, pro-West, pro-democracy, and
in some ways even pro-American, or at least the stereotyping
was there."[15]

Although Goenawan sometimes stayed in PSI student
housing, he was "never PSI". According to Arief Budiman, "there
was no formal membership, but it was not necessary. Yes,
informally we belonged to that group, but also at the same time
we belonged to other groups. Basically Goenawan associated with
the PSI because they had rooms. We didn't want to join the
radical Communist group, and PSI seemed to be the best fit at
that time."[16]

In my four years of doing research on the history of *Tempo*, I
never found one Indonesian intellectual who would admit to
"being PSI", although nearly everyone I interviewed had in one
way or another been influenced by the banned party's ideas. Perhaps
the most direct explanation of this apparent contradiction came
from former-KAMI leader Marsillam Simanjuntak. State Secretary
in the administration of President Abdurrahman Wahid, Marsillam
is a forthright person who never minces words. "Foreign scholars
are looking at the locus of the ideas and they find it in PSI," he
said, "but we [Indonesians] say 'I am not PSI' and it has a different
reason. Why? Because the old no-good PSI, they like to claim the

[13] Herbert Feith and Lance Castles, eds., *Indonesian Political Thinking 1945-1965*
(Ithaca: Cornell University Press, 1970), p. 227.
[14] Harold Crouch, *The Army and Politics in Indonesia* (Ithaca: Cornell University
Press, 1988), p. 179, fn. 1.
[15] Interview with Aristides Katoppo, June 21, 2003.
[16] Interview with Arief Budiman, December 4, 1999.

younger generation's success. So we, especially Goenawan, say, 'no I am not one of you.' But it's sometimes to no avail, this effort. Because you cannot disprove one way or the other not only your ideas, but that you were rubbing elbows with them."[17]

There was also a class aspect to PSI. They were generally from a wealthy elite, with Dutch educations, western orientation, and an interest in parliamentary democracy. Aristides Katoppo suggested that Goenawan wouldn't have fit in socially. "PSI people almost always had a car somewhere," he laughed, "and Goenawan didn't have a car." Aristides said that Goenawan was more comfortable with the "arty, Bohemian" crowd that was also part of Jakarta student life in the 1960s, and that while people from the PSI might temporarily join with that group, Goenawan was basically "moving in the other direction."[18]

Goenawan was not much of a student. According to Arief Budiman, Goenawan was preparing to be a poet, and this was more important to him than studying. "Goenawan went to Yogya," Arief said. "There was a competition; he won first place, I won third. He was glorified by everybody, and he forgot to come back. Everybody knows he is brilliant, but he doesn't have the discipline to complete his studies. He is enjoying himself, starting a new career. So he just forgot himself, and he preferred to stay in Yogya. He failed very badly. Especially statistics. Some of the professors admit that he's clever. But to pass a university degree you have to have discipline. And also he hates statistics."[19]

Goenawan himself recalled that his "disenchantment with school" began in 1963 during the Asian Games. "Everyone was busy and Jakarta was changing fast. So I left Jakarta and traveled with a group of painters from Yogya, from one small town to another...introducing people to modern art. So my schooling was very, very erratic."[20]

---

[17]   Interview with Marsillam Simanjuntak, July 18, 2002.
[18]   Interview with Aristides Katoppo, January 8, 2001.
[19]   Interview with Arief Budiman, December 4, 1999.

In a letter to H.B. Jassin, written from Yogyakarta when he was twenty-one years old, Goenawan accepted responsibility for his disappointing academic performance. He explained:

> On July 26, I left Jakarta. Destination: Surabaya, Yogya, Solo, Pasuran, and several other cities. The leave-taking from Jakarta was difficult, because I had to leave behind several obligations (examinations, etc.) But I couldn't stand it any longer. For some time my efforts to stick with it haven't been sincere. Perhaps it's because of laziness, or perhaps it's my own irresponsibility. Whatever the cause, the feeling that pushed me to go was powerful, and so I left. Fortunately I can share the expenses of the trip with Sanggarbambu, a group of painters with whom I feel a sense of shared vision.
>
> I spent one night in Solo. Perhaps in the future I can visit longer. Now that I'm free of Jakarta, rigid with upright buildings, I feel that Solo (if only temporarily) provides a degree of relaxation. Everything about Solo is attractive. Asian-Games fever has not yet reached here. Pekalongan is located in Central Java, but I never felt the Javanese-ness of that coastal city. In Solo I've found a world that slowly creeps from century to century, until it reaches the shape it has now.[21]

---

[20]   Interview with Goenawan Mohamad, July 12, 1999. Goenawan would later flesh out his criticism of the Asian Games into a more highly developed critique of the nationalism of Soekarno's Guided Democracy, which he characterized as an Orwellian "continuous frenzy." See Goenawan Mohamad, "Peristiwa 'Manikebu': Kesusastraan Indonesia dan Politik di Tahun 1960-an". in *Kesusastraan dan Kekuasaan* (Jakarta: Pustaka Firdaus, 1993), pp. 17.

[21]   Goenawan Mohamad to H.B. Jassin, August 3, 1962. Goenawan Mohamad file, H.B. Jassin documentary library. All translations unless otherwise noted are my own.

Although Goenawan did return to Jakarta for the new academic term, it was as a member of Arief Budiman's class. He had failed to be promoted.

In September 1963, both Goenawan and Arief became notorious as signers of the *Manifes Kebudayaan*, or the Cultural Manifesto. Derisively referred to by its enemies as "Manikebu", the manifesto grew out of an ideological conflict with the *Lembaga Kebudayaan Rakyat* (Lekra), or Institute of People's Culture.[22] Lekra was the cultural organization of the Indonesian Communist Party, or PKI. It was founded in 1950 as part of the "great debate" that had raged since before independence over the direction of Indonesian national culture.[23] Lekra called for the development of an "anti-imperialist" people's culture that would be an integral part of the struggle for social and economic change."[24] After President Soekarno proclaimed Guided Democracy in 1958, Lekra became even more insistent in its view that *Politik adalah Panglima*, or that "Politics is the Commander" – meaning that politics should guide all artistic activity and cultural endeavor.[25]

The signers of the *Manifes Kebudayaan* were mostly in their twenties. Sixteen were writers, three were painters, and one was a composer. Its three most famous signers were H.B. Jassin, Trisno Sumardjo (the translator of Shakespeare), and Radio Republik Indonesia's Wiratmo Soekito, who wrote the first draft.[26] Most of the signers were members of H.B. Jassin's informal group. The Manifesto was published in *Sastra*, and it stated:

> We, Indonesian artists and intellectuals, hereby present a cultural

---

[22] For an analysis of the conflict between Lekra and the Manikebuists, see A. Teeuw, *Modern Indonesian Literature*, pp. 27-39.

[23] For the historical context of the founding of Lekra, see Keith Foulcher, *Social Commitment in Literature and the Arts*, esp. pp. 13-26.

[24] Keith Foulcher, *Social Commitment in Literature and the Arts*, p. 19.

[25] See Keith Foulcher, *Social Commitment in Literature and the Arts*, chapter 5.

[26] See Goenawan Mohamad, "Peristiwa 'Manikebu'", in *Kesusastraan dan Kekuasaan*, pp. 11-54. This essay was first published in *Tempo*, May 21, 1988.

manifesto declaring our principles and ideals and our policy with respect to the National Culture. For us culture is the constant effort to bring the conditions of human existence to perfection. We do not regard any one sector of culture as superior to the others. All sectors act in correspondence to achieve this culture to the best of their ability. In this realization of a National Culture we strive to be truly and purely creative by way of our contribution to the struggle to defend and foster our dignity as Indonesians in the community of nations.[27]

Although the phrasing of the Cultural Manifesto does not sound overly combative today, within the ideological hothouse of Soekarno's Guided Democracy it was a clarion call for humanist art. Dutch literary scholar A. Teeuw highlighted the central point of the Cultural Manifesto when he wrote, "The emphasis on the diversity of culture and the accentuation of artistic creativity as a valuable end in itself, all political ideologies aside, constitute[d] unequivocal criticism of the monolithic cultural ideals of Lekra, where *politik* is asserted to be the *pemimpin*, or leader and everything else is made subservient to ultimate political goals."[28] The Manifesto was accompanied by a second article, entitled "*Sejarah Lahirnya Manifes Kebudayaan*" (The History of the Birth of the Cultural Manifesto) and written by Goenawan Mohamad. This essay focused on many of the themes that would occupy Goenawan for the next thirty-five years, including the absolute necessity of creative freedom.[29]

The Communists and Soekarnoist Nationalist parties reacted to the Cultural Manifesto as a shot across the bow. Goenawan writes that between September 1963 and May 1964, the opponents of the Cultural Manifesto launched a harsh and systematic

---

[27]   Translation by A. Teeuw, quoted in A. Teeuw, *Modern Indonesian Literature*, p. 35.
[28]   A. Teeuw, *Modern Indonesian Literature*, p. 36.
[29]   Goenawan Mohamad, "Peristiwa 'Manikebu'", pp. 16-17.

campaign of speeches and statements, which resulted in a presidential decree declaring the Manifesto illegal. The signatories were called "counter revolutionaries", and forbidden to publish. H.B. Jassin and Wiratmo Soekito lost their positions as civil servants.[30] According to Arief Budiman, it was actually Wiratmo Soekito and Jassin whom Lekra was trying to silence. "The target is for the big guy to be removed from office," he said. "RRI [Radio Republik Indonesia] was controlled by Wiratmo Soekito, so he was removed. For us there was no physical danger. The main target is Wiratmo and Jassin, who was head of the literature faculty. There were a lot of demonstrations. 'You have to retool,' they said. 'Remove and retool.' They succeeded in removing Wiratmo Soekito and Jassin. For us it was not dangerous at all. We are laughing, we are discussing."[31]

The signers of the Manifesto were accused of being *gelandangan*, or "vagabonds", because of their refusal to identify with any one of the established political parties. They were also accused of belonging to the PSI. Goenawan recalls that they were attacked regularly, even weekly, and that the attacks on Jassin and *Sastra* made them angry. "Jassin tried to defend himself, poorly, because he was not politically astute. But this created a kind of solidarity because we thought it was unfair to attack Jassin and the magazine."

Goenawan recalled that in some ways the group was energized by the attacks, reading books on law and philosophy and Marxist theory in order to strengthen their arguments. Most of the books available at that time were imported from either the Soviet Union or China. It was ironic, Goenawan noted, that while Lekra was becoming more and more dogmatic in its view that art should

[30] Goenawan Mohamad, "Peristiwa 'Manikebu'", p. 13.
[31] Interview with Arief Budiman, December 4, 1999. David Hill cites Wiratmo Soekito ("Mengapa Sebuah Pseudomanifes", *Horison*, Nov. 1987, pp. 380-1) as "refut[ing] the widely held belief that signatories were sacked from government positions; they were moved to less prominent posts on full salary." David Hill, "Mochtar Lubis: Author, Editor, Political Actor", fn. 78, p. 208.

serve politics, the Soviet Union itself was experiencing a thaw under Kruschev. "We started to learn more about what was happening in Russia," he said. "It was Kruschev's time, the thaw, and new writers were coming in who were very free in their expression. And we learned about this. And we started – look, even in Russia there was a change!"[32]

In addition to capturing the attention of their enemies in Lekra, the "counter-revolutionaries" of the Cultural Manifesto group also caught the eye of Western scholars and diplomats, who found much to admire in their opposition to Communism and commitment to "universal humanism." The Manikebuists were part of the political stream of democratic socialism.[33] And like their elders in the PSI – who, as David Hill has suggested, "provided the entree, the point of personal and intellectual contact for numerous foreign scholars (and journalists) whose subsequent analysis reflect this sympathy of orientation"[34] – the young leaders of the Manikebu group played an important role in shaping the thinking of the next generation of Western scholarship.

One group that was especially interested in the Manikebuists was the Congress for Cultural Freedom (CCF). The CCF was an organization of anti-Communist European liberal intellectuals and artists that included Albert Camus, Stephen Spender, and Isaiah Berlin, among others. Established in 1950, the Congress for Cultural Freedom "had offices in thirty-five countries, employed dozens of personnel, published over twenty prestige magazines, held art exhibitions, owned a news and features service, organized high-profile international conferences, and rewarded musicians and artists with prizes and public performances."[35] It also received

---

[32]   Interview with Goenawan Mohamad, July 12, 1999.

[33]   For an analysis of Democratic Socialism as one of five streams or "aliran" of Indonesian political thought see Herbert Feith and Lance Castles, eds., *Indonesian Political Thinking*, pp. 227-244.

[34]   David Hill, "Mochtar Lubis, Author, Editor, Political Actor", p. 12.

[35]   Frances Stoner Saunders, *The Cultural Cold War: The CIA and the World of Arts and Letters* (New York: New Press, 2000), p. 1.

considerable funding from the CIA, although this fact was not known to grantees at the time.[36] According to historian Frances Stoner Saunders:

> Whether they liked it or not, whether they knew it or not, there were few writers, poets, artists, historians, scientists, or critics in post-war Europe whose names were not in some way linked to this covert enterprise. Unchallenged, undetected for over twenty years, America's spying establishment operated a sophisticated, substantially endowed cultural front in the West, *for* the West, in the name of freedom of expression. Defining the Cold War as a 'battle for men's minds' it stockpiled a vast arsenal of cultural weapons: journals, books, conferences, seminars, art exhibitions, concerts, awards."[37]

The Congress for Cultural Freedom was dedicated to nurturing, building, supporting, and sustaining what came to be referred to as the "Non-Communist Left". In many cases made up of disillusioned former Communists, the "NCL" as it was known in Washington circles, was devoted to propagating the ideals of democratic socialism as an alternative to Communism. The enemy of the NCL was the Non-Aligned Movement.[38]

An "interim committee" of the Congress of Cultural Freedom was organized in Jakarta in 1956, and its members included such notable cultural figures as Mochtar Lubis and Sutan Takdir

---

[36] An April 1996 article in the *New York Times* exposed the funding link between the CIA and a variety of smaller philanthropic foundations that were funding CCF activities. See Frances Saunders, *The Cultural Cold War*, pp. 134-5.

[37] Frances Saunders, *The Cultural Cold War*, p. 2. For background on the American context of the activities of the Congress for Cultural Freedom, see Christopher Lasch, *The Agony of the American Left* (New York: Vintage books, 1969), pp. 63-114.

[38] Frances Saunders, *The Cultural Cold War*, pp. 63-89. Unfortunately, Saunders' book deals almost exclusively with the activities of the Congress for Cultural Freedom in the United States and Europe.

Alisjahbana.[39] The aims of the CCF were close enough to those of the PSI so that there was considerable overlap between the two groups. Indonesian intellectuals associated with the CCF included Wiratmo Soekito, Soedjatmoko (the brother-in-law of Sutan Sjahir), newspaper editors P.K. Ojong and Rosihan Anwar, Soe Hok Gie, and, as Arief Budiman later recalled, "all of the PSI."[40]

A number of intellectuals and student leaders who were active during this period remembered the Congress for Cultural Freedom primarily as a source of books. The CCF sponsored a book-translation program called Obor [Torch] under the leadership of Mochtar Lubis. It also assisted in providing scholarships. At one point the Congress told the Jakarta group that they had funding for one young person to go to Europe, and asked for a nomination. Arief Budiman was their choice, and he went to Paris in 1964. From there he was sent to the College of Europe in Bruges, Belgium. "It was the start of the European unification," Arief said, "so the idea is to send this young intellectual there to be associated with this non-Communist group. So I went to Bruges. This was my first time outside of the country. After a few months I asked to go back to Indonesia. I had a girlfriend at that time, who is now my wife. So I went back. I said no, I couldn't stay there any longer."[41]

When the Congress decided to continue the scholarship program for a second year, Goenawan Mohamad was chosen as its candidate.

One of the more interesting coincidences in Goenawan Mohamad's life is that his departure for Europe occurred almost immediately after the coup of September 30, 1965, when six army generals were kidnaped and killed. Goenawan remembers that he was at a friend's house that night. At 7 AM the next morning, he heard a radio announcement claiming that the "Thirtieth of

[39] For background on the activities of the CCF in Indonesia, see David Hill, "Mochtar Lubis: Author, Editor, Political Actor", pp. 197-200.
[40] Interview with Arief Budiman, December 4, 1999.
[41] Interview with Arief Budiman, December 4, 1999.

September Movement" had taken action to prevent a coup by a "Council of Generals" disloyal to the president. He said that he could tell from the way the announcement was made that it had come from the left. "We better go," he recalled thinking. He went to the New Zealand embassy, where he had a part-time translating job. They didn't yet know anything about the coup.

"By the evening of that day we had already produced pamphlets," Goenawan said. "No one knew who was in charge. That evening we knew Soeharto had taken over Halim airport. There were troop movements everywhere, but which side they were on, no one knew."[42]

At 9 PM that night, Major General Soeharto, the commander of the Army Strategic Reserve Command (Kostrad), announced over the radio that a "counterrevolutionary movement" had kidnaped the six generals in a coup attempt against President Soekarno. He further announced that he had taken over the command of the army, and that an understanding had been reached between the army, navy, and police to crush the Thirtieth of September Movement.[43]

A few days later, Goenawan left Jakarta for Europe. A young American diplomat, Paul Gardner, gave Goenawan $50 to pay a bribe for a passport. Goenawan and Paul Gardner were friends – Goenawan describes Gardner as having been lonely in Jakarta, and Gardner remembers Goenawan as having often dropped by his house to borrow American magazines, including *Time*. Years later, as a retired ambassador, Gardner joked that he had always wondered if he had been responsible for giving Goenawan the idea for *Tempo*.[44]

When asked if Goenawan's departure for Europe only a few days after the coup was a coincidence, Arief Budiman said, "It

---

[42]   Interview with Goenawan Mohamad, July 12, 1999.

[43]   Quoted in Harold Crouch, *The Army and Politics in Indonesia*, p. 99.

[44]   Conversation with Paul Gardner, January 2001, Washington, D.C.

was a pure coincidence. Nothing is really a conspiracy. History is full of coincidences."[45]

As is well known, the Communist Party of Indonesia was blamed for the kidnaping and murder of the six generals, and under the command of General Soeharto the army moved to crush the PKI. Assisted by anti-Communist organizations, the army launched a campaign of killings throughout Java and Bali that lasted for over a year, and resulted in the deaths of hundreds of thousands of Indonesians.

In Jakarta, many of Goenawan's friends were engaged with KAMI, the Indonesian Student Action Front. Established in October 1965, KAMI put pressure on the Soekarno government by organizing a series of demonstrations protesting price increases. Sympathetic army officers stayed in contact with student leaders and kept them informed of the views of General Soeharto. As Harold Crouch wrote, "when the students decided to hold massive demonstrations, they knew they had the backing of the army leadership."[46]

In January 1966, students gathering at the medical faculty of the University of Indonesia drew up the *Tritura*, or "Three Demands of the People". These included a reduction in the price of basic commodities, the dissolution of the Indonesian Communist Party, and a purging of the Cabinet. Their demands were followed by a series of demonstrations that once again appeared to have the army's tacit approval. Several years later, Arief Budiman described the role of KAMI:

> [The] student federation acted as a spearhead to open the path
> for the military to move further. Every time Soekarno tried to
> maintain the *status quo*, KAMI would provoke an open conflict.

45 Interview with Arief Budiman, December 4, 1999.
46 Harold Crouch, *The Army and Politics in Indonesia*, p. 166. For a discussion of the role of KAMI and other student "action fronts" and their relations with sympathetic army generals, see chapter six.

Marsillam Simanjuntak, Jakarta, 1971 [*Tempo*/Beng Bratanata]

The military would always come to reestablish a new order, at the same time renegotiating a new political *status quo* whereby Soekarno lost a bit. So it went on until Soekarno lost totally.[47]

Although Goenawan was acquainted with the student leaders who organized these demonstrations, according to Marsillam Simanjuntak, who was the head of the Jakarta "Presidium" of KAMI and a friend of Arief Budiman's brother Soe Hok Gie, there was a distinction between the "student activists" and the "literary group" associated with Goenawan and Arief. Marsillam said that before 1965, Goenawan had always been more of a "subterranean activist" than a student leader, active in "distributing pamphlets and so forth, meeting here and there and discussing gossip and information."

"Mostly he moved around the anti-Soekarno and anti-Communist movement," Marsillam said. "They kept themselves a little bit outside….After [Arief Budiman's brother] Soe Hok Gie died, Arief Budiman became a student activist. He became a substitute!"[48]

---

[47]   Arief Budiman, "The Student Movement in Indonesia: A Study of the Relationship between Culture and Structure", *Asian Survey*, vol. 18, no. 6 (June, 1978), p. 617.
[48]   Interview with Marsillam Simanjuntak, July 18, 2002.

In Bruges, far from the events that were unfolding in
Indonesia, Goenawan was hungry for news. "News from Indonesia
concerning the recent cabinet shuffle was in the headlines of the
continental and English papers yesterday," he wrote to Salim Said.
"I very much hope that you can send me a letter concerning this:
I can only guess at the real developments....The big student
demonstration I heard about from Radio Copenhagen; it was
translated by a Danish friend of mine."[49]

Letters posted from Jakarta suggested that while Goenawan's
friends were at first concerned with the soaring prices of basic
commodities, and the possibility that the remnants of the PKI
might use this inflation to their advantage, their concern rather
quickly turned to horror at the army-sponsored massacre.[50] One
friend described East Java as "the wild west", and wrote that the
PKI were being killed like rats, their bodies flung into the Brantas
River. Goenawan wrote to H.B. Jassin that the image of Indonesia
in Europe had been colored by these dramatic reports, and
questioned his own right to comment on the killings. "Have we
sinned?" he asked, "Or are we innocent?"

> In Europe, I feel I don't have the right to make such an
> evaluation. How should I, one who travels in safety from one
> place to another, evaluate those who struggle between life and
> death? My heart says that I must, but I can't. I don't have the
> right. This is why I became angry when I read (with help from
> a Danish friend) an editorial in a Copenhagen daily...that was
> protesting the "massacre" in Indonesia. I felt angry, because
> they are only spectators, and not participants. What do

---

[49] Goenawan Mohamad to Salim Said, February 23, 1966. Goenawan Mohamad
file, H.B. Jassin documentary library.

[50] See Marco Kartodikmo to Goenawan Mohamad, October 3, 1965, and Tjipto to
Goenawan Mohamad, December 5, 1965. Goenawan Mohamad file, H.B. Jassin
documentary library. I am very grateful to Henny Wati, who transcribed these
and many other handwritten letters.

they know? This is what causes me often to feel empty in Europe: here I am only a meaningless drop, and meaningless in my own nation, too.[51]

Arief Budiman wrote to Goenawan of his fear that right-wing Islamic and Catholic student groups were "inclining towards fascism," and beginning to act exactly like those whom they were seeking to eliminate. "We may not use the methods of Communists, it is our one and only capital," Arief quoted a friend as saying, "and I believe that this is true. Many groups have purged the PKI only to become PKI. It is only the people who suffer."[52]

Aside from the discussions of political developments, most of Goenawan Mohamad's correspondence from this period focused on the problem of freedom of expression, and the fervent hope that the new order would bring about the de-politicization of art. A symposium held at the University of Indonesia in May 1966 sparked discussion of a "new path", or *tracée baru* in the arts and culture as well as in economics. Arief Budiman described the symposium, and repeated to Goenawan the argument he had made against the revival of "cultural organizations" that were affiliated with political parties. "I declared," he wrote, "that it is the political parties that are shaping cultural organizations...[and that these] cultural organizations don't ever fulfill the function of culture, but rather the function of politics. And I pointed out that the artists in these organizations are 'former artists' who are no longer creative."[53] In the same letter, Arief told Goenawan of his plan to establish a new literary magazine to be called *Horison*. The magazine

[51]   Goenawan Mohamad to H.B. Jassin, January 30, 1966. Goenawan Mohamad file, H.B. Jassin documentary library.

[52]   Arief Budiman to Goenawan Mohamad, n.d., probably January, 1966. Goenawan Mohamad file, H.B. Jassin documentary library.

[53]   Arief Budiman to Goenawan Mohamad, May 16, 1966. Goenawan Mohamad file, H.B. Jassin documentary library. The proceedings of this symposium were published as *Simposium Kebangkitan Semangat '66: Mengjeladjah Tracee Baru*, (Djakarta: Universitas Indonesia, 1966).

had both the blessing of H.B. Jassin and the financial support of Mochtar Lubis, who would become its editor-in-chief.[54]

Despite the prodigious letter-writing, Goenawan appears to have been a somewhat indifferent student in Europe, spending his time reading, writing, traveling, and working on translation projects for Ivan Kats, who worked in the Congress for Cultural Freedom's Asia program. His correspondence from the period suggests that he was quite involved with Kats, helping him put together lists of those who should receive CCF materials such as *Encounter* and *China Quarterly*. Kats frequently wrote to Goenawan in a friendly, avuncular way, offering him advice, encouragement, praise, and at one time a portable typewriter. Although the depth of Kats' genuine affection for his young friend is evident from both their correspondence and lifelong friendship, it is also true that Goenawan was an invaluable Indonesian contact for the Congress for Cultural Freedom, precisely the kind of young liberal intellectual that the CCF wished to encourage.

By the end of the summer of 1966, Goenawan was ready to return home. His letters hinted at it, and answers from his friends were full of talk of what he could do once he returned to Jakarta. One possibility was to join the newspaper *Harian Kami*, which had begun to publish in June. In August Arief Budiman wrote:

> Yesterday I met with Nono [Makarim] who is now chief editor
> of *Harian Kami*, together with Zulharman and Ismid. Nono
> now puts into practice all of our earlier discussions and he is
> great. The editorials that he writes are sharp and strike at the
> issues. *Kompas* has got some heavy competition…Actually, we

---

54   David Hill suggests that *Horison* was the "nexus" between the young writers associated with the student movement and the signatories of the Cultural Manifesto. For a brief history of *Horison*, see David Hill, "'The Two Leading Institutions': Taman Ismail Marzuki and *Horison*", in Virginia Matheson Hooker, ed., *Culture and Society in New Order Indonesia* (Kuala Lumpur: Oxford University Press, 1993), p. 252.

Nono Makarim, Jakarta, 1975 [*Tempo*/Ed Zoelverdi]

really need you. I mentioned a "job". Ismid says it will be easy because Wiratmo is at RRI, Umar Kayam…has become the director general of RRI-TV, there's the newspaper *Kami*, and last but not least, there's *Indonesia Raya*, which Mochtar Lubis is quickly going to publish when his print machine comes. Thus I am optimistic concerning your "job", although I can't guarantee it's "fixed".[55]

When Goenawan returned to Indonesia in 1966, it was a different place. Soekarno was still president, but he was steadily losing ground against relentless pressure from the army and student groups. Many of Goenawan's friends, including Fikri Jufri, were now working for the anti-Communist newspaper *Harian Kami*, and Goenawan also gravitated towards their group.[56]

---

[55] Arief Budiman to Goenawan Mohamad, August 23, 1966. Goenawan Mohamad file, H.B. Jassin documentary library.

[56] KAMI was an acronym for Kesatuan Aksi Mahasiswa Indonesia (Indonesian Student Action Front), and also the word for "we," or "our." So *Harian Kami* can be read as either "Our Daily", or as the daily of the Indonesian Student Action Front. According to Marsillam Simanuntak, "*Harian Kami* was supposedly part of KAMI, but later on Nono [Makarim] said it was just *Harian Kami*." Interview with Marsillam Simanjuntak, July 18, 2002.

As former chief editor Nono Makarim explained, "after a year Goenawan came back and it was very natural that he played dominos with us. That was the game at *Harian Kami*; in the morning waiting for the reporters to come in, the editors played dominos. And Goenawan played dominos every day; sometimes he just saunters off to a manual typewriter. He says 'What's the news today?' And he starts writing, nothing formal."

"For reporting, it was Fikri," Nono added. "Fikri was the first one who felt the economic pressure and he left us to go to work for *Pedoman*. And the luxury that he got, of course, he was riding around on a Vespa, a motor scooter, and oh boy, that was fantastic."

Nono Makarim is an attractive man with a sturdy physique and a commanding presence. Born in Pekalongan, Central Java in 1939, he is the son of a wealthy lawyer of Arab descent. Nono describes himself as "family by marriage" with *Tempo* founder Fikri Jufri. "His family and my family were very, very close," he said. "So that when I was angry with my mother and didn't want to go home, I went home to Fikri's."

"Prior to G-30-S [the 30th of September] we had small discussions," Nono said. "Goenawan was part of that, Fikri was part of that...Wiratmo Soekito was there too. And you know, we were in our early twenties, we thought that we are fantastic. We can change the world. And the dropping of names is horrible, 'Rosa Luxemburg said this,' and we had these discussions in the coffee lean-tos, *warung kopi*. And out of those discussions, out of what we thought at the time, how a state must look like, how people must behave, a newspaper was born."

Nono described himself as "a watcher," and said that he wasn't involved in the formation of the Indonesian Student Action Front (KAMI). "But they were demonstrating left and right," he said. Instead of participating directly, he sent notes to the people who were organizing the actions in Jakarta "about what I think they did wrong and what I think should be corrected."

Goenawan Mohamad [left] and Fikri Jufri in
Tempo's office on Jl. Senen Raya, 1977 [*Tempo*/Ed Zoelverdi]

It went on for a month or two and then they said they don't
want to accept any more notes from me and they want me to
come. So I sort of came over and they appointed me to sit in
their central committee….I was in charge of pamphleteering.
Pamphleteering was done to prepare Jakarta and Bandung for
demonstrations to come so that the theme is known, [and] out
of the pamphlets grew the newspaper. It's a four-page newspaper.
And I borrowed Rp. 60,000 from a friend who was in business,
and lo and behold we published a newspaper. We were very,
very successful economically in the first years.[57]

Harian Kami was an unusual sort of newspaper. "We looked down
on journalists actually," Nono said. "This was just a means. We
were, the ethos about ourselves, the picture I had of myself was
the VW bug, and black turtleneck. That was the image of ourselves.
Pontificating wisdom and knowledge about politics. Disgustingly
arrogant. It was fun, although at a given moment I thought I was
running around in circles."

---

[57]   Interview with Nono Makarim, June 23, 2000.

One of the young men who gravitated towards Nono Makarim's group was a cartoonist for the newspaper *Merdeka* named Harmoko. Nono described the man who would later preside over the banning of *Tempo* as a close friend, adding that "we did all the naughty things that young men do together." Goenawan was never especially close to Harmoko, and later remembered him as having been more of a doer than a thinker. "He was a simple-minded anti-Communist."[58]

Although *Harian Kami*'s circulation was not large, it represented something significant at the beginning of the New Order. Along with Mochtar Lubis' *Indonesia Raya*, Rahman Tolleng's *Mahasiswa Indonesia*, and T.D. Hafas' *Nusantara*, *Harian Kami* was fearless in its revelation of corruption, which it saw as threatening the goals of the New Order.[59] "We did crazy things," Nono said. "A student activist died demonstrating in Bandung. The editorial page was black with one flower in the middle. And poetry sometimes on the editorial page. We were raised on magazines like *Encounter*. The writings of Melvin Lasky, Stephen Spender, *The God that Failed*, the whole CIA-sponsored thing."

When asked if the CIA was interested in *Harian Kami*, Nono laughed. "We didn't know," he said. "They should have been, but we didn't know."

In 1967, a split occurred within the student organization KAMI when some members were appointed to the provisional parliament, or MPR. For those who were opposed to the appointments, it seemed self-evident that if the student movement were to remain a "moral force", it could not become involved in practical politics.[60] Those who favored the appointments argued just the opposite, that KAMI had to carry on its struggle "from within". Marsillam

---

[58] Email correspondence, June 28, 2000.
[59] Harold Crouch, *The Army and Politics in Indonesia*, pp. 294-5.
[60] Arief Budiman defined the concept of the student movement as a "moral force" in

Simanjuntak, who counted himself among the "Puritans", later recalled saying that "if KAMI cannot be an instrument of the students and it is exploited by the military, let us bury the instrument." Marsillam said that for him, it took less than one year to begin to mistrust the military. "There was no more partnership," he said.[61]

Arief Budiman likewise became very quickly disenchanted with the military. "In 1966," he said, "after the 1965 tragedy happened, I was involved in fighting against the Communists, glorifying the military, hoping they would bring democracy to us. The expectation was that they would give power back to the civilians. At the time we were all very hopeful that the Soekarno dictatorship should be ended. Then in 1970 we started to doubt the military capacity to bring democracy. So I was in the first student group in 1970 that did a demonstration against the military."[62]

Harian Kami chief editor Nono Makarim said that he had similar doubts. "Very early on I started thinking that history has got to repeat itself because the infrastructure has remained the same. The style of government. While the demonstrations were still on, while the power structure was reorganizing, reinventing itself, it was still possible to make changes."

"I remember writing a series of editorials against the Jakarta commander because they closed down my enemy newspaper *Suluh Indonesia*," Nono said. "And I was called by Ali Moertopo. When

---

this way: "they disclaimed any interest whatsoever in power; their criticisms were based on moral considerations, not political interests." Arief Budiman, "The Student Movement in Indonesia," p. 618.

[61] Interview with Marsillam Simanjuntak, July 18, 2002.

[62] Interview with Arief Budiman, December 4, 1999. In 1971 Arief Budiman was arrested as a leader of the demonstration against First Lady Ibu Tien's "Beautiful Indonesia in Miniature", which to its opponents resembled all-too-closely the grandiose, state-sponsored prestige projects of the Soekarno years. He was detained for a month without charges being brought. See Arief Budiman to Nono Makarim, February 3, 1972, and Arief Budiman to Goenawan Mohamad, February 4, [1972], Goenawan Mohamad file, H.B. Jassin documentary library.

you got a call to Jl. Raden Saleh, you sort of say good bye to your friends. I wasn't married then, it was easier. He called me in, and I had my toothbrush with me, but that was all, just my toothbrush. And I had to sit in their guestroom and it took some time, but then a ray of hope appeared. I was offered tea or coffee. Ah – it can't be that bad. And after one or two sips I was called in."

> The general shook my hand in a *pro forma* way and said 'your friends are confused.' 'Oh,' I said. 'Impossible.' 'They are confused because I just killed your enemy and you should be dancing the war dance like a crazy person. You know, Nono, we're in a war against anything that smacks of Communism. And in a war, when your enemy gets killed, you should be rejoicing. You are not rejoicing. Your friends are confused.' I had to explain to him, 'General, you see *Harian Kami* has no permanent friends, it has no permanent enemies either. We do have a permanent editorial policy, and sometimes it attaches to friends. Sometimes it attaches to enemies. And that is why probably my quote unquote friends get confused. But you know,' I said, 'we don't do these things because we are brave. I am very much afraid. I don't mind telling you that coming here was frightening to me. But you see what I'm also doing is protecting myself. When I wrote those series of editorials I had *Harian Kami* in mind. Because what's happening now to my quote unquote enemy, tomorrow will happen to my quote unquote friend. Next week it happens to me.' And it did, in 1974 already it did.

As subsequent events have shown, these doubts about the military's capacity to bring about democracy were soon borne out. Once the army solidified its hold on power, suspected Communists who had survived the killings were imprisoned, in most cases without a trial. Many leftist writers, journalists, and members of Lekra who were suspected of Communism but deemed not to have been directly involved in the events of the 30th of September were exiled to the penal colony of Buru Island.

In 1970, Goenawan Mohamad and several other writers left *Harian Kami* to join with Fikri Jufri in founding their own magazine, to be called *Ekspres*. Although their departure from the newspaper was amicable, it was nevertheless a severe blow to Nono Makarim, who, in a gracious note to Goenawan, described him as "irreplaceable."

"I tried to imagine," Nono wrote, "a situation in which Nono Makarim worked for a daily that was led by Goenawan Mohamad. Then Nono got an offer to work for a publication that was 'exciting', and 'challenging'. I would have felt as bad as you have, nevertheless I would do as you did. The project is too exciting a challenge to merely let it pass you by, especially if you and I realize that it will only strengthen our argument for that brand of journalism that we are both trying to find and articulate. You must never doubt that you have my sincere support in this."[63]

The plan was to create a magazine like *Time* or *Newsweek*. But this required a lot of capital, and, according to media scholar and analyst Daniel Dhakidae, the "old timers" – like Auwjong Peng Koen, Mochtar Lubis, and Rosihan Anwar – were unwilling to put up the money for so ambitious a venture.[64] Finally, a young photographer named Marzuki Arifin, who had worked for *Harian Kami* and was employed by *Merdeka*, introduced them to his father-in-law B.M. Diah, who agreed to be their publisher.[65] Sixty percent of the magazine would be owned by B.M. Diah, forty percent by the *Ekspres* group.[66]

---

[63]   Nono Makarim to Goenawan Mohamad, April 8, 1970. Goenawan Mohamad file, H.B. Jassin documentary library. This letter used a combination of English and Indonesian.

[64]   Quoted in Daniel Dhakidae, "The State, The Rise of Capital and the Fall of Political Journalism", fn. 77, p. 257.

[65]   Daniel Dhakidae, "The State, the Rise of Capital and the Fall of Political Journalism", p. 257.

[66]   Interview with Christianto Wibisono, April 24, 2001.

Goenawan's partner in the new venture was Fikri Jufri, and the two couldn't be more different. Where Goenawan is shy and reserved, Fikri is warm and expressive. An Indonesian of Arab descent, Fikri "knows everyone". Fikri and Goenawan first met at the University of Indonesia, where Fikri was in the faculty of economics, studying with the economists who would become the architects of the New Order economic policy. In a 1977 interview, Fikri said that he first heard of Goenawan after reading his essay "Seribu Slogan dan Sebuah Puisi" (A Thousand Slogans and a Poem) which was published in 1963. Fikri said that upon reading the essay he searched for Goenawan for a week.[67]

Daniel Dhakidae has argued that *Ekspres* was born in an era of "huge anti-party sentiment" that coincided with a new model of capitalist development.[68] The previous generation of newspapers had been affiliated with and subsidized by the political parties; Goenawan and Fikri envisioned a new kind of news magazine that would be removed from partisan politics. Fikri Jufri told Daniel Dhakidae, "We were fed up with the daily newspapers, they were more like pamphlets." Goenawan echoed this sentiment when he told Daniel that they wanted *Ekspres* to be free of "sloganistic and partisan language".

"*Time* gave us the idea," he said, "since there was something lively, unfrozen and unfreezing."[69]

Marsillam Simanjuntak rejects the notion that Goenawan and his friends created *Ekspres* for ideological reasons, and says that

---

[67] *Asian Wall Street Journal*, 25 May 1977. The essay can be found in Goenawan Mohamad, *Kesuastraan dan Kukuasaan*, pp. 76-77.

[68] Daniel Dhakidae, "The State, The Rise of Capital and the Fall of Political Journalism," p. 255.

[69] Quoted in Daniel Dhakidae, "The State, The Rise of Capital and the Fall of Political Journalism," pp. 256-7. There are striking parallels between the founding of *Ekspres* and the development of non-partisan "penny papers" like the *New York Sun* in the United States in the 1830s. See Michael Schudson, *Discovering the News: A Social History of American Newspapers* (New York: Basic Books, 1978), esp. chapter 1, and Janet E. Steele, *The Sun Shines for All: Journalism and Ideology in the Life of Charles A. Dana* (Syracuse: Syracuse University Press, 1992).

what they really wanted to do was to make a name for themselves. "It had nothing to do with New Order or anti-Communism or anti-Old Order in which they found *Ekspres*," he said. "It was pure and simple to enhance their journalistic careers, or ambition, or ideas! In *Ekspres* was introduced money, capital, a modern way of publishing. You can then try to seek the explanation, oh yeah, they got fed up with activism. But for me that's not the explanation. Because they are not leaving activism, because [in 1970] *Harian Kami* was not activist any more."[70]

The introductory issue of *Ekspres* was published on May 26, 1970. It consisted of eight pages, but as the "Letter From the Editor" explained, subsequent editions would be 36 pages and in full color. The editors of *Ekspres* promised to provide readers with a weekly "that was informative enough without being either dry or complicated."

> We will serve up a cover story in every issue. The political situation, economics, religion, sports, art and science, city and village, entertainment, style, etc. will all be covered each week. We are aware that readers have both the right and the desire to understand what's happening. At the same time, we know that readers don't want to be bothered with trivial matters. The journalism we want to practice is journalism that won't make your blood pressure rise or cause your forehead to wrinkle up. Happy reading now and in the future![71]

---

[70]   Interview with Marsillam Simanjuntak, July 18, 2002.
[71]   *Ekspres*, 26 May, 1970. In this introductory issue the chief editor was listed as Goenawan Mohamad. The assistant chief editor was Fikri Jufri, and the managing editor was Usamah. The publisher was Marzuki Arifin, and the assistant publisher Christianto Wibisono. The business manager was Nurman Diah. Members of the editorial council were listed as Arief Budiman, Fikri Jufri, Christianto Wibisono, Usamah, Marzuki Arifin, and Goenawan Mohamad. Sri Atmakusumah, the wife of *Indonesia Raya*'s managing editor Atmakusumah Astraatmadja was listed as the head of "documentation and research", but Sri says that she never actually agreed to accept this position. Interview with Sri Atmakusumah, June 17, 2003.

Later, Goenawan said that never again during the New Order would he and his friends feel as free as they did when they were writing for *Ekspres*.

After having been in business for less than six months, Goenawan and Fikri were fired from *Ekspres* on November 3, 1970. Why? Because Goenawan had spoken out in response to a split within the Indonesian Journalists' Association that had occurred at the 1970 congress in Palembang. In an obvious effort to control the PWI, Army Special Operations (Opsus), had attempted to install its own man as the head of the organization. Unfortunately for Goenawan and the other writers at *Ekspres*, the man in question was B.M. Diah.

According to Atmakusumah, who was then managing editor at *Indonesia Raya* and the treasurer of the Jakarta chapter of the PWI, the choice of "most if not all professional journalists" for the head of the PWI was *Pedoman* editor Rosihan Anwar. "This was because he was a more independent-minded person than B.M. Diah," Atma said. "B.M. Diah was once Minister of Information, Ambassador to Thailand, and Ambassador to the U.K., so we thought he must be a government man."

"We in Jakarta had already decided that we should support Rosihan Anwar because he was a real journalist. So Rosihan Anwar got elected in Palembang, but the government and military didn't like that result. Then B.M. Diah, supported by leaders of military newspapers and some others, had a meeting in the same hotel, and decided to elect B.M. Diah as chairman of PWI. So after that for four months we had two PWI!"[72]

In Jakarta, Goenawan expressed his regret at B.M. Diah's refusal to negotiate to resolve the split. His statement was first published in *Sinar Harapan* newspaper, and then reprinted in the

---

[72]   Interview with Atmakusumah, June 21, 2003. See also Angela Romano, *Politics and the Press in Indonesia: Understanding an Evolving Political Culture* (London: RoutledgeCurzon, 2003), p. 93.

other Jakarta dailies. Although Goenawan had made it clear that this view was his private opinion and not that of *Ekspres*, publisher Marzuki Arifin said that Goenawan's comments nevertheless "contradicted *Ekspres*'s policy of not getting involved with the problems of the PWI."[73]

Goenawan, Fikri, and assistant publisher Christianto Wibisono were fired. Eight staff members signed a letter of support, but the experiment with *Ekspres* was over.[74]

By 1970, it was clear to anyone who was paying attention that what Nono Makarim had described as "history repeating itself" was happening. "Under Soekarno, of course, it was the Jakarta military command who first initiated the *Surat Izin Terbit* [Permit to Publish]" Atma said. The individuals were different, but the style was the same. Once again the military was looking for ways of bringing pro-government journalists to power.

After a "face-saving settlement" on March 6, 1971, the two competing PWI organizations were reintegrated, but the damage to freedom of expression was done.[75] According to Marsillam Simanjuntak, this was more than just a dispute over B.M. Diah. "It was not because we hate B. M. Diah that we take sides with Rosihan Anwar, no! It was us against Soeharto, actually. Opsus [Special Operations], Ali Moertopo. So this is a continuation of our political movement that was aborted by Ali Moertopo....You have to put this into a bigger picture of the political context at that time."[76]

As Marsillam said, "it's always a fight between two camps." This was the house into which *Tempo* was born.

---

[73]   *Kompas*, November 4, 1970. See also *Indonesia Raya*, November 4, 1970.

[74]   All eight of these signatories eventually moved to *Tempo*. The list included five members of the editorial staff: Toeti Kakiailatu, Syu'bah Asa, Zen Umar Purba, Isma Sawitri, Putu Widjaja, and three members of the artistic staff: Muchsin Zein, Fachruddin Jahja, and Mubarok. *Kompas*, November 6, 1970.

[75]   For details of this episode as well as other government efforts to secure sympathetic leadership of the PWI, see David Hill, *The Press in New Order Indonesia* (Jakarta: Pustaka Sinar Harapan, 1994), esp. pp. 67-73.

[76]   Interview with Marsillam Simanjuntak, July 18, 2002.

the new order

We need a development government that is strong, but it can't be forgotten that strength must also be shown by the authorities themselves in, among other things, their attitude towards receiving criticism.[1]

– Goenawan Mohamad, January 29, 1972

When *Tempo* was founded in 1971, the New Order was still new. Although the 1970 dispute over the leadership of the PWI raised concerns that the Army had an interest in controlling the leadership of the journalists' association, there was still a kind of euphoria among the press as it enjoyed a relatively high level of freedom. But how long would government willingness to tolerate criticism continue?

As officials warned that "the time is not yet right" for certain kinds of criticism, journalists began to check themselves. Those who did not faced dire consequences. When Aristides Katoppo, then managing editor of *Sinar Harapan* newspaper, published the results of the presidential "Commission of Four's" inquiry into corruption in July 1970, he was called to account by the *Dewan*

---

[1]   Goenawan Mohamad, "Melayani, Dengan Kritik", *Tempo*, January 29, 1972.

Kehormatan (Honorary Press Council) of the Indonesian Journalists' Association.[2] Although he argued convincingly that he had violated no press ethics and had obtained the documents by good journalistic means, he was nevertheless taken aside by a senior member of the Council and warned that he might still be charged under the state secrets law. Aristides' response, "Since when did corruption become a state secret?" was amusing at the time, but the president had the last laugh when eighteen months later Kopkamtib (the Operations Command to Restore Security and Order) withdrew *Sinar Harapan*'s SIC (Permit to Print) and made it clear that the paper would be permanently closed down if Aristides Katoppo was not removed.[3]

On January 19, 1972, General Soemitro, the deputy commander of the Indonesian Armed Forces and the commander of Kopkamtib, called a meeting with the editors of daily papers in Jakarta. Although the meeting was friendly enough, the general warned the editors to "watch your tongues." Ten days later, *Tempo* published an essay written by Goenawan Mohamad that addressed the question of "what kind of criticism is wished for and permitted by the authorities?" In answering the question, Goenawan reminded readers of an aphorism: your mouth is your tiger, splitting your head. "Anyone who doesn't want to have his head split needs to choose wisdom over audacity," he concluded.[4]

Goenawan's words turned out to be prescient. Within two years, twelve Indonesian newspapers and magazines would be shut down in the aftermath of the incident known as Malari, or the

---

[2]   For background on the growing public concern with corruption that led to the appointment of the Commission of Four, see Harold Crouch, *The Army and Politics in Indonesia*, pp. 293-9.

[3]   Aristides Katoppo believes that the president was personally responsible for this decision. Interview with Aristides Katoppo, June 21, 2003. See also David Hill, *The Press in New Order Indonesia*, p. 38.

[4]   Goenawan Mohamad, "Melayani, Dengan Kritik", *Tempo*, January 29, 1972.

15th of January calamity. Although *Tempo* would survive this "purge", there would nevertheless be a price to pay.

After the split with B.M. Diah, Goenawan and his splinter group from *Ekspres* were forced to find a new investor. According to Fikri Jufri, "We did not care about money, we did not even think about publishing a magazine that made money. What was in our head was to publish a tremendous news magazine, and the tremendous magazine got its example from *Time* and *Newsweek* and our experience in publishing *Ekspres* for seven months demonstrated that we were able to publish the impossible. And the most important thing was we had made our name."[5]

Perhaps Goenawan and Fikri did not care about making money, but they cared about finding another publisher. Arief Budiman was director of Yayasan Indonesia in Balai Budaya at the time, and he remembers Goenawan coming to his office, desperate to find new funding. "First I contacted Mochtar Lubis," Arief said. "We went together. Mochtar was so arrogant. Goenawan asked for some money as initial capital. He wanted color, good quality paper, etc. but this is read by Mochtar Lubis as arrogance by the young people. 'When I started *Indonesia Raya*…' he said. Goenawan said 'they don't understand. We are not starting from scratch.'"

"Lukman Setiawan was the one who was successful in getting the investor," Arief said. "So that's how the cooperation began. Goenawan was quite desperate."[6]

Lukman was a sports writer who had worked for *Kompas* newspaper, and the investor he found was Ciputra. Ciputra, or Tjie Tjin Hoan, was born in 1931 in Central Sulawesi. Although Ciputra became one of the wealthiest developers in Indonesia, his origins were modest. Ciputra's biography in *Apa & Siapa – Tempo*'s

5   Interview with Fikri Jufri, quoted in Daniel Dhakidae, "The State, The Rise of Capital, and the Fall of Political Journalism", p. 268. For a complete account of the founding of *Tempo*, see pages 255-272.
6   Interview with Arief Budiman, December 4, 1999.

equivalent of "Who's Who" – notes that as a boy, Ciputra walked seven kilometers to school each day, and that his mother sold cakes to support the family. With the same single-minded determination that would later govern his business career, he succeeded in entering the prestigious Bandung Institute of Technology, where he studied architecture.[7] When Ciputra met Goenawan Mohamad in 1970, he had already joined a group of capitalists who, together with Jakarta Governor Ali Sadikin, would change the face of Jakarta.

The group was called P.T. Pembangunan Ibukota Jakarta Raya, or the Jaya Development Group. It was established in 1961, and Ciputra was its CEO. Partly owned by the Special Province of Jakarta (DKI Jakarta), the Jaya Group controlled a portfolio of investment interests ranging from a soccer team to big-ticket road and bridge projects. The Jaya Development Group has been described as an important amalgam of state, Chinese, and indigenous capital.[8] In his memoirs, Ali Sadikin explained the connection between the city of Jakarta and the Jaya Development Group in this way:

> The Jaya Development Group had existed since 1961. When I was Governor, the metropolitan authority made an effort to rejuvenate sections of Jakarta that were no longer in keeping with the status and development of the city. Private and national capital were both used in this effort because the Jakarta city budget was too limited to undertake this kind of redevelopment. As a joint business venture, the Jaya Development Group could move with greater agility and enable private partners to involve their capital with more confidence.[9]

In addition to building public works projects such as bridges and

7   "Ciputra," *Apa & Siapa*, 1986, www.pdat.co.id.
8   Richard Robison, *Indonesia: The Rise of Capital* (North Sydney, Australia: Allen and Unwin, 1986), pp. 89-90.
9   K.H. Ramadhan, *Bang Ali: Demi Jakarta 1966-1977* (Jakarta: Pustaka Sinar Harapan, Jakarta 1995), p. 442.

toll roads, the Jaya Group also developed the Senen Market Project, City Hall, and the Ancol recreation center. Ali Sadikin wrote that by the end of his term as governor, "the Jaya Group owned about thirty smaller companies that were active in the fields of trade, development, construction, recreation, and other businesses."[10] A 1995 survey listed the Jaya Group as the 23rd largest conglomerate in Indonesia, with estimated annual revenues of 1,928 billion rupiah.[11]

The part of the Jaya Development Group that went into partnership with *Tempo* was the Jaya Raya Foundation, or Yayasan Jaya Raya. Established in 1970, the Jaya Raya Foundation was the "charity arm" of the Jaya Development Group, and it was also headed by Ciputra.[12] It was initially established to promote athletics, especially soccer and badminton, although its mandate was sufficiently broad to include social and cultural efforts such as the arts, education, and health.[13] The Jaya Raya Foundation was funded by contributions from its members, which were for the most part companies that did business with the city. Many of these businesses were part of either the Jaya Development Group or Ciputra's own Metropolitan Group.[14] Put another way, the Jaya Raya Foundation was a consortium of companies with the Jaya

---

[10] Ibid.

[11] *Warta Ekonomi*, November 25, 1996.

[12] Interview with Christianto Wibisono, April 24, 2001. Ciputra's title was Ketua Dewan Pengurus, or Chairman of the Board of Directors.

[13] Daniel Dhakidae, "The State, The Rise of Capital, and the Fall of Political Journalism", p. 260.

[14] A full list of members can be found in the introductory issue of *Tempo*. They include: P.T. Pembangunan Jaya, P.T. Philindo, P.T. IRTI, P.T. Jaya Bowling Indonesia, P.T. Jaya Bali Agung, Kantor Urusan Perusahaan Daerah, Jayasan Rehabilitasi Social, B.U. Lotto Jaya, Perusahaan Pengangkutan Djakarta, Perusahaan Terminal Bis dan Shelter DCI Djakarta, Bank Pembangunan Daerah Djakarta, PD Pasar Jaya, PD Dharma Jaya, Jayasan Pulo Mas, P.T. Southwest Investment and Development & Co, Djakarta Racing Management, P.T. New International Amusement Centre, P.T. Metropolitan Reality International, P.T. Metropolitan Development, P.T. Perentjana Djaja, Project Tjempaka Putih, Bank Bumi Daya, Perusahaan Tanah and Bangunan DCI Djakarta, P.T. Djakarta Motor company, and PN Pantja Niaga. *Tempo*, Nomor Perkenalan, 1971.

Development Group as its biggest shareholder. Jakarta Governor Ali Sadikin was the head of its Supervisory Board (Dewan Pengawas), and it is likely that many of these businesses joined the Jaya Raya Foundation because they wanted access to Ali Sadikin and the Jakarta city government.[15]

Aristides Katoppo, the editor of *Sinar Harapan* newspaper and a long-time observer of the Indonesian media scene, explained the relationship between the Jaya Development Group and the Jaya Raya Foundation in this way. Pointing to a new building under construction, still a dusty tangle of wire, pilings, and exposed concrete slabs, he said, "take that building, for example. Not only does it have a developer, but that developer has probably subcontracted with other companies that will provide the electricity, the plumbing, the cement. Imagine that the contractor went to each of the subcontractors and asked for a contribution of 5% of their earnings. He says he wants to establish a foundation." Aristides smiled. "And the developer gets these "voluntary" contributions, but they are not really so voluntary. That is how you create a *yayasan*."[16]

As head of the Jaya Raya Foundation, Ciputra had near total discretion with regard to the foundation's funds. Unlike the directors of a "P.T.", or limited liability corporation, the directors of a *yayasan* were not accountable to any external body. Under the law regulating foundations, it was "foundation directors [who were] responsible for guaranteeing that the profits would be evenly distributed to foundation members. Even donating members of the public had no control over the allocation of the money they had contributed."[17] Based on the model of the Dutch *stichting*,

---

[15]   Interview with Bambang Harymurti, March 17, 2001.

[16]   Interview with Aristides Katoppo, April 23, 2001.

[17]   During the New Order years, the Soeharto family controlled over twenty foundations, many of which conducted for-profit business activities despite their non-profit status, while their standing as "foundations" enabled them to evade the regulations concerning corporations – including the tax code. "Foundation Law," *Tempo* [English version], September 14-20, 2004.

the *yayasan* had obvious advantages in terms of lack of accountability and transparency.

Harjoko Trisnadi was one of the founders of *Tempo*, and also a representative of Ciputra and the Jaya Raya Foundation on *Tempo*'s board of directors. A slightly built man of Chinese descent, he is a journalist turned businessman. His movements are quick and nervous. Harjoko believes in saving documents, and he's eager to talk about the role of the Jaya Raya Foundation and the Jakarta city government in the history of *Tempo*.

"The Jaya Development Group was established to develop buildings in Jakarta," he said. "Now at that time the local government wasn't financially able to undertake these projects, so the governor established the Jaya Development Group, which worked as a private company, but actually its capital was in the name of the metropolitan government. Ciputra was the CEO."[18]

Harjoko explained that there was a precedent for the relationship between the City of Jakarta and *Tempo*. "Before *Tempo*, I already owned a magazine called *Star Weekly*," he said. "The chief editor was P.K. Ojong, who was also the founder of *Kompas* newspaper. But in 1959, it was banned by the government for various reasons. After that, Governor Soemarno Sosroatmodjo [the governor who preceded Ali Sadikin] decided that he wanted to have a publication – a magazine – which would support his idea of modernizing Jakarta. So in 1961 he called me, and this was what sparked the idea for *Jaya* magazine."

"The publisher of the magazine was the Jaya Development Group," Harjoko said, "and this was the beginning of my connection with Ciputra. Actually, in day-to-day affairs there was no connection with the Jaya Development Group, we found our own money, etc. We only borrowed the name from Jaya Development. And that magazine continued until 1969."

"In 1965, of course, came the New Order," he continued,

---

[18]   Interview with Harjoko Trisnadi, June 28, 2000.

"and *Jaya* magazine was no longer believed to reflect the aspirations of the new government. By that time, a new governor of Jakarta had been appointed – Ali Sadikin, a man of wide vision. In 1970, he called Ciputra and me. He had an idea. Our magazine had already been closed; we should publish a new magazine that expressed the aspirations of the New Order."

"Now, at the same time," Harjoko said, "Goenawan, Fikri, and friends who had recently been fired from *Ekspres* magazine because of an internal conflict, were looking for a new investor. Ciputra became that investor."

Ciputra has been called a "wonder boy" in the field of property development.[19] In addition to managing the Jaya Group – which, with its ties to the Jakarta city administration, would become one of the twenty largest Chinese-owned conglomerates in Indonesia[20] – Ciputra founded a second development group in 1971. The Metropolitan Group consists of forty-six companies in the hotel, trade, contracting, and real estate business, and is active in Singapore as well as Indonesia.[21] Christianto Wibisono, one of the founders of *Tempo* and an expert on Indonesian business organizations, points out that although Ciputra manages the Jaya Group, he owns the Metropolitan Group. Christianto said that Ciputra was often able to use his influence at P.T. Pembangunan Jaya to steer business towards the Metropolitan Group via subcontracts.[22]

In 1981 Ciputra established the Ciputra Group, which by the late 1990s consisted of forty businesses in the property and finance sectors. Christianto Wibisono described this conglomerate as Ciputra's "personal" business, emphasizing that he founded the company for his children. In this regard the Ciputra Group is a

---

[19]   "Wonder Boy dari Parigi", *Infobank* edisi November no. 218/1997, pp. 32-33.

[20]   Jamie Mackie, "Changing Patterns of Chinese Big Business", in Ruth McVey, ed., *Southeast Asian Capitalists* (Cornell: Southeast Asia Program Publications, 1992), p. 187.

[21]   Mucharor Djalil, "Ladang Bisnis Seorang Arsitek", *Infobank* edisi November no. 218/1997, pp. 32-35.

[22]   Interview with Christianto Wibisono, April 24, 2001.

classic example of the overseas Chinese "family firm", in which, as Robert Hefner writes, "the preferred strategy among successful business owners is to assign each son different spheres of influence in the business or, better yet (if one is especially successful), an entirely separate business."[23]

Ciputra is a tall, distinguished-looking man in his late sixties. An admirer of Singapore's Lee Kuan Yew, he greets a visitor in the cool wood-paneled waiting room of the Ciputra Group building on Jl. Prof. Dr. Satrio in Kuningan, Jakarta. The dim room is filled with dark leather furniture and models of building projects that radiate the glow of tiny lights. Proud of his achievements, Ciputra mentions his dream of creating a Jakarta version of Singapore's famed Orchard Road along Jl. Prof. Dr. Satrio. The shopping, office, and residential center would be anchored by the Citra Regency apartments, a luxury building that in 2001 reigned over a neighborhood of abandoned building projects languishing behind sheets of corrugated steel. Abruptly halted by the 1997 Indonesian economic crisis that after four years showed few signs of abating, the development sites along the busy thoroughfare were being reclaimed by rainwater and thick vegetation.

Immaculately dressed in a navy blue suit, Ciputra speaks in rapid and serviceable English. He recalls the establishment of the Jaya Raya Foundation this way: "Ali Sadikin asked me to help with sports. Football, badminton, and athletics." The governor was also interested in publishing works of literature. "Ali Sadikin has a friend, named Ajip Rosjidi, he is also in literature. So he says, 'Okay Ciputra, please, you develop these sports, you develop this literature. And why not join together with *Jaya* weekly to form one foundation to do this?' He is a great motivator. 'Okay, you do it!' he says."[24]

---

23   Hefner suggests that this inheritance strategy not only has the advantage of avoiding rivalries among sons, but that "the consequences…for growth cycles in Chinese business are enormous." Robert W. Hefner, ed., *Market Cultures: Society and Morality in the New Asian Capitalisms* (Boulder, Co.: Westview Press, 1998), p. 14.

24   Interview with Ciputra, March 12, 2001.

Explaining that it was Lukman Setiawan who first introduced him to Goenawan Mohamad, Ciputra says, "I didn't know Goenawan. But when *Ekspres* came, I really admired it. Wah, these are the best people. It was something new for me. I asked Lukman, 'Please, you find these people because you know them.'"

"My job is finding people, you know? Everything that happens in the market about people attracts my attention. Later I form all these new companies. In Jaya, I founded more than fifty companies. What I want in this publication I don't yet know, but what I need is people."

It was Ciputra himself who managed the negotiations. According to Fikri Jufri, Ciputra ended the conversation by saying "It is my job to negotiate things with Japan, with big businesses such as Mitsubishi, but it is not as complicated as the negotiation with you journalists. Gentlemen, who are you anyway?"[25]

The deal struck between the *Ekspres* group and the Jaya Raya Foundation was unique. The split in ownership would be 50-50, with Jaya Raya providing the capital and the journalists providing the skill. As the head of the Jaya Raya foundation, Ciputra brought eighteen million rupiah to the table.[26] The first publisher of *Tempo* was called Jaya Press, and it was a for-profit part of the Jaya Raya Foundation.

According to Goenawan, it is likely that no one expected *Tempo* to succeed. Laughing, he said that if Ciputra had anticipated that *Tempo* would become a financial success, he would have put his own money into it.[27] As it was, Ciputra owned no shares of *Tempo* as an individual. Instead the 50% he controlled was in his capacity as head of the Jaya Raya Foundation. His representative on the

[25] Daniel Dhakidae, "The State, The Rise of Capital, and the Fall of Political Journalism," p. 260.
[26] Interview with Harjoko Trisnadi, June 14, 2001. Christianto Wibisono disputes this number, saying that the figure was twenty-two million. Interview with Christianto Wibisono, April 24, 2001.
[27] Interview with Goenawan Mohamad, March 11, 2001.

Goenawan Mohamad in *Tempo*'s office in Jl. Senen Raya, 1971 [*Tempo*/Ed Zoelverdi]

board of directors was Eric Frits Samola, who came from the Jaya Development Group. Although Harjoko Trisnadi was Ciputra's original choice for director of the company, Harjoko demurred. As a result Eric Samola became the director and Harjoko was named assistant director.[28]

The relationship between Ciputra, the Jaya Raya Foundation, and *Tempo* magazine suggests a pattern that is familiar to students of Indonesian political economy. As is well known, during the days of colonial rule, immigrant Chinese occupied a middle stratum in the Indonesian economy, located somewhere between the colonial business elites on the top and indigenous petty entrepreneurs on the bottom. For much of the New Order period, private business enterprise in Indonesia was controlled by the local Chinese. During the early 1990s, for example, it was estimated that Chinese ownership of domestic private corporate capital was about 70 percent of the total.[29]

A key factor in this "inherited social system" is the reciprocal

---

28   Interview with Harjoko Trisnadi, June 28, 2000.
29   Richard Robison, "Industrialization and the Development of Capital", in Ruth McVey, ed., *Southeast Asian Capitalists* (Cornell: Southeast Asia Program Publications, 1992), p. 68.

relationship between Chinese entrepreneurs and bureaucratic elites. In Indonesia, as throughout much of Southeast Asia, the Chinese tend to be economically strong but politically vulnerable, and to depend on bureaucrats for political protection.[30] As Jamie Mackie explained:

> The prosperity of Chinese businessmen under the post-1965 regime has often been attributed to their political connections as *cukong* to the New Order power-holders. The term came into currency around 1970 to denote a close relationship between a Chinese who knew how to raise money and an Indonesian official (often an army officer) who could provide protection and influence. During the early days of the regime the government budget was quite inadequate to fund more than a small part of the routine expenditures of the armed forces and the regional civilian administration. 'Unconventional finances' had to be raised by any means whatever, at both the local and national levels.[31]

The ownership of *Tempo* was thus similar to many other business arrangements in the New Order in that it involved both Chinese entrepreneurial skill and, indirectly, state capital. Ciputra controlled a foundation that was partly owned by the City of Jakarta, and that, in turn, owned 50% of the magazine. Yet there were key differences as well. One was that Ciputra was not personally an "investor" in *Tempo*. Moreover, in the classic New Order relationship, the Chinese investor was protected by a politically powerful general, and this was not the case with *Tempo* – unless of course one wanted to count Jakarta Governor General Ali Sadikin.

---

[30]   Ruth McVey, "The Materialization of the Southeast Asian Entrepreneur," in Ruth McVey, ed., *Southeast Asian Capitalists*, p. 16. See also Fred W. Riggs, *Thailand: the Modernization of a Bureaucratic Polity* (Honolulu: East-West Centre Press, 1966).
[31]   Jamie Mackie, "Changing Patterns of Chinese Big Business", pp. 178-9.

Although the experience of the Chinese in Indonesia suggests that economic power is not synonymous with political power, the two are obviously related. For Goenawan Mohamad and the founders of *Tempo*, the primary goal of their financial arrangements with the Jaya Raya Foundation was editorial independence. As Christianto Wibisono said, one hard lesson they had learned from their experience with B.M. Diah and *Ekspres* was that if the journalists controlled less than 50% of the shares, they did not control the magazine.

The introductory issue of *Tempo* was eighteen pages long, and distributed for free. The cover story focused on Minarni, an Indonesian badminton star who suffered a tragic fall at the 1970 Asian Games in Bangkok. *Pantau* magazine writer Coen Husain Pontoh has described its headline, "Bunyi 'Kraak' dalam Tragedi Minarni" (A Craack-ing Sound in Minarni's Tragedy) as something that was likely to pique readers' interest.[32]

The editors devoted considerable space to explaining the new magazine's goals, scope, and approach towards language. *Tempo* would cover various rubrics, groups, and aspects of life with language that was "bright and fresh, smart and pleasurable." With words that echoed Goenawan Mohamad's letters from the early 1960s, *Tempo* criticized the language of conventional journalism as something that had become "half dead," full of worn-out slogans, empty words, and "sentences in shambles."[33] Perhaps the most famous section of the introductory edition was *Tempo*'s definition of good journalism, which has been reprinted many times over. It read:

> Our journalism will not be one-sided, or based on the politics
> of a single group. We believe that neither virtue nor the lack of

---

[32] Coen Husain Pontoh, "Konflik Tak Kunjung Padam", *Pantau*, Augustus 2001, p. 45.
[33] *Tempo*, Nomer Perkenalan, no date. [The magazine was actually published on March 1, 1971.]

virtue is the monopoly of any one side. We believe that the
duty of the press is not to spread prejudice, but rather to wipe
it out, not to sow the seeds of hatred, but rather to communicate
mutual understanding. The journalism of this magazine will
not be sneering or insulting, obsequious or slavish. What gives
us jurisdiction is not power or money, but rather good
intentions, a sense of justice and healthy thinking – all of which
will be the basic philosophy of this magazine.

In terms of layout, *Tempo* resembled *Time*, and the editors made
little secret of the fact that they had been influenced by the style
of the American magazine. Like its American counterpart, *Tempo*
was divided into departments, which included National,
Economics, Film, Photo, International, City and Village, and
People. Even the word "tempo" meant "time", and a brief section
on the choice of a name asserted that "'time'…in its many variations
is commonly used by journalistic publications throughout the
world."[34] The similarity in appearance of the two magazines –
and especially *Tempo*'s use of *Time*'s "trademark" red border – would
be a factor in the lawsuit that *Time* brought against *Tempo* in
1973.[35] Although the case was ultimately dropped, it was
nevertheless a cause of consternation among Goenawan and his
friends.[36]

The early editions of *Tempo* covered the arts, lifestyle, and
behavior in ways that were fresh and new. There were stories about
nightclubs in Jakarta, the prostitution trade, and the development

---

[34]   *Tempo*, Nomer Perkenalan.
[35]   In 1973, an Indonesian law firm representing *Time* sued *Tempo* in Jakarta's Central
District Court. The suit declared that "at a glance *Tempo* looked exactly the same
as *Time* magazine." The case was dropped in the middle of 1974. Apparently there
had been some "mis-coordination" between *Time*'s central office in New York and
local representatives, who later stated that "the suit had happened because of a
mistake and without instruction from *Time*, Inc." Coen Husain Pontoh, "Konflik
Tak Kunjung Padam", *Pantau*, Augustus 2001, p. 46.
[36]   See for example Aristides Katoppo to Goenawan Mohamad, January 12, 1974,
Goenawan Mohamad file, H.B. Jassin documentary library.

of cheap hotels for backpackers along Jl. Jaksa. There were articles on the press, including a proclamation signed by the editors of seven papers stating that their reporters would refuse to accept "envelopes" at press conferences. A feature on "the wives of the Republic" – including President Soeharto's wife Ibu Tien – served up the interesting tidbit that the first lady did not sleep with her husband. And an article on the "Your Next Destination Indonesia" campaign pointed out the pros and cons of the development of tourism in Bali, the latter including the arrival of "hippies" (or "tourists without money") and the commercialization of Balinese religion.[37]

The stories that people remember from the early days of *Tempo*, or "the ones that still stick," as Goenawan once said, are the articles on the arts, culture, and literature. For example, there was a memorable piece on theater in New York, written by Syu'bah Asa. There was playwright Putu Wijaya's story on the cost of developing tourism in Bali. And there was Goenawan's own piece on *Ngaben*, the Balinese ritual of cremation, as well as his cover story on W.S. Rendra that compared the poet's theatre workshop in Yogyakarta to a *pesantren*, or Muslim boarding school.[38]

Whatever the subject matter, *Tempo* stories were written in a style that was always *"enak dibaca"* – a pleasure to read. This style, which utilized both a facility with language and a story-like format, prompted a team of Indonesian university students who systematically read and coded a selection of magazines to conclude that in its early days *Tempo* was almost like a "gossip magazine."

"Public officials were described in great detail," one student

---

[37]   *Tempo*, May 10, 1971. For the cover story on nightclubs, see *Tempo*, March 20, 1971. For "envelopes," see *Tempo*, April 3, 1971; for the prostitution trade, see *Tempo*, September 11, 1971. For the development of Jl. Jaksa, see *Tempo*, April 10, 1971. For Ibu Tien and the other ladies of the Republic, see *Tempo*, April 24, 1971. For the tourism campaign and its affect on Bali, see *Tempo*, May 10, 1971.
[38]   "Teater Amerika, Ada Iklan dan...", *Tempo*, February 19, 1977; "Bila Waktu Menjamah Bali", *Tempo*, May 27, 1972; "Jalan Lain ke Surga", *Tempo*, August 31, 1985; "Rendra, Dimanakah Kau, Saudaraku?" *Tempo*, March 27, 1971.

remarked. "Maybe an official had two wives, four houses, like what we find in gossip magazines today. The lives of high officials were very interesting to people. At that time there weren't yet any tabloids. The people had a desire to read, and *Tempo* could see a market."[39]

The students may have been struck by the "gossipy" subject matter, but what *Tempo* quickly became noted for was its use of language. Linguist Dede Oetomo suggested that much of what was new about the use of the Indonesian language in *Tempo* is actually related to the syntax and structure of Javanese.

An extraordinary man by any measure, Dede Oetomo is Indonesia's foremost gay activist. He is also a teacher, writer, and scholar. Dede's imposing figure – tall and of rather princely bearing – belies both his good-natured friendliness and his generosity of spirit. His Surabaya home was a kind of salon for students and other activists in the early days of the pro-democracy movement, and doubled as the headquarters for Indonesia's largest gay organization, Gaya Nusantara.

"I grew up in a family that read a lot," Dede recalled, "and when I came to Surabaya when I was in high school, that was early New Order, and there were all these wonderful publications. There was no censorship yet. You had *Indonesia Raya* blasting [state-owned oil company] Pertamina, it was wonderful, and *Tempo* was definitely something, even from the very beginning. I started buying *Tempo* regularly when I was a student in Malang; that was 1976. I would actually ride my motorbike to the town square where there was a newsstand. One evening, usually a Thursday evening, *Tempo* would be there."[40]

"*Tempo* played around with language in a very interesting way," he said. "They would use words that were only used in poetry, but not to make it sound quaint or highbrow. It's a fresh way of using Indonesian that you wouldn't find in other Indonesian magazines or newspapers."

[39] Focus group interview with coders, June 2, 2000.
[40] Interview with Dede Oetomo, May 8, 1998.

For many years *Tempo* had a column on language that was written by Slamet Djabarudi, a man who was at the forefront of this language development.[41] Slamet's column focused on language usage and spelling, and was widely renowned. But for Dede, most of *Tempo*'s contribution to the development of the Indonesian language stems from its relationship with Javanese, not only in terms of the different levels of language, but also in terms of playfulness. "One thing about Javanese folk culture," he said, "is that it's very witty, it's very playful. You play all the time, you laugh all the time, you giggle all the time. You're very rarely serious." According to Dede, *Tempo* also had a tongue-in-cheek quality, an in-the-know way of saying "*I* know what you're doing there."

Asked for an example of *Tempo*'s playing around with language, Dede explained "there's a two-word phrase in Indonesian – *kacau balau*, which means in total chaos. So the original Indonesian overlay expression is *kacau balau*. And *kacau* can exist by itself, but not *balau* until *Tempo* actually played with it. And then *balau* became acceptable."

"As a linguist, I would say that the way young people [today] use language by replacing words with words that are unusual started with *Tempo*. But that's not so surprising, because remember that many of the people at *Tempo* were raised speaking Javanese, and in Javanese the way you play with the levels is actually just to change the words and the ending. So it's like the word for chaotic was *kacau*, and you just change it to another word and make it a level higher, more interesting, more critical, cuter. If you look at the syntax, I think the mechanism of *Tempo* is based on changing these words."[42]

---

[41]   See "Slamet Djabarudi", in the 15th anniversary issue of *Tempo*, March 1986, p. 70.

[42]   Benedict Anderson has made a similar argument in "Politics of Language and Javanese Culture", writing that "the invisible presence of Javanese language and literature has been very important for the creativity of Javanese writing in Indonesian. In this sense, it is like a black hole – something one knows is there even if one cannot see it." Benedict R. O'G. Anderson, "Politics of Language and Javanese Culture," in *Language and Power*, p. 235.

According to Dede, *Tempo* also experimented with spelling, especially after 1972 when the Indonesian spelling was changed. "*Tempo* didn't just turn around, they would spell things their own way sometimes," he said. "And that was another way the language of *Tempo* had such an attraction for people like me."

Another important aspect of the early writing in *Tempo* was its narrative quality. Far from utilizing the "inverted pyramid" style, in which a lead paragraph contains the most important elements of "who, what, where, when, why and how," articles in *Tempo* in the early years had a story-like quality, sometimes meandering from one topic to another. As one of my coders observed, "it was like reading a novel. Sometimes it was funny. If they were supposed to be writing about development, instead they would write about architecture. Maybe they only had a little bit of news, but they still had to fill the column. We can see that there really wasn't much of a connection."[43]

Since the beginning of *Tempo*, Goenawan has told young writers that their articles should read "like stories." The writer and novelist Bur Rasuanto went even further, saying that in the early 1970s he and other *Tempo* writers had been influenced by the work of Tom Wolfe and the other "new journalists" from America who applied literary techniques to the practice of journalism.[44] As he said, they were interested in "lots of detail", but they weren't just "playing around".[45] It is probably not surprising that a group of poets and writers with backgrounds in literature would be more interested in setting a scene or developing characters than they were in adhering to conventional guidelines of what made a story newsworthy. These sorts of guidelines, including a strict numerical system of "deciding what's news", would be developed later. But in the early days of *Tempo*, it was the artists and writers who ran the magazine.

---

[43]   Focus group interview with coders, June 2, 2000.
[44]   See Tom Wolfe and E. W. Johnson, eds., *The New Journalism* (New York: Harper and Row, 1973).
[45]   Interview with Bur Rasuanto, June 19, 2002.

When *Tempo* celebrated its fifteenth anniversary in 1986 with a special edition, it included a list of all the cover stories that had ever been published. The vast majority of these stories fell under the rubrics of the Nation or Economy. Not surprisingly, these departments were also the focus of the early years of the magazine, as *Tempo* devoted considerable space to national affairs and the development of the Indonesian economy under the guidance of the American-trained Indonesian economists known as the "technocrats".

From a global perspective, the technocrats can be seen as part of the vast "modernization project" of the 1960s. They were influenced by Western development theorists like W.W. Rostow, Daniel Lerner, and Samuel Huntington who energetically espoused programs designed to develop the economies of the world's poorer nations, and bring them in line with the capitalism of the West.[46] The specter of Communism was never far from this Cold War vision, and Southeast Asia was of particular concern to modernization theorists, who hoped to prove the superiority of American liberalism over Marxism in guiding "undeveloped" countries like Indonesia along the road to modernity.[47]

Soeharto's New Order government, with its vigorous opposition to Communism and desperate need to jumpstart the economy, was thus ripe for developmentalism. To the technocrats, many of whom had been affiliated with the economics department at the University of Indonesia, it seemed obvious that rational economic planning was the only way to end the chaos of the Soekarno years and bring about the possibility of growth and

[46] For an excellent overview of these and other theorists, see J. Timmons Roberts and Amy Hite, *From Modernization to Globalization: Perspectives on Development and Social Change* (Oxford: Blackwell Publishers, 2000).

[47] Jonathan Nashel, "The Road to Vietnam: Modernization Theory in Fact and Fiction", in Christian G. Appy, ed., *Cold War Constructions: The Political Culture of United States Imperialism, 1945-1966* (Amherst: University of Massachusetts Press, 2000), p. 134.

prosperity.[48] At the May 1966 *Tracée Baru* symposium, senior economist Widjojo Nitisastro had criticized the "neglect" of the Soekarno years, arguing that under Guided Democracy rational economic principles were considered "unnecessary" and "too conventional". All too often, he said, "the management of the economy had been based on catch-phrases and [revolutionary] slogans."[49]

Once Soeharto came to power, his team of economic advisors launched an ambitious economic development plan along the lines set out by Rostow and the other modernizers. In 1968, Soeharto appointed his first "Development Cabinet", giving the Department of Trade to Professor Soemitro Djojohadikusumo, and the Department of Finance to Ali Wardhana. In 1971, four more technocrats joined the cabinet, including Widjojo Nitisastro.[50] Under their leadership, Soeharto undertook an ambitious program of *pembangunan* or development, building infrastructure such as schools, clinics, roads, and markets.[51]

Tempo gave thorough coverage to the cabinet, and was generally supportive of the technocrats. Its story on the president's announcement of his new cabinet in September 1971 pointed out the reduction in the number of ministers who were also army officers, and concluded that "it would now be difficult to accuse Indonesia of being a military state."[52] The article acknowledged, however, that the technocrats were not without critics, and quoted

[48]   John James MacDougall, "The Technocratic Model of Modernization: The Case of Indonesia's New Order", *Asian Survey*, Vol. 16. No. 12 (Dec. 1976), 1166-1183.

[49]   Widjojo Nitisastro, "Kata Pengantar", *Simposium Kebangkitan Semangat '66: Mendjeladjah Tracée Baru*, (Djakarta: Universitas Indonesia, 1966).

[50]   Harold Crouch, *The Army and Politics in Indonesia*, p. 242.

[51]   For a fascinating discussion of the linguistic origins of the word "pembangunan" see Ariel Heryanto, *Language of Development and Development of Language: The Case of Indonesia*, Pacific Linguistics, Series D-86, 1995, esp. pp. 11-19.

[52]   *Tempo*, September 18, 1971. Harold Crouch has likewise pointed out that as the army tightened its grip on power in the period of "consolidation" between 1968 and the 1971 elections, its representation in the cabinet actually declined. Harold Crouch, *The Army and Politics in Indonesia*, pp. 241-2.

B.M. Diah's newspaper *Merdeka* as saying that the technocrats were more interested in seeking foreign capital than they were in fighting for small native (*bumiputera*) businesses.

One of the most searing attacks on the technocrats came from an American named David Ransom, and was published in the October 1970 issue of the California-based magazine *Ramparts*. Ransom's article linked the economic policies of the technocrats with Ford Foundation-sponsored training at Berkeley, Harvard, Kentucky and Cornell, as well as other "CIA-fed" exchanges dating back to the 1950s. "But it is the foreign-investment plan that is the payoff of Ford's twenty-year strategy in Indonesia and the pot of gold that the Ford modernizers – both American and Indonesian – are paid to protect," Ransom wrote. "The nineteenth-century Colonial Dutch strategy built an agricultural export economy. The Americans are interested primarily in resources, mainly mineral....A corps of 'qualified' native technocrats formally make economic decisions, kept in hand by the best American advisors the Ford Foundation's millions can buy."[53]

Goenawan Mohamad responded to Ransom's attack on the technocrats in a signed essay. Accusing Ransom and the editorial staff of *Ramparts* of having "made up their minds...long before they did their interviews or collected their data," Goenawan argued that they "had already determined their enemy to be the institutions of the American Establishment." Worse yet, by characterizing the technocrats as "traitors" or "cheap peons" of the CIA, Ransom was refusing to give them credit for having a "dynamic" of their own. "This young man who pretends to be so revolutionary is actually among the most reactionary in the West," Goenawan wrote, "seeing the people of Indonesia, people of color in a backward country, as no more than water buffalos, whom the wise men of America can easily lead by the nose."

---

[53]   David Ransom, "Ford Country: Building an Elite for Indonesia", in Steve Weissman, ed., *The Trojan Horse: A Radical Look at Foreign Aid* (Palo Alto California: Ramparts Press, 1975), revised edition, pp. 93-116.

In language reminiscent of his criticism of sensational European news reports of the 1965-66 massacre of the PKI, Goenawan questioned the moral validity of Ransom's argument. Although Goenawan acknowledged that it was appropriate to have a national debate on the role of foreign capital in economic development, the stakes were not "academic conclusions", but rather the fate of millions of Indonesians who were living in poverty:

> Many among the New Left in the West have noble hearts and a lofty humanitarianism, only they don't have to take the risks that haunt the majority of the Indonesian people right now.... [They] can declare their love for Indonesia, its people and its culture. But if...they prefer that Indonesia follows the path that they choose for it, are they also prepared to shoulder the burden that is now being borne by the Indonesian people? This is where the problem of moral responsibility emerges; something that is appropriately asked of one who declares himself to be nervous about foreign investment, but who lives off of foreign capital, someone who says he hates capitalism, but who lives as a capitalist.[54]

Ransom's critique of the technocrats as tools of the CIA may have resonated with the American "New Left", but the argument that their policies favored growth at the expense of distribution, and foreign capital and Chinese-Indonesian entrepreneurs at the expense of "native" businesses was more convincing in Indonesia. By the early 1970s, the technocrats faced growing opposition, especially from students, who were unhappy with what they saw as discriminatory policies and growing indications of corruption among the political and military elite. Student discontent was met with sympathy by some of the more professional military leaders,

---

[54]   Goenawan Mohamad, "Dari Kisah 'The Berkeley Mafia'", *Tempo*, September 25, 1971.

who were likewise afraid that the achievements of the New Order would be undermined by the blatant profiteering of those whom Harold Crouch has called the "financial" generals. These generals, along with their foreign or Chinese-Indonesian business partners, were popularly perceived to be the exclusive beneficiaries of the influx of foreign capital.[55]

By 1973, students opposed to the business activities of the "financial" generals began to pin their hopes on Lieutenant General Soemitro, the deputy commander of the Armed Forces and the commander of Kopkamtib. General Soemitro's primary political opponent was Ali Moertopo, the head of Opsus (Special Operations) and one of the president's personal assistants, or *aspri*. Ali Moertopo's Opsus was widely believed to have been responsible for having ensured a favorable outcome for Golkar in the election of 1971, and his special position as *aspri* was a particular target of student protest. The convergence of political rivalry within the army with popular dissatisfaction over corruption and what were felt to be narrowing opportunities for indigenous businesses made for an explosive combination.

Late in 1973, a series of incidents occurred that brought the crisis to a head. On August 5, Bandung experienced the worst anti-Chinese riots of the New Order, as a mob rampaged through the city center, destroying hundreds of vehicles and over a thousand shops and homes. Army units were not sent in until late in the afternoon, and once they arrived, the soldiers did little to quell the fires and looting, thus raising suspicions that they sympathized with the rioters.[56] In September, Muslim students stormed

---

55   See Harold Crouch, *The Army and Politics in Indonesia*, especially chapter 12, "Policies and the Struggle for Power", pp. 304-343.

56   Atmakusumah, then managing editor of *Indonesia Raya*, remembered that the Minister of Information called a meeting of newspaper editors and warned them not to "exaggerate" reports of the riot, but that his paper nevertheless devoted three-quarters of its front page to coverage of what had happened in Bandung. "I already felt that we might be banned," he said. "In the morning I got a call from Pusat Penerangan ABRI [the Armed Forces Information Center], asking me who

Parliament in protest of a government-backed "marriage law" that they saw as a threat to political Islam. On October 24, a group of students at the University of Indonesia petitioned the government in protest of "the violation of law, raging corruption, the abuse of authority, rising prices, and unemployment" and a strategy of economic development that they claimed benefitted only the rich.[57] And in November and December, delegations of students demonstrated at Bappenas, the Japanese embassy, and Bank Indonesia in protest of corruption, foreign capital, and "Japanese economic imperialism".

While these events were occurring in Jakarta and elsewhere, General Soemitro, the head of Kopkamtib, the agency charged with security and the restoration of order, toured university campuses in Surabaya, Bandung, and Yogyakarta, and pledged a "new pattern of leadership" and "two-way communication". As *Tempo* noted, what was "interesting" was the attitude of Kopkamtib Jakarta. "Maybe because it wants to be consistent with the 'new face' of authority, they have taken no action against these demonstrations," the magazine suggested.[58] Or, as editor Nono Makarim elliptically explained many years later:

> The government's indecisiveness in the face of widespread displays of discontent, its hesitation to act when the sporadic student protests were growing into huge demonstrations on the eve of the Japanese prime minister's visit to Jakarta, were clear signs that heavy infighting was taking place among the most powerful factions in the government. With one of the adversaries

---

had attended the meeting. I said 'myself.' 'Didn't you hear what the minister said?' 'Yes of course.' 'Why did you print this report like this?' 'Look,' I said, 'we don't exaggerate it, we just put the story as it is!' I myself edited it. Of course I was very very careful. I still had the original reports in my file." Interview, June 21, 2003.

[57]   Quoted in Harold Crouch, *The Army and Politics in Indonesia*, p. 311.
[58]   "Mahasiswa, Arah Apa?" *Tempo*, December 8, 1973. See also "Dilema Komunikasi Timbal-Balik", *Tempo*, December 8, 1973.

The Malari incident, Jakarta, January 15, 1974 [*Tempo*/Syahrir Wahab]

clearly supporting the protest movement in a bid for popular support, a fatal choosing of sides by student leaders as well as some editors was inevitable.[59]

On January 14, 1974, the Japanese prime minister Tanaka arrived in Jakarta for a state visit. Harold Crouch has concluded that both General Soemitro and his rivals intended to use the visit for a showdown, arguing that "it can be surmised that Soemitro hoped that the student protest against Tanaka's visit could be used to weaken the position of [presidential assistants] Ali Moertopo and Sudjono Humardhani, both of whom were identified in the public mind with a pro-Japan outlook."[60] On the 15th, the day after Tanaka's arrival, students demonstrated throughout the city, declaring their dissatisfaction with foreign capital – especially Japanese capital – and Japanese business practices. By late in the day, however, the situation had gotten out of hand. *Tempo* reported that the student protestors had been overtaken by a wave of rioters.

[59] Nono Makarim, "The Indonesian Press: An Editor's Perspective", in Karl P. Jackson and Lucien W. Pye, eds., *Political Power and Communications in Indonesia* (Berkeley: University of California Press, 1978), p. 280.
[60] Harold Crouch, *The Army and Politics in Indonesia*, p. 314.

Cars burning during the Malari incident, Jakarta,
January 15, 1974 [*Tempo*/Syahrir Wahab]

These youths with "tattered" and "dirty clothes" set fire to Japanese cars, destroyed buildings and shops, attacked the showroom of the Astra Motor Company and the Coca Cola plant, and burned and looted the Senen market in the "biggest and most widespread rioting that has occurred in [Jakarta] during peace time."[61] As spirals of thick, black smoke hung in the cloudy sky, the army took no immediate action. On the second day of the rioting, troops opened fire on the looters. About eleven people were killed, and hundreds wounded.

When order was finally restored, it was not entirely clear what had caused the "Malapetaka Januari" or Fifteenth of January Disaster – usually shortened to "Malari". Officially, the riot was blamed on remnants of the banned parties PSI and Masyumi. Many of those arrested were former student leaders, including Fahmi Idris, Dorodjatun Kuntjoro Jakti, Marsillam Simanjuntak, Hariman Siregar, and Adnan Buyung Nasution. General Soemitro was dismissed from his position as commander of the Kopkamtib, and "resigned" from his position as deputy commander of the armed forces. As Nono Makarim wrote, "A massive wave of arrests

---

61   "Musibah Bagi Golongan Menengah & Bawah", *Tempo*, January 26, 1974.

was followed by the deposition of the second most powerful man in the country, and with him an awe-inspiring power-bloc 'mysteriously' disappeared. With the demise of one of the contending groups, of necessity came the time for reckoning with its supporters."[62]

Although it was clear that General Soemitro had "lost" in the intra-army rivalry, it was not equally clear that Ali Moertopo had "won". Ali Moertopo had been a vocal critic of the technocrats, setting up his own research institute, the Center for Strategic and International Studies, which often criticized the technocrats for their alleged subservience to Western aid donors such as the IMF.[63] As Aristides Katoppo explained, "Soeharto used Ali to countervail against Soemitro. But if Ali Moertopo is the winner of this, then he becomes a major threat to Soeharto."[64] And indeed, within a few years Ali Moertopo was himself sidelined to the Department of Information.

If the political implications were not immediately clear, the implications for the press were immediate and catastrophic. In the aftermath of Malari, twelve publications had their SIC and SIT (printing and publication licenses) withdrawn. They were *Nusantara, Harian Kami, Indonesia Raya, Abadi, The Jakarta Times, Mingguan Wenang, Pemuda Indonesia, Ekspres* weekly news magazine, *Pedoman, Suluh Berita, Mahasiswa Indonesia,* and *Indonesia Pos.* Of these, *Abadi* and *The Jakarta Times* were eventually permitted to return to publication, but only after their names and editorial staffs were changed.[65]

---

[62] Nono Makarim, "The Indonesian Press, An Editor's Perspective", p. 280.

[63] Harold Crouch, *The Army and Politics in Indonesia*, p. 326.

[64] Interview with Aristides Katoppo, June 21, 2003.

[65] *Abadi* was permitted to return as *Pelita, The Jakarta Times* returned to publication as *The Indonesian Times.* David Hill, *The Press in the New Order*, p. 37. For a detailed chronology of the bannings after Malari, see Abdurrachman Surjomihardjo, ed., *Beberapa Segi Perkembangan Sejarah Pers di Indonesia*, 2nd printing, (Jakarta: Kompas, 2002), pp. 289-297.

Why were some publications banned and others not? According to Bur Rasuanto, who had written *Tempo*'s cover story on Malari, certain papers were banned not so much because of what they published, but rather because of who edited them and the views with which they were associated. Goenawan Mohamad agreed with this assessment. "It was a purge," he said.[66]

Nono Makarim, the former editor of *Harian Kami* who had left the newspaper several months before Malari to study at Harvard, said that had he seen the emerging showdown between General Soemitro and Ali Moertopo, and had warned Zulharman Said, the acting editor, "When the elephants fight, move out, don't choose sides. Because mind you they don't fight about principles, they fight about turf." According to Nono, Zulharman chose sides with Gen. Soemitro against Ali Moertopo, and "the mistake was made."[67]

According to Bur Rasuanto, *Tempo* had seen the potential danger, and tried to be fair to both sides. He believes that what saved *Tempo* was a cover story they had done on the technocrats, and specifically on Widjojo, on December 1, 1973. This story examined the criticisms of the technocrats that had been raised by "students, intellectuals, and the younger generation."[68] As Bur explained, "Widjojo was the enemy of Ali Moertopo. Widjojo wanted foreign capital to enter, including Japanese. Therefore we criticized both sides." He emphasized, however, that *Tempo*'s criticism of Widjojo had been fair. "It was responsible criticism," he said. "We were not going to support one person. We criticized him because we usually supported him. We would frequently invite him to lunch to find out what was going on."[69]

Goenawan agreed with Bur's assessment, adding that Ali

---

[66]   Interview with Bur Rasuanto, June 19, 2002. Interview with Goenawan Mohamad, July 25, 2002.
[67]   Interview with Nono Makarim, June 23, 2000.
[68]   "Kini Teknokrat Sebagai Tergugat", *Tempo,* December 1, 1973.
[69]   Interview with Bur Rasuanto, June 19, 2002.

Moertopo had wanted to get rid of Widjojo and put Daoed Joesoef in Bappenas instead. "Although Ali Moertopo won the battle with Soemitro, he didn't win with Widjojo," Goenawan said. "Soeharto loved Widjojo."

Yet according to Goenawan, there was another possible factor in the survival of *Tempo*. In the months leading up to Malari, there had been a group of editors who met regularly with General Soemitro. The group included Rosihan Anwar and Mochtar Lubis (the editors of *Pedoman* and *Indonesia Raya*), as well as writers from *Harian Kami*. Goenawan recalls having attended these meetings once or twice, but not as a regular. It is possible, Goenawan said, that this is what saved *Tempo*. The magazine may have been viewed as neutral. Aristides Katoppo, who viewed Malari from a kind of exile in the United States, agreed with this assessment, suggesting that *Tempo* may have survived partly because Goenawan was considered to be more of an intellectual than a political figure.

In remembering Malari, Marsillam Simanjuntak says that he was arrested "by association". As he explained, he had tried to stop the students. "I tried to say 'don't do that,'" he said, "because what they are doing is based on the assumption that they are speeding the process of Ali Moertopo against Soemitro. To which I said, 'no, don't ever think that you are speeding or accelerating the process.' [Instead] you create a situation where both parties cannot do anything but just clash."

And what about the papers that were banned? Also "by association," according to Marsillam. "But I can tell you this," he added, "although I am always a friend of Goenawan Mohamad, and Fikri Jufri and of *Tempo*, there was something of a disappointment with *Tempo* here and there." People expect more from *Tempo*, he said, "because they look at Goenawan. This is the problem, actually. Goenawan is not the single owner and decision-maker for the whole."[70]

This was exactly the problem. The lesson of Malari was clear: if a newspaper or magazine wished to survive, it would have to make certain compromises. As Goenawan had once asked H.B. Jassin, how can one who travels in safety evaluate those who struggle between life and death? For *Tempo* and the rest of the Indonesian press, compromise would become a matter of survival.

---

70 Interview with Marsillam Simanjuntak, July 18, 2002. Marsillam said that "in 1974, Goenawan helped us, not through *Tempo*, but by writing pamphlets...underground leaflets speaking the unspeakable to the military and to Soeharto and so forth. That's quite a feat; it's brave to do that. It was after I was arrested. Probably GM wants to assuage his conscience."

CHAPTER FOUR

the strategies

"We had many strategies."
— *Susanto Pudjomartono, February 18, 2000*

One of the first pieces of legislation passed by President Soeharto's New Order government was the Press Act of 1966. Although the law explicitly stated that "freedom of the press is guaranteed in accordance with the fundamental rights of citizens," this was hardly the case.[1] Despite guarantees that there would be no censorship or press bannings, would-be press entrepreneurs were required to obtain two permits before they could publish a newspaper or magazine: the Permit to Publish (SIT) from the Department of Information, and the Permit to Print (SIC) from the military security authority (Kopkamtib).[2] As the military's response to Malari demonstrated, a newspaper could be effectively banned by the withdrawal of either one.

Tempo survived Malari, but after 1974 the magazine's relationship with the New Order became increasingly complex, and the editors developed a set of strategies designed to protect the magazine that reveal much about the practice of journalism

---

[1] Translation by David Hill, *The Press in New Order Indonesia*, p. 25.

[2] The Permit to Publish (SIT) was subsequently renamed the Press Publication Enterprise Permit (SIUPP) in the revised Press Law of 1982.

during the Soeharto years. One of the most important of these strategies was economic independence, which was evident in the 1974 reorganization of the magazine's ownership, a move designed to minimize political pressure from outside. Another involved knowing when to accommodate to the development aims of what was known as the "Pancasila press". Like all Indonesian media, *Tempo* was obliged to report favorably upon government activities and announcements, but there were also subtle ways of undermining the government's point of view. In some cases, *Tempo* journalists used narrative devices to question what public officials were saying, while at other times they drew upon the norms of journalistic professionalism to argue that they had to "cover both sides."[3]

In Indonesia, news is much more than what appears on the printed page. Journalism is also a network of relationships, and *Tempo*'s efforts at "lobbying" government officials suggest the ambiguity of the magazine's relationship with power. In the lounges of five-star hotels and under the dim flourescent lights of military office buildings, *Tempo* journalists cultivated close professional connections with government and military sources. In many instances these connections were based on ties that dated back to the 1960s – when, as student activists, many of *Tempo*'s founders had worked with allies in the military to bring down Soekarno. When *Tempo* was banned for the first time in 1982, it may have even been these ties that saved the magazine.

Goenawan Mohamad always believed that *Tempo* had to be economically independent. At the time of its founding in 1971, *Tempo*'s financial backing had come solely from the Jaya Raya Foundation, a consortium of businesses loosely tied to the city of Jakarta. Three years later, Goenawan and the other founders drew

---

3   See Joseph C. Manzella, "Negotiating the News: Indonesian press culture and power during the political crises of 1997-8", *Journalism* 1 no. 3 (2000): 305-328.

up a new agreement with foundation director Ciputra that gave the magazine even greater autonomy.

In the beginning, *Tempo*'s arrangement with the Jaya Raya Foundation had been somewhat informal. "There was no written agreement," explained founding director Harjoko Trisnadi.[4] But by the end of 1973 *Tempo* was doing well, and Harjoko was able to report to the Jaya Raya Foundation that there was a surplus. Because the founders of *Tempo* were now in a position to return the money, they met with Ciputra in hopes of creating a new company: P.T. Grafiti Pers, or Grafiti Press. "Goenawan wanted the employees to have a role," Harjoko said, "so he asked Ciputra if 50% of the shares of Grafiti could be owned by the journalists, and 50% by the Jaya Raya Foundation."

Before Ciputra would agree to the deal, however, he asked that Goenawan and his friends establish a second company of their own. "Ciputra said 'I don't want to deal with dozens of employees, therefore you need to form one legal body,'" Harjoko explained. The result was P.T. Pikatan, which was established on December 11, 1973. Grafiti Pers, the joint venture between this company and the Jaya Raya Foundation, was founded two months later on February 4, 1974.[5]

P.T. Pikatan had twenty-two shareholders who owned shares as individuals. Five of these shareholders – Goenawan Mohamad, Harjoko Trisnadi, Fikri Jufri, Lukman Setiawan, and Bur Rasuanto – were the "founders" of *Tempo*.[6] Each of these individuals was given seventy shares of the total one thousand shares.[7] Seventeen

---

4   Interview with Harjoko Trisnadi, June 14, 2001.
5   Interview with Harjoko Trisnadi, June 14, 2001.
6   *Tempo* journalists routinely use the word *pendiri* or founder to describe these five individuals. The term would become particularly significant after the *Editor* "exodus". See chapter 8.
7   According to Christianto Wibisono, there was "absolutely no question" as to who the founders of *Tempo* were: they were the ones who negotiated with Ciputra. Christianto left *Tempo* before the re-negotiation of the shares, but says that if he had stayed on at *Tempo*, he would also have been considered a "founder". Interview with Christianto Wibisono, April 24, 2001.

additional employees (*karyawan*) were each given twenty shares. In order to be included in the group of seventeen, employees had to meet two criteria. They had to have been with *Tempo* when it was founded, and they still had to be working for the company three years later when P.T. Pikatan was established. Provided that an individual met these criteria, it didn't matter what kind of position he or she held at the magazine. As Goenawan is fond of pointing out, one of the seventeen original shareholders was the office boy.[8] Thirty-five shares of P.T. Pikatan were given to Eric Samola, and the remaining 275 were given to the *Tempo* employees as a group. Anyone who joined *Tempo* after 1973 would own shares as part of this collectivity.[9]

In 1985 Minister of Information Harmoko instituted a new regulation requiring that 20% of each press company be owned by the employees. The 275 shares of P.T. Pikatan that were already owned collectively equaled 13.5% of Grafiti Pers, so Harjoko Trisnadi asked Ciputra to make up the difference between that and 20%. Ciputra agreed, and the Jaya Raya Foundation contributed sixty-five additional shares (or 6.5% of the total) to the Yayasan Karyawan *Tempo*, or the *Tempo* Employees' Foundation.[10] As a result of the 1985 agreement, *Tempo* employees now owned a majority of the shares of Grafiti Pers. Goenawan had attained his goal of financial independence.[11]

---

[8]   The seventeen were: Harun Musawa, Mahtum, Herry Komar, Toeti Kakiailatu, Zen Umar Purba, Putu Wijaya, Zainal Abidin, Bambang Soemaryo, Syahir Wahab, Salim Said, Budianto, Yunus Kasim, D.S. Karma, Fachruddin Jahya, Syu'bah Asa, Yusril Djalinus, and Wage Minarno. I am grateful to Harjoko Trisnadi for giving me this list.

[9]   These arrangements still left 725 shares of P.T. Pikatan in the hands of twenty-two individuals. After a few years, this ownership of 36.5% of Grafiti Pers by a relatively small group of individuals would become problematic. See chapter 8.

[10] According to Harjoko, Ciputra first suggested that the 65 additional shares come from P.T. Pikatan, but "I told him that it would be difficult to take away the shares of individuals. Finally he agreed." Interview with Harjoko Trisnadi, June 14, 2001.

[11] Of the 1000 total shares of Grafiti Pers, P.T. Pikatan now owned 365, the Jaya Raya Foundation owned 435, and the *Tempo* Employees' Foundation owned 200.

Yet the story is actually more complicated than these numbers would suggest. In the late 1970s, Grafiti Pers created seventy new "priority shares". Of these, ten went to each of the directors: Goenawan Mohamad, Fikri Jufri, Harjoko Trisnadi, and Lukman Setiawan. Another thirty priority shares went to Eric Samola as the representative of the Jaya Raya Foundation. Of the thirty shares in Eric Samola's name, ten actually belonged to Ciputra, and ten to Budiman Kusika, who represented the interests of the city within the Jaya Raya Foundation. Significantly, new company directors could not be appointed without the consent of the holders of the priority shares – who were thereby given a veto power.

Goenawan makes no secret of the fact that the priority shares were created as a way to maintain control of *Tempo* after 1977, when Ali Sadikin stepped down as the governor of Jakarta. The governor of Jakarta was the titular head of the Jaya Raya foundation, and Goenawan described the new governor, Tjokropranolo, as "not friendly".

"Ali Sadikin protected everybody," Goenawan said. "We were afraid that the new governor could pressure Ciputra into taking out Eric Samola and putting in somebody new."[12]

Why did Eric Samola hold Ciputra's shares? Because Ciputra did not want to own shares in his own name. Goenawan often says that as an Indonesian of Chinese descent, Ciputra preferred to stay in the background. Ciputra himself confirmed this, saying simply "because I'm not indigenous, I had to use his name." Later the controversy over the true ownership of Eric Samola's thirty shares would become what Goenawan called an "embarrassment" to *Tempo*, as Samola refused to return the shares to Ciputra. To this day, Ciputra owns no shares in *Tempo* as an individual.

By all accounts, Ciputra seems almost never to have interfered

---

12   Interview with Goenawan Mohamad, June 1, 2001. Christianto Wibisono said that Ali Sadikin's resignation forced Ciputra to find a new "protector", thereby leading to his alliance with Liem Sioe Liong, the Soeharto crony and builder of Krakatau Steel. Interview with Christianto Wibisono, April 24, 2001.

in the day to day activities of *Tempo*.[13] When asked about the extent of his involvement, Ciputra said "Once or twice a year we had a meeting, a meeting of the board of trustees, or the board of directors. We discussed all the planning. Sometimes small things. Sometimes people complained about *Tempo*. But I leave it to them, they make the decision. Because I will not mix with business like this. If I know something, I will only make suggestions. But I have no right to tell them about the content of the magazine. I gave them a commitment."

Goenawan's recollections are slightly different. "Ciputra wanted to be involved, but he was scared. He made an effort, but he never succeeded," Goenawan said. "I should give him credit. He was very careful." Goenawan added that sometimes Ciputra would talk to Harjoko. "Ciputra would always talk to him," he said, "expecting that he would talk to me. It was not easy to talk to me. And Harjoko never did – he laughed and said 'forget about it.'"[14]

But Ciputra did call Goenawan on at least one occasion. It happened in 1987 after an incident at the North Jakarta amusement complex called Taman Impian Jaya Ancol, in which four young children drowned in a man-made lake. *Tempo* sent reporters to Ancol to cover the story. Ciputra, who was the managing director of the Jaya Group that had developed Ancol, telephoned Goenawan and asked that the story not be included. Goenawan refused.[15] The March 14th National section of *Tempo* contained an article on the incident, and included a lengthy quotation from Ciputra.[16]

---

[13] Toeti Kakiailatu said that although there had also been discussions with Sofian Alisjahbana about becoming the publisher of *Tempo*, the group favored Ciputra because they felt he would not try to interfere with the magazine's contents. Interview with Toeti Kakiailatu, January 8, 2002.

[14] Interview with Goenawan Mohamad, June 20, 2000.

[15] For an account of this incident, see "Gong! *Tempo*, Majalah & Mitos", *Jakarta-Jakarta*, July 24, 1987.

[16] "Musibah di Taman Impian", *Tempo* March 14, 1987.

Although this story is often repeated as a measure of *Tempo*'s editorial independence from the economic interests of Ciputra, given the newsworthiness of the event, *Tempo* probably had little choice but to publish. What is more interesting is the number of stories involving the Jaya Group that were never published at all. As a builder of toll roads, markets, and real estate projects, the Jaya Group was involved in many instances of *penggusuran*, or confiscation of land in the name of development. In most cases, those who were already living on the land were simply evicted. Although there was usually compensation, it was not always adequate – and it sometimes ended up in the pockets of corrupt local officials. Likewise, when older markets were condemned to make way for new shopping complexes, tenants with expired leases were forced to move their kiosks to other locations. With a handful of exceptions, stories in which Jakarta residents or small traders were evicted by the Jaya Development Group did not appear in *Tempo*.[17]

Although Goenawan managed to ensure that *Tempo* was free of direct pressure from its owners, keeping a polite but firm distance from government officials who wished to influence the magazine's content was more problematic. In the New Order, journalistic "professionalism" was understood to mean functioning as a mouthpiece for the dissemination of government programs and plans. It was not understood to mean challenging government authorities, or otherwise acting as a watchdog for citizens in the style of the "liberal" Western media. The "Pancasila press", named after the state ideology of the New Order, was expected to be a

---

[17]   A search of *Tempo*'s *Kota* or City section found approximately thirty stories with the keywords *gusur* or *tergusur* in which the condemnation of land occurred in Jakarta. The Jaya Development Group was not mentioned in connection with any of them. A second search for keyword "Jaya" led to the discovery of three stories involving *penggusuran* in which P.T. Jaya was the main actor. "Membunuh Ular dan Buaya", *Tempo* August 4, 1973; "Di Pasar Pagi Tanpa Tawar-Menawar", *Tempo*, September 30, 1978; and "Hilang Jejak Kapitan Djamin", *Tempo* July 25, 1981.

partner in economic development. In this way it strongly resembled "development journalism" as practiced elsewhere in Asia.[18]

The Indonesian press was supposed to be "free and responsible". Yet unlike the Western concept of press freedom, which emphasizes freedom *from* government control, press freedom in the New Order was understood to mean freedom *to* assist the state in carrying out programs for social and economic development. Although the phrase "a free and responsible press" was almost certainly borrowed from the 1947 Hutchins Commission Report, in the New Order it was stripped of any liberal or progressive meaning. In the Hutchins Commission Report, "responsible" meant providing the public with a truthful and comprehensive account of the day's events, serving as a forum for the exchange of comment and criticism, and projecting a representative picture of constituent groups in society.[19] In the New Order, "responsible" meant adhering to a set of guidelines prohibiting the reporting of anything that was likely to inflame ethnic, religious, racial, or group (class) tensions.[20] In practice, this meant that the press couldn't report openly on religious clashes, church burnings, race riots, labor unrest, or separatist movements. Nor could it criticize the first family, senior government officials or military leaders.

As Angela Romano has noted, "exposés on corruption, collusion and mismanagement were…often criticized for being negative, socially disruptive and damaging to public faith in the

---

[18]   For an excellent discussion of the meaning of the "Pancasila press", see Angela Romano, *Politics and the Press in Indonesia*, pp. 37-52. For a discussion of "development journalism," see William A. Hachten, *The Third World News Prism: Changing Media, Clashing Ideologies* (Ames: Iowa State University Press, 1987).

[19]   Theodore Peterson, "The Social Responsibility Theory of the Press", in Fred S. Siebert, ed., *Four Theories of the Press* (Urbana: University of Illinois Press, 1963), pp. 73-103.

[20]   These were the infamous "SARA" guidelines. The mnemonic SARA stood for Suku, Agama, Ras, and Antar-golongan. See David Hill, *The Press in New Order Indonesia*, pp. 44-47.

delicate and still-developing institutions of state. The ambivalence surrounding the journalists' role and the uncertainty about what issues were worth taking risks for thus emerged as enormous disincentives to intrepid journalism."[21] Or as Nono Makarim, the former editor of *Harian Kami*, wrote:

> An editor must identify himself squarely with the existing system to be given the opportunity to work at all. And as a rule he is basically in support of stands taken and objectives pursued by the powers that be. His critical appraisals are directed most of the time to marginal aspects of policy and rarely touch the basic tenets of the regime.[22]

Given such a climate, news stories relied on veiled language, innuendo, and sometimes saying "the complete opposite" of what was intended.[23] As David Hill has written, "for the newspaper-reading public, interpreting such articles takes a sensitive political instinct, a knack for reading between the lines (or 'reading between the lies') as former editor of *Sinar Harapan*, Aristides Katoppo has claimed."[24]

Working as a journalist under such restrictions was difficult enough, but being an editor who was responsible for the fates of dozens of employees, as well as the livelihoods of hundreds of agents, distributors, and newsboys was even worse. No one knew this better than *Sinar Harapan* editor Aristides Katoppo, who in 1973 was forced to go into a kind of exile in the United States – ostensibly because his newspaper had published the state budget before it was endorsed by the Parliament. Rather than resigning from *Sinar Harapan*, Aristides allowed himself to be "reassigned" to studying abroad. Alighting first at Stanford University and then

21 Angela Romano, *Politics and the Press in Indonesia*, p. 80.
22 Nono Makarim, "The Indonesian Press: An Editor's Perspective", p. 270.
23 Nono Makarim, "The Indonesian Press: An Editor's Perspective", p. 261.
24 David Hill, *The Press in New Order Indonesia*, p. 46.

at Harvard, Aristides became part of a lively community of Indonesian expatriates, which included both Nono Makarim and Arief Budiman.

From the United States, Aristides kept a close eye on developments in Indonesia, and one of his primary correspondents was Goenawan Mohamad. Aristides' frequent letters to Goenawan reflect both his eagerness for news of family and friends, and his frustration at having been cut off from an eyewitness view of events. In early January 1973, when General Soemitro was promising a new pattern of leadership and two-way communication between the government and the people, Aristides wrote of his skepticism, suggesting that the "new face" of the military was only a mask, or "cosmetic powder." "A sweet face now," he wrote, "but "what next, after a hundred flowers bloom?"[25]

In the same letter, Aristides expressed his "astonishment" at the news that Goenawan had been elected to the board of directors of the PWI, or Indonesian Journalists' Association. Since 1969, a ministerial regulation from the Department of Information had made it obligatory for anyone who wished to work as a journalist to become a member of "an Indonesian journalists' association which is authorized by the government." Given that the only authorized journalists' association was the PWI, the regulation had become a "circuitous path" to making PWI membership mandatory.[26] The regulation had been vigorously opposed by a number of journalists, including both Goenawan and Aristides. Aristides wrote:

> I'm astonished that you are brave enough to jump into the PWI
> kettle. Certainly you are aware of how in the current constellation
> of political developments, even the PWI is becoming a battlefield
> for persons or forces who use the name of the profession as a

[25] Aristides Katoppo to Goenawan Mohamad, January 12, 1974. Goenawan Mohamad file, H.B. Jassin documentary library.
[26] Angela Romano, *Politics and the Press in Indonesia*, p. 89.

ladder to power….In this matter the risk is being splashed with stinking mud. I can understand your dilemma, and it's a pity that I haven't mastered the science of how to get in the water without getting wet; I await your experiment.

Only days later, Aristides' doubts about the new face of the military were borne out. As a result of Malari, twelve newspapers had been banned, and many of his friends had been jailed. Afraid that history was "repeating itself", Aristides' frustration spilled over in a letter to Goenawan:

> Maybe as a member of the board of PWI you can explain why there is not forgiveness for *Harian Kami*, *Indonesia Raya* and the other newspapers that were muzzled. What actually was their mistake?…Reading the serious accusations that are thrown about, I become nervous that history is quickly repeating itself. Apparently truth and justice only move the conscience of the majority if they are supported by the strength of those in power.[27]

Although in earlier letters Aristides had teased Goenawan about his change of heart in joining the PWI, after Malari he was quick to defend his friend. On May 15, 1974 he wrote another letter to Goenawan, this time reassuring him that doing what was necessary to protect *Tempo* and its employees was an act of bravery:

> Don't be upset by an anonymous letter that accuses you of being an 'opportunist', a 'coward', etc….Sometimes keeping quiet is in fact an act of courage itself, courage to confront the risk of being stamped a 'coward' by people who don't understand your responsibility as the leader of a publication. Who can appreciate how difficult it is to swallow our anger and take a position that others may consider cowardly, only because we want to protect

---

[27]   Aristides Katoppo to Goenawan Mohamad, March 7, 1974. Goenawan Mohamad file, H.B. Jassin documentary library.

those who work for us, and their families, from losing their livelihoods as the result of our "bravery"? Making a sort of sacrifice in a private way in the awareness that it is one's own choice is different from dragging along people who maybe don't have that choice.[28]

As Aristides would later say, such sacrifice was "the price you had to pay," and for Goenawan there was indeed no other choice. Goenawan served out his term as a member of the board of directors of the PWI, and in 1978 was elected to a five-year term as a member of its Dewan Kehormatan, or Honorary Council.[29]

After Malari, how did *Tempo* writers manage to avoid being paralyzed by fear of censorship? *Tempo*'s policy was that reporters should report and that writers should write. Let the editors "take the fear," Goenawan always said. Yet this was sometimes easier said than done. At weekly planning meetings, *Tempo* journalists had to decide exactly what would appear in the magazine. Goenawan believes that one advantage *Tempo* had was that as a weekly, even "hot" stories were less "hot" after a few days. "The magazine pushed ahead when the government was weak, but was more restrained when it was strong," he said.[30] Even so, many of *Tempo*'s editors remembered the debates over how many pages should be allotted to a story – or if a particular event should even be covered at all. Disputes within the government had to be reported with particular caution. Government and military officials made frequent use of the telephone, encouraging journalists to emphasize "harmony", and not to include reports of conflict. One

---

[28]   Aristides Katoppo to Goenawan Mohamad, May 15, 1974. Goenawan Mohamad file, H.B. Jassin documentary library.

[29]   For a complete list of PWI office holders from the organization's founding in 1946, see H.K. Soeherman, "Catatan Selintas Pertumbuhan PWI, 9 Februari 1946 - 2 Oktober 2003", http://www.pwi.or.id/dokumen_detail.php?artikel_id =27&lang=in.

[30]   Interview with Goenawan Mohamad, February 9, 1998.

of the more insidious aspects of this "telephone culture" was that because the warning was oral, there was no written record of the occurrence. As David Hill has written, "only if a paper [was] recalcitrant enough to breach such instructions [was] it sent written warnings. The last resort [was] the revocation of the company's license, representing a total ban and often financial collapse."[31]

Senior editor Leila Chudori recalled the frequent arguments over the "angle" of a story, including several incidents in which writers argued with their editors over how far to push in questioning the government's point of view. Assistant chief editor Toriq Hadad likewise remembered how particular generals or high public officials had the power to block the inclusion of a story simply by refusing to be interviewed. In the case of a 1993 incident in Sampang, Madura, in which the army shot dead four villagers who were protesting the building of a reservoir that would destroy their farmlands, *Tempo* editors decided that it would only be safe to publish the story if the commander in the field agreed to be interviewed. "Today I wouldn't include such a lengthy interview," Toriq said. "Just a few quotes. The interview wasn't all that interesting, but at the time we had to do it."[32]

In some ways *Tempo*'s reliance on quotes from high-ranking government and military officials is not surprising. It is a convention of journalism that reporters will seek out the most authoritative sources available, even if lower-ranking officials might be able to provide a more complete picture.[33] Yet Indonesian journalists working under the political restraints of the New Order had to rely on the views of government sources for reasons that were quite different from those of their Western counterparts. As Susanto Pudjomartono said, "We had to publish the official version first. That was the first rule. Otherwise, I am banned."[34]

---

[31]   David Hill, *The Press in New Order Indonesia*, p. 45.

[32]   "Nyo'on Odik, Lalu Robohlah Mereka", *Tempo*, October 9, 1993

[33]   Leon Sigel, "Who? Sources Make the News", in *Reading the News* (New York: Pantheon Books, 1986), pp. 9-37.

[34]   Interview with Susanto Pudjomartono, February 18, 2000.

Toriq Hadad agreed. "Our fear was only one: that the military would be angry," he said. "We always had to begin stories with the military's version. If there are two versions, we must start with the military's version. Only later can we slip in the rest."

"There was always this risk," he added. "We always felt this fear. The fear that perhaps *Tempo* might be closed because of a quote of mine. Mas Goen [Goenawan Mohamad] used to say 'we can be afraid but never subjugated.'"[35]

Yet despite these pressures, *Tempo* journalists were not without the power to challenge the government's point of view, or to "slip in the rest," as Toriq put it. One of their most effective rhetorical devices was the *pelacakan* or re-tracing of events. The *pelacakan* reconstructed an event by placing facts in a time-line. Although journalism is supposed to be based on verifiable facts, the choice of which facts to use is a subjective one – and a carefully arranged chronology can present readers with an alternative view that might even undermine what the authorities are saying.[36] Examples of controversial stories in which *Tempo* utilized time lines to subtly challenge the military's view of events include the 1981 hijacking of the Garuda Indonesia airplane "Woyla", the 1991 "incident" at the Santa Cruz cemetery in Dili, East Timor, and the 1993 shooting of protesters over the construction of the Nipah dam in Sampang, Madura.[37]

In addition to the time-line, *Tempo* used a number of other narrative devices, including the rhetorical question and passive sentence structure. In his story on the shootings at Nipah Dam, writer Toriq Hadad asked "is it true that the citizens were armed?" Although the story answered this question first with the authorities' allegation that an investigative team had found machetes, sickles, sharpened bamboo spears, and stones at the scene of the incident,

---

[35] "*Kita boleh takut tapi jangan takluk*", Interview with Toriq Hadad, February 15, 2000.

[36] For a fascinating discussion of the slippery nature of "facts" in news, see Carlin Romano, "The Grisly Truth About Bare Facts", in *Reading the News*, pp. 38-78.

[37] For *Tempo*'s chronology of the Garuda Woyla hijacking see *Tempo*, April 4, 1981;

it also contained the contradictory claim that "eye witnesses and victims interviewed by *Tempo* said that none of the citizens were carrying weapons." Toriq's assessment of the two competing accounts – "which is true, *wallahualam* [only God knows]" – was not likely to be challenged.[38]

Passive structure also allowed *Tempo* to make the subject of a sentence invisible. The magazine's account of the Nipah Dam shootings concluded with the statement: "they say, in several cities, that acts of solidarity are also likely to take place. What they are demanding, among other things, is that the army quickly shape an investigatory commission." Who was making these assertions? It was not clear from the article. Expressions like *kabarnya* or *konon* ("reportedly", or "they say") provided ways of including statements without assigning responsibility for them. Although passive construction is quite common in the Indonesian language, there were also good political reasons for using it. If a sentence – or even a story – had no subject, it also had no one who could be held accountable for the action.

Another device that *Tempo* frequently used was the publication of lengthy quotations from testimony given in open court. Even the thoughts of a dissident could be printed if they were already a matter of public record. In 1985, *Tempo* included nearly all of Governor Ali Sadikin's electrifying testimony in the subversion trial of retired General H.R. Dharsono. Ali Sadikin's testimony enabled *Tempo* to publish much of the material that had previously appeared in the Petition of Fifty's infamous *White Paper* – a document which itself had been declared illegal.[39]

---

for the Santa Cruz incident, see November 23, 1991; for the shootings at the Nipah Dam project, see *Tempo*, October 9, 1993. Chapter 5 analyzes the use of *Tempo*'s *pelacakan* in the Tanjung Priok incident.

[38] "Nyo'on Odik, Lalu Robohlah Mereka", *Tempo,* October 9, 1993.

[39] *Tempo*, November 9, 1985. For a discussion of the Petition of Fifty and the "White Paper", see John Bresnan, *Managing Indonesia: The Modern Political Economy* (New York: Columbia University Press, 1993).

In addition to utilizing a wide range of narrative and rhetorical devices, *Tempo* also protected itself by drawing upon the professional ideology of journalism. Despite the restrictions of the New Order press system, it was widely understood that a good story had to be "balanced" and to "cover both sides". As Adam Jones has suggested, in even the most restrictive press systems, there is nevertheless a "moral economy" of journalism, in which norms such as journalists' responsibility to the truth exist beneath the surface, waiting to emerge when conditions permit.[40] In several important instances *Tempo* editors managed to include a critique of official viewpoints by arguing that as responsible journalists they were obligated to comply with professional standards. In 1992, for example, *Tempo* journalist Dewi Anggraeni was permitted to accompany a group of international protestors on the voyage of the Lusitania Expresso from Darwin, Australia to East Timor, because her bosses had convinced the military authorities that it was imperative *Tempo* "cover both sides" of the controversial event.[41]

American media scholar James C. Carey has written that explanation – or the "why" of news – is what readers most want to get out of a story and are least likely to find.[42] The search for deeper meaning and the need to make sense out of occurrences is basic to the human condition. In American journalism, "why" is revealed over time, and readers seldom get a satisfying explanation from a single story. Some of the reasons for this are obvious; events unfold over time, and why something happened is not always immediately apparent. As Bill Kovach has written, truth in

---

[40] For a fascinating discussion of professionalism and the "moral economy of journalism" in the case of Nicaragua, see Adam Jones, *Beyond the Barricades: Nicaragua and the Struggle for the Sandinista Press, 1979-1998* (Athens: Ohio University Press, 2002), pp. 38-40. I am grateful to Chelsy Knight for bringing this book to my attention.

[41] Interview with Dewi Anggraeni, January 14, 2001. See also *Tempo*, March 14, 1992.

[42] James C. Carey, "Why and How: The Dark Continent of American Journalism", in *Reading the News*, chapter 6.

journalism is a "process", and journalists can only report the truth as best they see it at any given moment.[43]

If there is a dearth of explanation in American journalism, this was even more the case in New Order Indonesia. A story that explains things is dangerous, and *Tempo* writers were often able to reveal very little of what they actually knew. As Susanto Pudjomartono said, "usually at that time we could write only twenty, twenty-five percent of what we know. Sometimes only ten percent."[44]

One way in which *Tempo* managed to provide explanations of events was to *pinjam mulut*, or "borrow the mouth" of a high-ranking official. Although this technique is also used in Western journalism, in Indonesia the context was radically different. In the United States, journalists look for sources who will express a particular point of view because the conventions of objectivity bar them from inserting their own opinions into the news.[45] In New Order Indonesia, journalists had an even more compelling reason to find sources who would say what they themselves could not: a newspaper or magazine was far less likely to be reprimanded by the Armed Forces Information Center (Pusat Penerangan ABRI, or Puspen) if a controversial point of view was expressed by a general or other high-ranking official. *Tempo* writers frequently quoted foreign media, or international figures whose views contradicted those of Indonesian government officials for this same reason.[46]

---

43   Bill Kovach and Tom Rosenstiel, *The Elements of Journalism: What Newspeople Should Know and the Public Should Expect* (New York: Three Rivers Press, 2001), pp. 36-49.

44   Interview with Susanto Pudjomartono, February 18, 2000.

45   For an analysis of how journalists use expert sources in the United States, see Janet Steele, "Don't Ask, Don't Tell, Don't Explain: Unofficial Sources and Television Coverage of the Dispute Over Gays in the Military", *Political Communication*, Spring 1997, and "Experts and the Operational Bias of Television News: The Case of the Persian Gulf War", *Journalism and Mass Communication Quarterly*, Vol. 72, No. 4, Winter 1995, pp. 799-812.

46   See "Jika PBB Datang ke Dili", an account of international reaction to the Santa Cruz incident. *Tempo*, December 7, 1991.

Susanto Pudjomartono recalled one particularly dramatic case in which he had "borrowed the mouth" of a source to write a story that could never otherwise have appeared in *Tempo*. The story was based on an interview with the military governor of East Timor, and the headline was "The Timorese People are Dissatisfied".[47] Explaining that Puspen had organized the visit to Dili, Susanto said that one of the officials accompanying the journalists was an intelligence officer who, like Susanto, was a graduate of the University of Gadjah Madah. The two became friendly, and Susanto convinced him to help *Tempo* get an exclusive interview with the governor. After the story was published, Susanto received a summons. He explained:

> The chief of the Puspen said, 'Your article has caused some ripples among the officials because you wrote that the East Timorese are disappointed with the Indonesians. Why did you do it like this? We invited you to write an objective report on what is happening in East Timor, and yet you write like that.' Because Puspen checked, and according to them the governor never mentioned this sentence.
>
> I told him, 'It's not during the press conference. I have an exclusive interview.'
>
> 'We did not hear about that,' said the chief of Puspen. And he was surprised. But I did not tell him I went there with the intelligence officer. It would be embarrassing and unfair to him because he helped me to secure this special interview. So I came prepared. 'I have a transcript of this interview and a copy of this tape if you want, I can give you this.' And again he was surprised. And he said, 'I don't have to hear the tape, but I can read the transcript.'
>
> And after a few minutes he said, 'Yes, it is true. You should not do this, but this is a quotation, I can not argue with you.'[48]

47   "Rakyat Timor Timur Tidak Berbahagia", *Tempo*, August 27, 1988.
48   Interview with Susanto Pudjomartono, May 24, 2000.

In addition to demonstrating the technique of *pinjam mulut*, this story also illustrates the effectiveness of what Indonesian journalists refer to as *lobi*, or "lobbying". Susanto was able to get an exclusive interview with the governor of East Timor because he had drawn on a personal connection with the intelligence officer. Susanto said that "lobbying" was a deliberate strategy that *Tempo* began to utilize in the 1970s. "I became convinced that lobbying is most important for a news weekly like *Tempo*," he said. "Lobbying should be planned. So when I was national news editor I have a regular meeting with reporters and we plan who will contact who, who will approach who, and how to develop relations with them. The main objective of course is to get the best stories for *Tempo*."

Angela Romano has written extensively of the difficulty of cultivating news sources during the New Order.[49] President Soeharto almost never spoke directly with journalists, preferring instead to issue statements through his ministers. Public officials likewise preferred speaking with groups of journalists to granting private interviews, and were usually reluctant to steer too far from standardized responses.

Susanto readily admits that throughout the 1970s and 80s he had a particularly strong *lobi* with Armed Forces Commander General Benny Moerdani, but this was only one of the special relationships *Tempo* journalists had with government sources. *Tempo* founder Fikri Jufri emphasized much the same point when he said, "It was a decision in *Tempo* that we decide who will be close to whom. So Eric Samola, because he is Golkar, he will make the lobby to [Golkar Chair] Sudharmono; Goenawan we decide will lobby to [State Secretary and General] Moerdiono. Me, to CSIS [Center for Strategic and International Studies]. That is the decision of the staff."[50]

On the most basic level, "lobbying" meant that when something controversial happened, *Tempo* reporters were able to

49   See Angela Romano, *Politics and the Press in Indonesia*, pp. 117-133.
50   Interview with Fikri Jufri, March 11, 1998.

get the "inside story". But Susanto also acknowledged that there could be "excesses." "Because some reporters became very close with sources," he said. "And sometimes so close that they could not distinguish between the role of reporter and friend. It is actually a tragedy. For, example, I ordered Amran Nasution to be very close to [Soeharto son-in-law and Colonel] Prabowo. And he became very close and became a confidante."[51]

In situations like this one, it was easy to be seduced. But even for those who were not so easily seduced, *Tempo*'s relationship with power was complex. As Goenawan said, during the New Order there were always "people in the government [with whom] you could communicate." As part of the "Generation of '66", the founders of *Tempo* were acquainted with many of the founders of the New Order. Although the army had long since betrayed its alliance with the young activists who had helped bring the regime to power, *Tempo*'s editors were nevertheless able occasionally to draw upon their connections inside the government and military. For example "[General] Moerdiono always protected *Tempo*," Goenawan said. "He called, 'Be careful – I don't want *Tempo*, *Kompas*, and *Sinar Harapan* banned. So be careful.'" These ties would be tested in 1982, when *Tempo* was banned for the first time.

The cause of the 1982 banning was never entirely clear. Although the letter from the Department of Information stated that *Tempo*'s SIT (Permit to Publish) had been frozen because *Tempo* had violated the code of ethics of a "free and responsible" press, most people

---

51   Interview with Susanto Pudjomartono, February 18, 2000.
52   Surat Keputusan Menteri Penerangan Republik Indonesia, no. 7.6/Kep/Menpen/ 1982 tentang Pembekuan Untuk Sementara Waktu Surat Izin Terbit Majalah Mingguan Berita Tempo Berkedudukan di Jakarta. Archives, Serikat Penerbit Suratkabar Pusat-Jakarta. Sadly, after the Department of Information was dissolved in 1999 by President Abdurrahman Wahid, its archives were sold as scrap paper. Fortunately much of its correspondence was copied to SPS, the Newspaper

Fikri Jufri [seated]; *Tempo* employees reading letter freezing
Tempo's Permit to Publish, 1982 [*Tempo*/Ed Zoelverdi]

believed that the real reason *Tempo* was banned was that it had broken the prohibition against reporting on conflict during the general election.[52] Although Soeharto's government had for some time been trying to weaken the political power of Islam, in the 1982 campaign about a million people turned out for a rally of the Development Unity Party (PPP) in Jakarta. When Golkar tried to match this show of support with a counter-rally in Banteng Square, the demonstration was disrupted by members of the PPP. In the ensuing violence, seven people were reported killed and ninety-seven people injured, many by gunfire from security forces.[53]

Susanto Pudjomartono remembers the incident very clearly. When the riot occurred, he and several other *Tempo* journalists were previewing a new foreign film at a theater near Banteng Square. As he described it:

Publishers' Association, which still has copies in its archives. I am grateful to Karaniya Dharmasaputra for obtaining these documents for me. See also cover story "Kemarahan di Awal Kampanye", *Tempo*, March 27, 1982.
[53] John Bresnan, *Managing Indonesia: The Modern Political Economy*, p. 236.

In the middle of the film it was stopped. There are riots! So we went straight to Banteng Square, and of course we have our reporters and photographers there…So after that, we get that warning. And then someone said it's been decided in the cabinet meeting, the official reason is because we disrupt the national stability. But later on we really want to know which article has triggered this decision? And we found out that it is very confusing because different officials say different things. And we heard that the banning is only for two weeks. And later on there is no decision until four weeks.[54]

For the writers and reporters, who were certain that *Tempo* would be permitted to resume publication after two weeks, the atmosphere was relaxed. Former managing editor Bambang Bujono remembers that it was fun, like *cuti* or leave. They joked and played ping-pong to pass the time. As he said, maybe the editors and financial department were worried, but for the reporters and writers it was like a vacation.[55]

While the writers and reporters were enjoying a "vacation", behind the scenes there were furious negotiations between *Tempo*'s directors and government officials. Eric Samola and Goenawan met with Soekarno, Director General of Press and Graphics; Goenawan and Fikri met with Minister of Information Ali Moertopo. Susanto met with State Secretary Moerdiono. Eric Samola met with Golkar's Sudharmono. Because, as Fikri Jufri said, "We didn't know. Two weeks can become two months, so we have to be careful. You have to know when this happened, a lot of people up there, politicians, they don't like *Tempo*."[56]

Although Goenawan has no proof, he believes that the banning may have been initiated by Harmoko, the cartoonist-turned-publisher who was by then the head of the Indonesian Journalists'

54   Interview with Susanto Pudjomartono, May 24, 2000.
55   Interview with Bambang Bujono, May 22, 2000.
56   Interview with Fikri Jufri, May 30, 2000.

Ceremony marking *Tempo*'s return to publication, 1982 [*Tempo*/Yohannes Batubara]

Association. There were reports that it had been Harmoko who had pressed the government to "reign in" *Tempo*; an allegation that was borne out by the fact that Minister of Information Ali Moertopo was out of the country when the decision to ban *Tempo* was made.[57] Eric Samola was told that Harmoko was angry that *Tempo* was "always able to get away" with more than the other media did. Moreover, as Harjoko Trisnadi pointed out, *Tempo* was one of the few media institutions in which Harmoko didn't own shares.[58]

According to Goenawan, it is possible that Harmoko had a business interest in wanting to see *Tempo* shut down. "Because he wanted to establish a rival magazine, or he wanted to get rid of *Tempo*," Goenawan said. "The government had no reason at all to ban *Tempo*. Normally *Tempo* came out after the event was over and the situation was under control. So that's why *Tempo* always 'got away with it'."[59]

After four weeks, *Tempo*'s editors and owners began to get

[57]   Coen Husain Pontoh, "Konflik Tak Kunjng Padam", *Pantau,* August 2001, p. 48.
[58]   Interview with Harjoko Trisnadi, June 28, 2000.
[59]   Interview with Goenawan Mohamad, June 20, 2000.

seriously worried. Fikri Jufri learned that Minister of Information Ali Moertopo had gone to eastern Indonesia – first to Ambon, and then to Bali. Ali Moertopo had the power to return *Tempo* to publication. So Fikri followed him to Bali.

"I went to the Garuda Hotel," Fikri recalled. "I told one of the workers, 'if you see Pak Ali you tell me.' Then the elevator door opens and Pak Ali comes out. He was with a lady. The next morning I try again. He doesn't want to meet me. 'I have a deadline, I have to go,' he says."

"I go to his adjutant," Fikri continued. "'Look, you talk to him. Just follow my words: I want to meet the man I knew when he was captain. I want to meet the Ali Moertopo I knew in 1966, 1967.'"

Later, Fikri tried again to meet with the general, but was turned away. "He's already left sir. He's already checked out."

But then Fikri saw that Ali Moertopo was actually in the lobby. "I'm going back to Jakarta," he told Fikri.

According to Fikri, Ali Moertopo was a man who liked to have an audience, and at this point several other people had joined them in the lobby. "'Fikri, you're my boy. Goenawan's my boy [*anak buah saya*],'" Ali Moertopo said, his words claiming a connection with *Tempo*.

"He was showing off," Fikri concluded.

After the encounter in the hotel, Fikri called Sabam Siagian, the deputy editor at *Sinar Harapan*. "Who is your reporter at the Palace?" Fikri asked. "I met Ali. At his press conference later today, ask your reporter to ask him about *Tempo*, when it will come out again."

The answer? "*Tempo* will come out again at the latest in two weeks."

Fikri explained that he and Goenawan really began to know Ali Moertopo in 1967, when the office of the "Special Operations man" was close by to that of *Harian Kami*. "The relation is not a bad relation then," Fikri said. "Not yet. It began to get bad when the power begins to be more repressive. When it becomes really bad is after Malari."

When I asked Goenawan about his reaction to Fikri's meeting with Ali Moertopo, he said "*Anak buah saya* [my boy]? Well, it was his claim. I was never close to him. I met him twice or three times. We were friendly because we came from the same town. Of course from different generations. He liked to use the local dialect with me. And actually he was a very open person, not like a stiff general. Very accessible."

But wasn't there also something humiliating about this story? "There was, of course there was," Goenawan said. "But there was no other way to get the license back. So Fikri came there to try to find a way to do it. And he was not that close I think to Ali Moertopo. But he may have known him in the '60s. Fikri was among the student leaders then, in the demonstrations. So Moertopo was kind of bragging also, to claim him."

"But he claimed you, too," I said.

"Of course!" Goenawan said. "He would claim anybody."

"Look," Goenawan said, "let's review history. In 1966 the students were in the street. Ali Moertopo was in the military. Maybe manipulating some of the students, but they were equal. So then maybe Fikri could claim this because he was part of the New Order history. And it was quite daring for Fikri to do that, for Fikri to meet Ali Moertopo. Ali Moertopo was very high. What he said, it was kind of reminding Ali Moertopo, 'who are you?' It was quite daring. To verify, to remind him that you had a claim on him, when you were equal."[60]

Within a few weeks after the meeting between Fikri and Ali Moertopo, the Department of Information unfroze *Tempo*'s license, and the magazine was allowed to return to publication – but not before Goenawan was asked to sign a letter admitting the magazine's error. Goenawan remembers it this way.

---

[60]   Interview with Goenawan Mohamad, June 20, 2000.

"It was funny. Because the banning was initiated by Harmoko, Soekarno [Director General of Press and Graphics] was rather upstaged. He was not very happy. And he was somebody we respected. So when he tried to present the issue, it was a very *pro forma* kind of thing."

"So what shall I do?" Goenawan said he asked him.

"The usual thing," Soekarno said, "the usual thing. Why don't you do something like *Kompas* did? Sign a statement you won't attack the first family, Pancasila."

"So where is the document?" Goenawan asked.

They tried to find the document but they didn't have it in their files. "'Okay, why don't you borrow it from *Kompas?*'" Goenawan said, quoting Soekarno. So they called *Kompas*. "Okay, Jakob [Oetomo, chief editor of *Kompas*] or somebody sent it over and we signed it, just like that. Without passion. So the government, it's not so very – as Soekarno said, there is nothing wrong with *Tempo*."[61]

As this and many, many other stories suggest, power in the New Order was not monolithic. At Puspen and in the State Secretariat and even at the Department of Information there were generals, directors general, and public officials who respected *Tempo* and the journalists who had created it. Each of the senior editors whom I interviewed told of countless meetings with sympathetic public officials in which they had to "go through the motions" of a formal reprimand with each party fully aware that the interaction was *pro forma* only. As Susanto said, "many officials after summoning us said 'don't take it personally. Because I am an official

---

61   Interview with Goenawan Mohamad, June 20, 2000. *Tempo*'s SIT was "unfrozen" in a letter dated June 7, 1982. Surat Keputusan Menteri Penerangan Republik Indonesia No. 104/Kep/Menpen/1982 tentang Pencairan Kembali Surat Izin Terbit (SIT) Majalah Berita Mingguan Tempo di Jakarta, SPS archives. The letter from the Department of Information refers to a May 1, 1982 letter from *Tempo* that promised to maintain national security, orderliness, and the public interest, practice introspection, and guard the good names of government authorities and the national leadership.

I have to do my job. Because I was requested to serve you a warning. So I did that. It's okay. Let's shake hands.' Something like that."

Susanto added, "Some officials were embarrassed because it was against their conscience."[62]

Were these relationships among equals? No, because one side held all the power. And in June of 1982, when *Tempo*'s license was "unfrozen", there were many young reporters and writers at the magazine who were angry that Goenawan had signed the letter. Some believed he had done so only because he was a shareholder of *Tempo*, and had wanted to protect his financial interest. Others took a broader view, arguing that Goenawan had done what was necessary to save the magazine, and that there had been no other choice.

In August 2000, during a conversation on the exercise of power in the New Order, former *Tempo* writer Syu'bah Asa also brought up the story of Fikri Jufri and Ali Moertopo. "Fikri said something great when *Tempo* was banned the first time in 1982," Syu'bah said. "'I am going to go to Bali,' he said, 'and I am going to meet with Ali Moertopo. And I am going to suck up to him [*menjilat*]. Because if you have to suck up to someone, it's far better to do it face to face than in print.'"

"These were great words," Syu'bah told me. "This became a kind of credo. Don't ever suck up to power in our stories."[63]

---

[62]   Interview with Susanto Pudjomartono, May 24, 2000.
[63]   Interview with Syu'bah Asa, August 2, 2000.

the incident

"The more daily Islam becomes, the less problematic."
— *Nurcholish Madjid, November 10, 2001*

It was September, 1984, and *Tempo* had just published a four-page account of the "incident" at Tanjung Priok, in which according to official reports, nine Muslim rioters were shot dead by Indonesian soldiers and fifty-three more were wounded.[1] Several Chinese-owned shops had been burned by rioters, and eight bodies were found in the rubble. *Tempo*'s account of the incident, which challenged the official version and raised the death toll to twenty-eight, was considered so daring that many people thought the magazine was going to be banned. The story caused *Tempo*'s street price to sky rocket, and earned the magazine the gratitude of the Muslim community. "They even put copies of the article in the mosque," said Bambang Harymurti, who was a reporter at the time.[2]

Tempo editors' primary goal was to publish a story that was both "complete and fair," and to strike a balance between competing social forces in such a way that the magazine would not be reprimanded or worse.[3] The magazine's coverage of the

---

[1] *Tempo*, September 22, 1984.
[2] Interview with Bambang Harymurti, January 21, 2000. This observation was confirmed by others as well.
[3] "Priok & Bom BCA",15th anniversary issue of *Tempo*, March 1986, p. 61.

Tanjung Priok incident illustrates nearly all of the strategies that *Tempo* editors routinely used to keep the magazine from being banned. A look behind the scenes at the way in which the Tanjung Priok story was actually reported, written, and edited likewise reveals how *Tempo* journalists interacted with one another in covering sensitive issues. *Tempo* journalists' ability to negotiate the thicket of religious identity demonstrated not only the magazine's spirit of ecumenicalism, but also the power of the ideology of journalistic professionalism.

Tempo's attitude of democratic pluralism both inside and outside the magazine was especially significant during the New Order period, when devout Muslims were first marginalized by the regime and then cynically exploited in an effort to undermine the embryonic pro-democracy movement.[4] In the mid-1980s, in the months before and after the Tanjung Priok incident, *Tempo* published a stunning series of articles on the "renewal in Islamic thought" that articulated the magazine's tolerant views. By publicizing the efforts of liberal Muslim intellectuals to promote an Islamic society rather than an Islamic state, *Tempo* played a significant role in the development of what anthropologist Robert Hefner has called "civil Islam". In *Tempo*, under the leadership of Goenawan Mohamad, Islam has always been compatible with democratic values.

The best way to enter the Tanjung Priok area is via Jl. Raya Pelabuhan, a broad, busy street that runs parallel to the port and the container ships docked there.[5] Smaller numbered alleyways branch off the main road like fish bones off a central spine. These streets are narrow, and crowded with small homes, shops, and

---

4   See Robert Hefner, *Civil Islam: Muslims and Democratization in Indonesia* (Princeton: Princeton University Press, 2000).
5   I am grateful to *Tempo*'s Choirul Aminuddin for giving up a Saturday afternoon to take me to Tanjung Priok, and also for sharing with me his insights into the 1984 incident.

vendors. The majority of residents of Tanjung Priok are *Pribumi* or indigenous, and most of them work in the port. The bigger shops are on the main thoroughfare of Jl. Raya Pelabuhan, and many of them are owned by Indonesian Chinese. These are the shops that were burned during the riot.

The *musholla* Assa'adah, where the Tanjung Priok incident began, is on a quiet street branching off the main road. The green and white paint of the small prayer house reflects the hard bright heat of the midday sun. When I visited the *musholla* on an ordinary Saturday afternoon in July 2000, my presence drew a crowd, along with friendly reminders to take off my shoes before entering the small walled courtyard. Ahmad Sahi is still the head of the prayer house. He is in his fifties now, with cloudy eyes, straight brown hair, and a dignified demeanor. It was Ahmad Sahi who in 1984 tried to get Sergeant Hermanu to apologize for entering the *musholla* without removing his shoes, the event that sparked the Tanjung Priok incident. Achmad was one of the four men who were arrested after the sergeant's motorcycle was burned, and it was his arrest that prompted Amir Biki to lead a crowd of demonstrators to the police station the night of September 8.[6] We sat on a cool, white-tiled floor, and I showed the men who had gathered a photocopy of the article that had appeared in *Tempo* seventeen years ago. A fruit vendor pulled up to the curb, and the jingle of the Wall's ice cream cart attracted a flock of small children. The men in the courtyard passed around the photocopied story, studying it as carefully as if it had been written yesterday.

The Tanjung Priok incident has become a symbol of frustration. For some Muslims, it represents the feeling of being marginalized in their own country, a nation in which they make up eighty-eight percent of the population. For others, it represents the gross breakdown of the system of justice, in which abuses of human rights by the military are allowed to go unchallenged. Yet

---

6   Interview with Ahmad Sahi, July 22, 2000.

the Tanjung Priok incident cannot be viewed in isolation. Since 1966, the alliance between the army and Muslim groups that brought the New Order to power had been characterized by mutual suspicion and accusations of betrayal. The army had depended on the Nahdlatul Ulama (NU) and its youth wing Ansor to carry out the anti-Communist pogrom that took place in East Java, but Muslim leaders who were expecting to be rewarded for their loyalty were sorely disappointed.[7] It quickly became clear that the New Order government had no intention of reviving the Jakarta Charter or implementing Islamic law. Soeharto's refusal to allow for the return of the banned political party Masyumi, as well his 1973 forced "simplification" of the Muslim political parties into the government-approved grouping of the Development Unity Party (PPP) only added to the feelings of anger and resentment. As Robert Hefner has written,

> In the face of government repression, the Muslim community split into two camps. Some sought to defend the faith through a program of Islamic appeal (*dakwah*), intended over the long run to revive the Islamic parties and recapture the state. Another group in the Muslim community, however, criticized this reduction of Muslim interests to state-centered struggle....What was really needed [they said] was not another campaign to capture the state but a vigorous program of education and renewal in society. The ultimate goal of this program should be the creation of a Muslim civil society to counterbalance the state and promote a public culture of pluralism and participation.[8]

---

[7] For details on the NU's collaboration with the army, see Robert Hefner, *Civil Islam*, chapter 3. For an overview of the killings, see Robert Cribb, ed., *The Indonesian Killings, 1965-1966: Studies from Java and Bali* (Clayton, Victoria, Australia: Monash University, Center of Southeast Asian Studies, Monash Papers no. 21, 1990).

[8] Robert Hefner, *Civil Islam*, p. 16.

A 1984 government-sponsored initiative in Parliament to make Pancasila the sole basis of all social and political organizations rubbed even more salt into the wounds of already aggrieved Muslims. The five draft laws that would force even religious-based organizations to change their charters were opposed by many Christians as well as Muslims.[9] Many Muslims believed that the laws were heretical, and accused the government of attempting to destroy Islam as a political force. It was within this context that the act of a non-commissioned security officer in the Assa'adah *musholla* sparked one of the deadliest riots of the New Order.[10]

As Sergeant Hermanu later testified, on the afternoon of Friday September 7, 1984, he and a colleague saw several pamphlets on the outside wall of the prayer house, in an area where people washed before praying. One of the pamphlets urged Muslim women to wear head scarves or *jilbab* – something which at the time was considered to be a security threat as well as a dangerous protest. Although Sergeant Hermanu insisted that he had removed his shoes before entering the prayer house, eyewitnesses were equally insistent that he had not. When he asked the young men who were in the *musholla* to take down the posters, they refused. When he came back the next day, he found that even more fliers had been affixed to the walls. Because they were hard to remove, Sergeant Hermanu picked up a piece of newspaper and doused the posters with "black water" from a nearby gutter. Almost immediately, rumors started to spread of the "Christian soldier" who had failed to remove his shoes before entering a *musholla* and had sprayed the walls with sewer water.[11]

---

[9]   Robert Hefner, *Civil Islam*, pp. 121-2.

[10]   *Tempo*'s initial report as well as a cover story published several months later are still among the most complete accounts of the incident. *Tempo*, September 22, 1984, and *Tempo*, January 19, 1984. Another chronology can be found in John Bresnan, *Managing Indonesia*, pp. 218-244.

[11]   Hermanu told Bambang Harymurti of *Tempo* that he was a Muslim. Bambang said "People were under the impression that he was a Christian. I met him and I think it is mostly because of the way he speaks. It is like from the eastern part of Indonesia, and most people from the eastern part are not Muslim." Interview with Bambang Harymurti, January 21, 2000.

Two days later, on Monday, Sergeant Hermanu and a colleague were passing through the same small alley when they were approached by two youths who asked them to come to a local administrative office to apologize. Although the soldiers refused to apologize, they nonetheless agreed to accompany the men to the office. Meanwhile, a crowd gathered. Some threw sand and stones at the two men, who later charged that they had also been pushed and shoved. Several people dragged the soldiers' motorcycle into the middle of the street and pushed it over, breaking the gas tank and setting it on fire. Three youths were arrested by the police, along with Ahmad Sahi, the head of the *musholla*.

As the story of the incident spread, there was considerable sympathy for the four men who had been arrested. At this point Amir Biki, a respected community leader, appealed to the police to release the four detainees. Although he had had some success with similar episodes in the past, this time he was unsuccessful.

Two days later, on Wednesday, September 12, a platform was set up in Jl. Sindang several blocks away from the *musholla*. Jl. Sindang is broader than the other streets of Tanjung Priok, and runs perpendicular to where the mosque is located. The stage was built at the point where the two roads intersect. Loudspeakers were strung from the light poles in anticipation of an 8 PM event that would involve sermons from several well-known Muslim teachers. After prayers were finished, people spilled out of the *mesjid* to hear the speeches. One of the speakers was Amir Biki.

Biki's speech covered a wide range of topics, criticizing the government for its condemnation of land, family planning program, and draft laws that would establish Pancasila as the sole basis of all political and social organizations. It climaxed with the demand that if the authorities didn't release the four detainees by 11 PM, he would mobilize the crowd to attack the police station and set the prisoners free.

By 11 PM, the men had not been released. Led by Biki, the crowd began the 1.5km march to police headquarters, bearing green flags – the symbolic color of Islam – and chanting *Allahu Akbar*, or "God is great." At the same time another group of people started to move in the opposite direction, towards Jl. Jampea, the extension of Jl. Pelabuhan Raya, where they began setting fire to cars and Chinese-owned shops.

The part of the crowd led by Biki was about halfway to its destination when it was suddenly blocked by armed troops. The soldiers fired warning shots, but the crowd kept coming. According to witnesses, Biki cried "forward and attack," and was shot dead at close range. The crowd tried to scatter and fall back, but armored vehicles blocked their way. Later it was determined that the troops were not anti-riot police, but rather an air defense regiment. A White Paper later published by the Petition of Fifty group stated that the troops were armed with M-16 automatic weapons.[12] The situation was brought under control within less than an hour, but not before dozens of people had been killed or wounded.

Thursday afternoon, about fourteen hours after the incident, General Benny Moerdani held a press conference in which he said that the authorities had not anticipated the blow-up. "We didn't plan anything," he told the press. "We were trapped."[13]

For twenty-seven-year old *Tempo* reporter Bambang Harymurti, who was one of the first journalists on the scene, the most memorable image was the blood. "When I came there," he said, "the fire brigade was still washing down the street, because there was blood. They were washing down the street."[14]

---

[12] John Bresnan, *Managing Indonesia*, p. 223. The *White Paper* also relied on *Tempo*'s account. Bambang Harymurti recalls that former Jakarta Governor Ali Sadikin went to his mother's house and asked to use his tapes and interview notes as evidence in their investigation. He refused, saying that the governor would have to talk to his bosses at *Tempo* about this. Interview with Bambang Harymurti, January 21, 2000.

[13] Quoted in John Bresnan, *Managing Indonesia*, p. 224.

[14] Unless otherwise noted, Bambang Harymurti's account of how he reported on the Tanjung Priok incident is based on an interview conducted on January 21, 2000.

Sixteen years later Susanto Pudjumartono – who in 1984 was *Tempo*'s national desk editor and the writer of the Tanjung Priok stories – remembered the same image from Bambang Harymurti's report, but it didn't make it into the magazine. The editors of *Tempo* knew that as a news weekly they had a certain latitude to report on events with more depth after they had cooled down, but the occurrence at Tanjung Priok was still white hot, and the image of the fire brigade hosing down blood-washed streets was too provocative to publish.

Bambang arrived in Tanjung Priok early Thursday morning. "Some of the soldiers were still shooting up in the air," he said, "and they were still taking bodies out of buildings." Journalists from daily papers *Kompas* and *Sinar Harapan* were also there, he said, "but they were so sure that they were not going to be allowed to print this story anyway that they didn't write the report. But at *Tempo*, we are always operating that a reporter should report. Just report. And then the editor will decide whether it can be printed. So we have to do this job."

For Bambang and Agus Basri, the two *Tempo* reporters assigned to the story, doing the job entailed the usual admonition to check and recheck. But it was very difficult to find eyewitnesses. Thus they had to "follow the chain" of sources in what was still a very dangerous and unstable situation. "[Eyewitnesses] would say 'I was there, but it happened earlier and my friend was there' and so you go to that friend," Bambang said. "They would say 'a thousand people were shot dead – my brother saw the bodies.' And then I went to the brother and asked 'were you really there?' And he would say 'no, actually I was not there, I heard this from my neighbor.' So you keep following the line. We thought the best thing to do was a sort of chronological order of what really happened."

National news editor Susanto Pudjumartono had a different concern. "Tanjung Priok happened on Wednesday night," he said, "Our deadline was on Monday. So by Thursday morning, I gave assignments to the reporters. Agus Basri and Bambang Harymurti and several others. Photographers. Everyone had to go Priok and gather as much of a report as possible. And reports, they came in the afternoon and the evening and by that time I got a kind of general idea of what really had happened, and it was very frightening. But you know, there are certain tendencies among the reporters. For example Agus Basri is a member of Muhammadiyah. And he tends to defend Islam. So I had to be very careful when reading his reports. The title of his report is *Umat Islam Dibantai* [Massacre of Muslims]. So it shows his tendency. But I always double checked. The reporters had to submit written and oral reports. I checked all sentences very carefully. And the general picture was very frightening."[15]

Susanto's comment about Agus Basri's "tendency" to defend Islam is especially significant in an organization in which the vast majority of employees were nominal Muslims. Since its founding in 1971, *Tempo* has had a reputation for being "nonconfessional" or secular in orientation. Although the magazine is known to be non-confessional, religious devotion is, paradoxically, both so ordinary and so pervasive at *Tempo* that nobody even notices it. Prayer rugs hang over the back of desk cubicles, and although the *Tempo* building has a small *musholla*, there are also spaces in both the newsroom and library that are used for praying. When someone is late for a meeting or appointment, "he is praying" is an understandable explanation. Some reporters or writers are known to be more devout than others, and they are the ones who are asked to give a prayer at the beginning of a ceremony or event. Statements such as "he is close to NU [Nahdlatul Ulama]," or "he is *abangan*" are common.[16]

---

[15]   Unless otherwise noted, Susanto Pudjomartono's recollections of how he wrote the Tanjung Priok story are based on an interview conducted on February 18, 2000.

[16]   The classical study of the distinction between Indonesian *santri* (or devout) and *abangan* (or nominal) Muslims is Clifford Geertz, *The Religion of Java* (New York: The Free Press, 1960).

Although everyone's religion is a matter of public knowledge, there is nevertheless a broad spirit of ecumenicalism at *Tempo*. During Ramadhan, for example, non-Muslims are sensitive about eating or drinking in front of their co-workers.[17] Some Christians even fast out of solidarity with their Muslim friends – or perhaps in the hope of losing weight. Traditionally, *Tempo* holds a special meal to *berbuka puasa*, or mark the end of the fast on the first day of Ramadhan, and everyone attends. Likewise, at the end of the fasting month, the company sponsors a Halal Bihalal, or gathering in which co-workers – Christians and Muslims alike – greet one another and ask forgiveness.

As a young reporter, Bambang Harymurti had to keep these considerations in mind when he obtained a document that was at once shocking and a significant scoop for *Tempo*: a tape recording of Amir Biki's last speech. A student at Perguruan Tinggi Dakwah Islam (PTDI), a Muslim evangelical school in Tanjung Priok, had invited Bambang to come to the attic of the place where he and his friends were hiding and to listen to the tape recording. One of the students acted as a lookout, and whenever he saw a soldier, he would order his friends to shut off the tape. "There were still a lot of soldiers there," Bambang said. "We would have to put it on and off because any time a soldier would come around we would have to hide." As soon as he heard the tape, Bambang knew that he had something that was both very important and very damaging to Biki. When I asked Bambang why the students would want to give so incriminating a recording to a reporter, he explained, "if you are a true believer of Amir Biki, it is all true."

---

[17] I have been told by several sources that this changed somewhat in the early 1990s, when the elevation of Margana (a Catholic) to the position of Coordinator of Reporters launched rumors of Christianization. In an interview with Coen Husain Pontoh, Goenawan Mohamad confirmed these rumors, and described the gossip about religion as "unhealthy". Although he tried to put a stop to it, he said that there was only so much he could do, especially given that he wasn't about to remove Margana. Coen Husain Pontoh, "Konflik Tak Kunjung Padam", *Pantau*, August 2001, p. 50.

Friday prayers one day after the incident at Tanjung Priok, Jakarta, 1984
[*Tempo*/Bambang Harymurti]

Bambang managed to make a recording of the tape, but then he faced a dilemma. "When I went to the office with that tape and everybody heard it, some of my Muslim friends thought it was planted. Because it made Amir Biki look bad." At a time when everyone was afraid of being accused of being a military informer, the tape looked as if it might be part of "a ploy by the Christians."

"I gave it to Syu'bah Asa," Bambang said, because Syu'bah "is considered to be in the Muslim section of *Tempo*. Because at the time a lot of people thought that Susanto was too close with Benny Moerdani [a Catholic]. So I thought I didn't want to be a part of this, so I gave it to Syu'bah Asa. But I think that Syu'bah thought it was such a hot thing that he gave it to Susanto."

Bambang's comment suggests the difficulty of trying to generalize about religious identity in Indonesia. Each of the journalists involved in the story – Bambang Harymurti, Susanto Pudjomartono, and Syu'bah Asa – is a professed Muslim. Moreover, Bambang has said that in the early 1980s he was quite devout, usually praying five times a day. The difference is that whereas Bambang and Susanto are described by their friends as either *abangan* or "somewhat secular" Muslims, Syu'bah is "known by everybody" to be *santri*.[18] Bambang's decision was also based on political considerations. He knew that if he first gave the tape to Syu'bah Asa, that he could not be accused by the other devout Muslims in the office of handing the tape over to Susanto – who it was believed might possibly show it to Benny Moerdani.[19]

When I asked Susanto if he thought it was significant that Bambang initially gave the tape to Syu'bah and not to him, he replied "No. Syu'bah was one of the managing editors at that time and an expert on Islam. Everybody knows about that. And we used to consult him on Islamic problems. So I think it is natural for Harymurti to go to him. Later on everybody listened, and then we discussed about it, openly."

Given the obvious overtones of inter-religious conflict in what had just taken place at Tanjung Priok, it is significant that Syu'bah Asa's professional journalistic values and sense of what makes news "hot" trumped any reservations that he as a devout Muslim might have had about the tape. Syu'bah confirmed that at *Tempo* he was known as a person who was close to Islamic organizations. And he remembered recognizing at the time that if excerpts from the tape were included in the story they could be used to condemn Amir Biki. "But for me," he said, "Islamic organizations are not as important as Islamic values. Therefore, okay. If it is news, it is news."[20]

In addition to the conflict between the military and the Muslim community, there was another aspect of religious conflict in the backdrop to the Tanjung Priok incident. As Bambang Harymurti explained, the issue of "Christianization" [*Kristenisasi*] made the

---

[18]   When I asked Bambang if he considered himself to be *abangan*, he said that when he first joined *Tempo*, the term implied more of a cosmopolitan, intellectual outlook than that of the *santri*, who were considered to be *kampungan,* or "hicks". Bambang said that in recent years the connotations of the term had changed, and that many Muslims like himself who in earlier years might have called themselves *abangan* were now more likely to call themselves "liberal Muslims". Conversation, July 19, 2004.

[19]   Interview with Bambang Harymurti, August 4, 2001.

[20]   Interview with Syu'bah Asa, August 2, 2000.

incident even more difficult to cover. One of the things that "everyone knew" about Tanjung Priok was that a number of churches had been built without legal permits in the overwhelmingly Muslim area, most likely as the result of bribes to the local authorities. Inter-religious conflict was considered to be an extremely sensitive topic during the New Order years; in fact *agama,* or religion, was one of the four areas of conflict that the SARA prohibitions warned editors not to inflame. Thus Christianization was an aspect of the story that *Tempo* could not include – at least not in the immediate aftermath of the event.[21]

Tempo's coverage of the incident took up four pages. It consisted of a main story, "Huru-Hara di Tanjung Priok", or "Riot at Tanjung Priok", and a sidebar or box entitled "Malam Terakhir buat Amir", "Amir's Final Night".

Like journalists everywhere, *Tempo* writers pay particular attention to the leads of their stories. As Susanto said, "we used to joke about ten thousand rupiah for a lead. Can you give me a lead? I can give you then thousand rupiah, or something like that." In this case, Susanto's lead began with an image of whitewash – a thick coat of lime covering the provocative slogans hidden beneath. Although his lead emphasized the restoration of order, it also alluded to the instability of the situation. Life in the port community may appear to have returned to normal (*telah kembali normal*), but only if one ignored both the panzers in the school parking lot and the sentiments that sparked the incident in the first place:

> Since Sunday morning, the graffiti in several streets in Tanjung Priok has been wiped clean. Thick white lime covers writing that is racist and anti-government in tone.

---

[21] *Tempo* was able to explain some of this background in a follow-up cover story that was published four months later. "Religious issues were also rather successful in heightening mass emotions. Among these were the building of churches in the middle of Muslim neighborhoods "without consultation" with the people who lived there." See "Menyingkap Peristiwa Priok", *Tempo*, January 19, 1985.

The atmosphere in Tanjung Priok has recovered. In several areas that last Wednesday night were run amok with riots, the watchful presence of troops is still evident. On Sunday night of this week two panzers were still parked in front of the PTDI [an Islamic tertiary school] on Jl. Tawes, which has been closed since Friday night. Yet daily life can be said to have returned to normal.[22]

Immediately following the two-paragraph lead is the official government view of the incident. As Leon Sigel writes, "news is not what happens, but is what someone says has happened or will happen."[23] The first source *Tempo* quotes is Armed Forces commander General L.B. "Benny" Moerdani. Even when operating under tight restraints, reporters and writers still have the power to decide how events will be "framed". Through their selection of sources and their arrangement of quotations, journalists put news into a particular context.[24] The context that *Tempo* chose to emphasize in this story was Benny Moerdani's unwillingness to scapegoat Islam.

The *Tempo* story began with praise for the general's decision to hold a press conference only fourteen hours after the event, thereby "letting the wind out of the rumors" that had inevitably developed. But *Tempo* then signaled to the careful reader that something significant was to follow. "Even more interesting, General Benny didn't accuse one side or group at all in masterminding this event. He also didn't connect it with any subversive activity."

As Bambang Harymurti explained, this sentence was

---

[22]   "Huru-Hara di Tanjung Priok", *Tempo* September 22, 1984.

[23]   Leon Sigel, "Sources Make the News", in Robert Manoff and Michael Schudson, eds., *Reading the News*, chapter 1.

[24]   As Todd Gitlin has written, "frames are principles of selection, emphasis, and presentation composed of…theories about what exists, what happens, and what matters." Todd Gitlin, *The Whole World is Watching: Mass Media and the Making and the Unmaking of the new Left* (Berkeley: University of California Press, 1980), p. 67.

significant in that it indirectly revealed a change in government policy. In the mid-1970s, the Soeharto regime had begun to characterize political Islam as a threat from the "extreme right". In 1977, just weeks prior to the presidential election, Admiral Soedomo, the commander of Kopkamtib, had announced the discovery of an anti-government conspiracy called "*Komando Jihad*". The timing of this announcement, as well as what were later shown to be ties between the leader of the plot and Soeharto's personal aide Gen. Ali Moertopo, lent credence to the accusation that "*Komando Jihad*" was a government-sponsored effort to discredit political Islam prior to the election.[25] Although the term "*Komando Jihad*" offended many Muslims, the government's accusations seemed to be at least partially vindicated in 1981, when a group of followers of a shadowy figure calling himself Imran hijacked a Garuda Indonesia passenger plane.[26]

Bambang Harymurti said that careful readers would understand that Benny Moerdani was not "blaming" Islam for the Tanjung Priok incident. "Because they [the government] always blamed the Muslims," he said, "Benny was making sure that he was not against Islam. So this is a major change in policy."

According to General Moerdani's statement of what had happened, at around 11 PM, fifteen army troops in Tanjung Priok faced an angry mob of fifteen hundred men armed with sickles. After warning shots failed to stop the surging crowd, the troops were forced to shoot in the direction of the attackers, who were attempting to seize their weapons. Moerdani explained that Amir Biki and the other masterminds of the event were "*oknum-oknum*," or bad apples – rogue elements who had fired up the people of

[25] John Bresnan, *Managing Indonesia: The Modern Political Economy* (New York: Columbia University Press, 1993), pp.195-6. Sidney Jones, in her masterful report on the "Ngruki network" in Indonesia, has flatly concluded "In reality, the *Komando Jihad* was Ali Moertopo's creation." Sidney Jones, *Al-Qaeda in Southeast Asia: The case of the "Ngruki Network" in Indonesia* (Jakarta/Brussels: International Crisis Group, August 8, 2002).
[26] *Tempo*, April 4, 1981.

Tanjung Priok with their "one-sided and unhealthy criticism of the government." His use of the term *oknum* was significant because, as Bambang explained, "it is used to disassociate the person from the group, or the organization. The implication here is that these are not Muslims, this has nothing to do with Muslims. This is not normal, this is an operation."

The last part of Benny Moerdani's statement dealt with the number of casualties. *Tempo* reported that "when asked about the number of victims, Benny, glancing at and whispering with Try Soetrisno, said that there were nine dead and fifty-three wounded." In addition to conveying the impression that the two generals were trying to get their stories straight, the "glancing and whispering" raised doubts about both the figures and Moerdani's conclusion that many of the victims were hurt not as a result of the actions of the armed forces but rather of the riot itself.

After the six paragraphs reporting on Benny Moerdani's statement, *Tempo* then devoted eighteen paragraphs to its own *pelacakan* or retracing of the event. Susanto explained that this was deliberate. "I wrote the official version," he said, "and then I continued with 'according to *Tempo* investigations,' this is our version." *Tempo*'s chronology, which comprised about two-thirds of the story, relied mostly on eyewitness accounts. When there were areas of conflict or disagreement, *Tempo* was careful to include the views of each side. For example, Sergeant Hermanu's denial that he had entered the *musholla* without removing his shoes was immediately contradicted by eyewitnesses, who added that they doubted Hermanu was the Muslim he claimed to be. "'When he was asked his religion, Hermanu said his religion was Islam. But he said the word Allah (Alloh) with the sound Alah. Therefore, he certainly isn't a Muslim,' said several eyewitnesses."

Tempo also carefully balanced its description of the "racist" speeches that "stirred up" the masses on the night of the 12th. Of Amir Biki's speech, Susanto Pudjomartono wrote, "his speech criticized [the government] on several matters, from the

The funeral of Amir Biki, Jakarta, 1984 [Bambang Harymurti]

confiscation of land to family planning and the draft law on mass organizations. He also vilified the government. Apparently he was planning something, because several times he ordered the crowd to 'wait instructions,' and said 'this speech of mine is maybe the first and the last.'" Because it was possible that some readers might have agreed with the anti-government sentiments expressed by Biki and others, *Tempo* framed the speeches in such a way as to distance the magazine from this conclusion. Susanto did this with a comment from an unidentified source (probably Benny Moerdani) who concluded that by goading the masses, "the speakers recklessly and clearly violated the teachings of Islam." The paragraph that described the actual confrontation between the ABRI forces and the mob led by Biki demonstrated the same careful balancing of opposing views. One of the sources quoted was an eyewitness and friend of Biki's who had survived the gunfire; the other source, an unnamed "official", was Benny Moerdani himself.

In the final section of the chronology, two short paragraphs described somewhat obliquely what was happening with the "other" part of the crowd – that which had been headed towards the Chinese-owned shops on Jl. Jampea. Here *Tempo*'s primary source was a twenty-year old servant at a Chinese-owned automotive store who had been awakened by the chaos. Although he and four other servants survived the fire, the next day eight bodies were found, including those of another servant and the Tan Kio Liem family. Bambang noted that in these two paragraphs *Tempo* had taken pains to point out that the owners of a nearby apothecary, which was spared, were Chinese Muslims.

The final section of *Tempo*'s story included statements of regret from the three major political parties, and a comment from a Golkar official expressing appreciation to General Benny Moerdani for "putting the matter into the appropriate perspective" of "opposition to Pancasila." Major General Try Soetrisno was given the final word, in which he reiterated the theme that the government wasn't going to accuse "a certain group" [Muslims] of masterminding the event. "'We must persist in keeping religion pure,' he said."

   Tempo thus provided two contradictory frames for the story. In the first frame, the primary "who" was Benny Moerdani, whom *Tempo* praised for the speed with which he spoke to the press and for his refusal to blame Muslims for what had happened. In this version Benny Moerdani was allowed to define "what" had happened (the successful restoration of order after racist and anti-government activity by *oknum-oknum* or bad apples), and to explain "why" the event had occurred (opposition to Pancasila). Yet *Tempo* also subtly undermined this view by providing readers with its own chronology and an alternative frame, one in which the main "who" was Amir Biki, the "what" was protest, and the "why" was the grievances of Muslims in the Tanjung Priok area.

   At first glance it might seem that the most glaring contradiction to Benny Moerdani's view of events was the challenge to the official number of dead. Yet the most dangerous challenge to the government's perspective, and the one that made explicit the alternative frame, was actually hidden in the sidebar or "box" on the life of Amir Biki. This second story, called "Final Night for Amir", opened with a description of the atmosphere at Amir Biki's home in Jl. Simpang. It mentioned his job as the director of P.T. Irajaya, an oil bunker business subcontracting with the state-owned oil company Pertamina, and his background as a student activist in 1966. The box described Amir Biki's strength as a community leader, his string of successes in getting the police to release other Muslim leaders who had been arrested, and his increasingly hardline views. But the most dangerous sentence, and the one that Bambang Harymurti said "made a lot of people think that *Tempo* was going to be banned," was the final sentence of the final paragraph:

> Thursday morning at 5:30, Dewi answered the telephone. The message: her husband had been shot to death. His body, already wrapped in burial clothes, arrived at their home two hours later. His family decided not to open the shroud. "Wholeheartedly we ask, why should it be opened?" said Boddy Biki. Without undergoing the final burial rites, the body of Amir Biki was interred. He is believed to have died a martyr's death.

As Bambang explained, "in the Muslim tradition you should open the shroud, except if he died in a battle. So it says here that he is a martyr, lifted to heaven."

But what exactly does the final sentence say? "*Ia dianggap mati syahid.*" He is believed to have died a martyr's death. Who says that Amir Biki is a martyr? Amir Biki's family? Or *Tempo*? It is hard to tell from the sentence, which was written in the passive voice. As Bambang said, "This was actually very smart. It is also a way to survive." Referring back to Benny Moerdani's reference to Amir Biki as *oknum*, Bambang explained, "from the government standpoint this was not done by Muslims, but by bad people. The '*oknum*'. So Amir Biki is '*oknum*'. But here we say he might be '*mati syahid*'. A martyr. This is basically changing him from being bad into a hero."

When I asked Susanto about this final sentence, he said, "Yes, I did it deliberately. And you know this issue was sold out. And it was photocopied and it was distributed and sold on the street. And it was distributed in hundreds of mosques after the Friday prayers. And to tell you the truth I was a little bit afraid. Everybody talked about *Tempo*'s version, and the last line gave a very big push to *Tempo*."

The last sentence of the story was so controversial that fifteen years later there was some disagreement as to who had actually written it. Bambang thought that perhaps Susanto had written it in active voice and that Fikri Jufri – a friend of Amir Biki's since 1966 – had changed it to passive. But Susanto insisted that he had written it as published, with no edits. Fikri agreed that Susanto had written the sentence, but felt that the real question was "did he check with somebody first? 'I want to write this, what do you think?' [Susanto's] check point was Benny Moerdani, because Benny was the man."[27]

"Everyone" knew that Susanto was close to Benny, and some people felt he was "too close." Susanto doesn't deny that he had a special relationship with Benny Moerdani, but in his eyes it was a professional one only. He explained the origins of the relationship this way:

> In 1977, I and six other journalists agreed to group ourselves into the so-called Seven Samurai, and we decided it was very important to monitor the news. And so we approached government officials. So we would attract his confidence and we would have regular chat. One of our most successful was to approach Benny Moerdani. Benny Moerdani was the

---

27   Interview with Fikri Jufri, May 30, 2000.

intelligence chief of the armed forces at that time. He was very close-mouthed and unapproachable. And we succeeded to approach him and later had regular meetings at least once a month with him. Sometimes alone, and sometimes with five or six of his assistants, who later on became very important persons. After several years we developed a kind of relationship. I could talk in common Javanese. This thing is very important in Indonesia.

This lobbying of highly placed government officials was one of *Tempo*'s most important strategies during the New Order. "There was so much information coming that we could not report," Susanto said. "Only five or ten percent we could report. Monitoring news was more important than writing."[28]

With regard to Tanjung Priok, Susanto said he knew from the very beginning that he could not write the whole story. "But I had a very good relation with Benny Moerdani," he said, "and on Thursday or Friday he had a press conference. And then after that I lingered on and asked him, this is the official version of the Tanjung Priok incident. Do we have to report the official version? Or can we report also our own investigations? 'It's a free country,'" he answered. 'Of course! You have the freedom to write whatever you think!'"

"On Friday and Saturday I met personally with Benny," Susanto said. "I asked him about his version, and he told me how the rioters were so angry that they tried to seize the weapons, and in that situation you have to shoot. It's a rule of the army. You do not give your weapons to demonstrators."

Susanto started to write on Monday morning. "So everybody is waiting for me to write," he said. "Usually the length of the story is decided on Monday. When I started to write I said it is impossible for me to write in two pages, so I plan to divide it into

28   Interview with Susanto Pudjomartono, May 24, 2000.

two sections. One is about the burial of Amir Biki." But even then it wasn't so easy. One of the key issues was how many people had been killed in the melee? Susanto recalled that before they closed the magazine everyone involved with the story met to discuss the number they should use. "Agus Basri, of course, he wants thirty or forty or fifty? Or even one hundred?" Susanto laughs. "We could not write about that. There is no evidence about that. Goenawan and Fikri said, 'It's up to you.'"

"So we could not write forty or fifty because there is no evidence," Susanto said. "And there is a possibility that if we make a mistake we will be banned. We will be closed."

Bambang also remembered that they had to be able to document the names of the people who had died. "At that time," he said, "people said there must be more. So we tried to – but of course we can only say what we are sure of. We had problems because the official number of people who died was nine, and here we said twenty-eight. But we can say that because we can give the names of those twenty-eight people. The number of Chinese people who got burned is already more than nine."

Tempo did get a sort of reprimand for its story in the form of a call from Puspen, the Armed Forces Information Center. Fikri Jufri was summoned to explain why *Tempo* had published the version it did. Yet as Susanto explained, "one reason we can dare to write the unofficial version is because I assured Goenawan and Fikri that I got an assurance from Benny Moerdani that we can write what we want. Puspen is very powerful, more powerful than the Department of Information. They are actually the ones who control the press. And the Puspen knows I was close to Benny."

What happened next was high stakes political theater. While Fikri was being reprimanded by Puspen, back at the office *Tempo* journalists were placing bets on who Fikri would call on the carpet. "Who will it be?" Susanto laughed. "We make a joke among ourselves who is going to be blamed by Fikri after he is summoned." Susanto knows that Fikri will not dare to blame him. "So people say, he will blame Agus Basri or Bambang Harymurti, or Margana."

Fikri did call the office, and he blamed Margana. "Fikri is a very good actor, you know," Susanto said. "In front of the chief of the Armed Forces Information Center he took a phone and dialed and talked to Margana. He said, 'Margana, how can you make this mistake?' For the sake of appearance! He is very good."

Susanto hastens to point out, however, that there was still a lot of danger. "We never see or believe that Benny was our protector," he said. "Never. And Benny has a lot of enemies. If he is designated as our protector, it is a disadvantage, not an advantage. Benny is also a professional soldier. If he had to kill me, then he would kill me without any hesitation. He is a real soldier, believing he could not violate his soldier's oath."[29]

Although Susanto is quick to say that his relationship with Benny Moerdani was a professional one, there are others who disagreed. "Susanto was seduced by Benny," Goenawan Mohamad later told me. "Fikri too was like that. He was seduced. It was very hard to find a military man like Benny then. Bright witty, English speaking, very informed. He was very friendly. He could be very friendly. He was very friendly to me every time we met. And you could be seduced."[30]

It was indeed possible for a writer to be "seduced", but there were also a number of controls put into place at *Tempo* that were designed to prevent it from happening. One of these controls was the process by which editors and writers decided which events would become news.[31] Before a story went into the magazine, it had to make it through at least two planning meetings and a "checking" meeting. All *Tempo* editors and writers were required to attend these meetings, and thus had a say in how a particular story would be played.

[29]   Interview with Susanto Pudjomartono, May 24, 2000.
[30]   Interview with Goenawan Mohamad, June 20, 2000.
[31]   The process that *Tempo* followed strongly resembled what was done at the American news magazines *Time* and *Newsweek*. This was not completely coincidental. Goenawan Mohamad had a friend at *Time,* and he visited the news magazine for several weeks in the mid-1970s.

Syu'bah Asa, *Tempo*'s office in Jl. Senen Raya, 1980 [*Tempo*/Eddy Herwanto]

Although each writer had to submit his story to a managing editor who would do the final edits, the writer nevertheless had a great deal of power to frame the final version of the piece. In most cases the writer had developed an expertise in the area, and was presumed to know more about the topic than his or her managing editor. Moreover, with the exception of Fikri Jufri, who was known for his reporting abilities, most of the managing editors in the 1980s were considered to be "word smiths" rather than journalists, and were thus unlikely to tamper with the content of the stories. And finally, there was the matter of timing. On deadline, there simply wasn't enough time for the managing editors to check and make sure that the original story outline was being followed. "I don't think there is so much supervising," Bambang said, " because by the time [a story is being edited] we are already planning for the next week."

Bambang Harymurti said that only later – in a follow-up story published four months after the event – was *Tempo* able to make the "real" cause of the incident more explicit. A key paragraph in this second story quoted a government official (Benny Moerdani) as referring to Tanjung Priok as a kind of "ashtray". His statement reinforced the view already common among many Muslims that Tanjung Priok was an "Intel" or intelligence operation, in which Islamic extremists were permitted to express themselves, thereby "magnetizing" or drawing out others and making it all the more easy for the army to crush them.

> "It's like when people smoke. The ashes certainly can't be thrown any old place. Ashtrays are needed. Tanjung Priok was indeed intentionally used as a kind of 'ashtray', a place to channel emotion," the official said.[32]

Moerdani's statement confirmed the belief of many Muslims that the ultimate goal of the state was to "corner" and destroy those who shared their beliefs.

Tempo's carefully balanced coverage of the Tanjung Priok incident not only demonstrated the magazine's ability to challenge subtly the "official" version of events put forth by the military, but it also suggested the editors' sensitivity to the aspirations of competing groups within Indonesia's diverse Islamic community. At the very time that some Muslim leaders were rejecting Pancasila and calling for the creation of an Islamic state, other Muslim intellectuals dismissed these notions altogether. During the 1980s, *Tempo* carefully balanced its coverage of those who called for an Islamic state with a series of articles that highlighted the thinking of those who argued instead that what was really needed in Indonesia was a renewal in Islamic thought.

Although the term "renewal in Islam" is usually associated with Nurcholish Madjid, as Robert Hefner points out, Nurcholish was one shining star among a constellation of other like-minded

---

[32] "Dari Perkara Priok dan Bom BCA", *Tempo*, January 19, 1985. Susanto Pudjomartono confirmed that his source was Benny Moerdani.

intellectuals.[33] In the early 1970s a group of young modernist Muslim scholars, most of whom had been associated with the banned Masyumi party, developed a new strategy for social change. Suspicious of mass politics, they argued that Indonesian Muslims had been sidetracked by the debate over the creation of an Islamic state. Not only was this impractical given the realities of the New Order, but it was also not in keeping with the teachings of the *Qur'an*, which they argued never mandated the creation of an Islamic state. What was important, they said, was that Muslims preserve what is sacred in Islam, while distinguishing the divine from what is merely human. Nurcholish concluded that Islam needed to "secularize" (or rather "desacralize") Muslim political parties and the drive for an Islamic state. "Islam itself, if examined truthfully," Nurcholish wrote, "was begun with a process of secularization. Indeed, the principle of *Tauhid* [the uncompromised oneness of God] represents the starting point for a much larger secularization."[34]

After the Soeharto regime passed laws requiring Pancasila to become the sole basis of all social and political organizations in the mid-1980s, renewal in Islamic thought became even more salient. *Tempo* did a number of cover stories on the challenges facing Islam, most of which were written by Syu'bah Asa. According to Ulil Abshar-Abdalla, the founder of the Liberal Islamic Network (*Jaringan Islam Liberal*), *Tempo*'s stories had an enormous impact on Islamic discourse in Indonesia. *Tempo* became known for advocating a variety of Islam that was compatible with the modern urge to create democracy and pluralism.[35] These stories also had the effect of creating some enemies for the magazine. As William Liddle noted, the scripturalist Islamic publication *Media Dakwah*

---

[33] For a superb discussion of the significance of renewal in Islamic thought, see Robert Hefner, *Civil Islam*, esp. pp. 96-7 and 113-4. See also R. William Liddle, "Improvising Political Cultural Change", in *Leadership and Culture in Indonesian Politics* (Sydney: Allen and Unwin, 1996), pp. 149-153.

[34] Quoted in Robert Hefner, *Civil Islam*, p. 117. I have drawn heavily on Hefner's analysis of the significance of renewal in Indonesian Islamic thought.

[35] Interview with Ulil Abshar-Abdalla, January 4, 2000.

saw *Tempo* as one of the "enemies of Islam, largely because of its promotion of Nurcholish Madjid, whom *Media Dakwah* view[ed] as an 'apostate.'"[36]

An example of the kind of story of which "scripturalist" Muslims disapproved ran in *Tempo* in December 1984, just two months after the Tanjung Priok incident. An article called "Does Islam Include a Concept of Statehood?" summarized a series of interviews with prominent Muslim scholars, including both Nurcholish Madjid and Abdurrahman Wahid, and concluded:

> Based on the statements of those who were interviewed by *Tempo*, it can be affirmed that in neither the *Qur'an* nor the Hadis – or even more generally in the laws pertaining to ritual obligations – is there a command for an Islamic state. At least not in the sense of requiring a particular shape or model. 'The problem with Iran,' said Abdurrahman Wahid, for example, 'is that because they believe their state is the one and only model of Islam, they then attack the form of the state of Saudi Arabia, etc.'
>
> Generally speaking, it can be agreed that Islam contains regulations for society, and not for the state itself. Certainly the ideal Islamic society will reflect the teachings of Islam, and at maximum, Islamic law. And indeed Islamic law requires the protection of the state, in whatever form that protection might take. But what is going on here right now is actually an even more fundamental discussion: the issue is how far Islamic law can change.[37]

Significantly, Syu'bah gives Goenawan full credit for this series of articles.[38] "Okay, in a technical sense, I may have known more

---

36   R. William Liddle, "Media Dakwah Scripturalism", in *Leadership and Culture in Indonesian Politics*, p. 271.

37   "Islam Punya Konsep Kenegaraan?", *Tempo*, December 29, 1984.

38   Examples of these stories include "Menghadapi Ide Pembaruan Islam", *Tempo*, January 13, 1973; Sebuah Masa Yang Berubah Sebuah", and Nurcholish Yang Menarik Gerbong", *Tempo*, June 14, 1986. Interview with Syu'bah Asa, August 2, 2000.

about the issues compared with Goenawan," Syu'bah said. But on topics like secularization, "Islamic vision," and the conviction that the thoughts of Nurcholish had to be included in *Tempo*, "we were the same." Although Syu'bah wrote the articles, he says that Goenawan Mohamad was the "visionary."

"Goenawan said we must defend the Islamic community because they have been treated unjustly," Syu'bah said. "And if it turns out that Islam treats others unfairly, then we'll strike at Islam." Syu'bah concluded that *Tempo* was safe because the magazine treated each branch of Islamic thought fairly. "We defended them all," he said. "It was Goenawan's design. I only implemented it."

In their stories on renewal in Islam, as in their stories on Tanjung Priok, *Tempo* writers and editors strove for balance in covering this war within the Indonesian Muslim community. The goal of lobbying different groups in power was to make sure that *Tempo* would never be seen as tilting towards one side or another.[39] *Tempo* had a strong lobby with Benny Moerdani, but with Muslim preachers as well.[40] As Syu'bah said, sometimes *Tempo* defended *umat* Islam, and sometimes *Tempo* criticized it.

Tempo always followed a very careful path to remain balanced. It was not until the early 1990s that *Tempo* was no longer perceived to be neutral – and when this happened, the consequences were disastrous.

---

[39] The effort at balance pervaded all aspects of *Tempo*'s coverage – extending even to political prisoners. Susanto Pudjomartono recalled that when a reporter once proposed giving Muslims who were detained in Jakarta's Cipinang prison a gift of *peci* (a fez-like cap) and sarongs at Lebaran, he asked "why only Muslim prisoners? We should give them to all the political prisoners. There are two sections there, *kiri* and *kanan*. Extreme leftists and extreme rightists. So we had developed a very strong relationship with all the prisoners there, and they were willing to help us." Interview, February 18, 2000.

[40] Susanto told me that he regularly met A.M. Fatwa, who warned him that there had been a "radicalization" of the Muslims in Tanjung Priok. Fatwa, who later went to prison for his alleged involvement in stirring up the Tanjung Priok incident, told Susanto, "I am a Muslim preacher. If I go there, nobody will want to hear me. Because I am not a hardliner."

CHAPTER SIX

the nation

Tempo was indeed born in the New Order. But *Tempo* itself,
not only the editors, but also within the institution, defended
critical thought. It has to be said.
Tempo was miraculous.

— *Amarzan Loebis, August 26, 2004*

When Amarzan Loebis was released from Buru Island in 1979, he
was thirty-eight years old. He was with the last group of detainees
to be released from the penal colony, and once he was freed, he
went straight to *Tempo*. There he met with national editor Susanto
Pudjomartono, who said that the magazine was going to do a cover
story on the release of the political prisoners, many of whom had
been imprisoned at Buru since its creation in 1969. The detainees
were accused of having belonged to the Indonesian Communist
Party (PKI), or to one of its affiliated organizations. At Buru, they
lived – and in many cases died – under conditions that were
shockingly brutal. The vast majority had never been charged with
a crime.

Amarzan asked if *Tempo* would be sending a reporter to Buru,
and the answer was no. "Do you want a story, a report from the
field?" Amarzan asked. "A report of what happened during the
last days?"

"Who *are* you?" Amarzan recalls that Susanto asked in
amazement.

Political prisoners, Buru Island, no date [*Tempo*/Amarzan Loebis]

Amarzan told Susanto he had been at Buru. "I was part of the last group to come home," he said.[1]

Amarzan Loebis was not his real name. He had been born in Medan, North Sumatra, with the name Amarzan Ismail Hamid. The son of a man who also worked in newspapers, Amarzan became a journalist while still in high school. After he moved to Jakarta, he studied journalism at the Perguruan Tinggi Ilmu Jurnalistik (College of Journalism), and in 1963 joined *Harian Rakyat,* where he wrote about culture. *Harian Rakyat* was "The People's Daily", and it was the newspaper of the Indonesian Communist Party.

Amarzan was a poet as well as a journalist. In Jakarta he joined Lekra, the Institute of the Peoples' Culture, which was the cultural wing of the Indonesian Communist Party. Amarzan wrote many different kinds of poetry, including lyrical, story-like ballads that led literary critic Keith Foulcher to describe him "as perhaps the

---

[1]   Amarzan Loebis' story is drawn from an interview on August 26, 2004. For an account of life at Buru Island Penal Colony, see Pramoedya Ananta Toer, *The Mute's Soliloquy: A Memoir*, translated by Willem Samuels (Jakarta: Hasta Mitra in cooperation with the Lontar Foundation, 1999).

most significant Lekra poet of all."[2] As a young man, he was friendly with Fikri Jufri and Nono Makarim, meeting with them and other "free thinking" students in an informal political discussion group held in a house that was also a girls' dormitory. Together they enjoyed the discussions – and the chance to see the pretty girls – until 1965, when their lives suddenly and dramatically diverged.

During the 1960s, Amarzan never met Goenawan Mohamad, although he knew of him and admired his poetry. As Amarzan explained, Lekra wasn't strong at the University of Indonesia, and Goenawan was a "campus kid" [*anak kampus*]. "Leftist thinkers at the University of Indonesia didn't come from the literature department," he said.

After the 30th of September, 1965, Amarzan went into hiding. "Maybe they forgot about me, or maybe I was good at hiding," he laughs. He sold gasoline and lived in a kiosk on the streets of Jakarta until 1968, when he was arrested. He was interned for two years in Jakarta's Salemba prison, one year at Nusa Kambangan Island off the South Java coast, and then eight more years at Buru Island in the Moluccas. Buru's most famous detainee was Pramoedya Ananta Toer, whom Amarzan had known from Lekra. When I asked Amarzan why he was imprisoned, he said simply "Lekra. All Lekra people, everyone close to Lekra was either captured or killed."

"Were you a member of PKI?" I asked.

"No," he answered. "I always had questions."

To the Soeharto regime, such distinctions were unimportant. In 1971, Amarzan was sent to Buru Island. There, exiled and forgotten, he joined the other political detainees or *tapol* who were no longer considered to be a part of the nation of Indonesia.

---

[2]   For more on Amarzan Ismail Hamid's poetry, see Keith Foulcher, *Social Commitment in Literature and the Arts*, pp. 138-140. Several of Amarzan Ismail Hamid's poems can be found, with English translations, in Foulcher on pp. 148-165.

What is the "nation" of Indonesia? This is a question that has confounded Indonesians and scholars of Indonesia alike, since long before Benedict Anderson gave a name to the problem of imagining a community with as much ethnic, religious, and cultural diversity as Indonesia.[3] Aside from the shared history of Dutch colonialism and the lingua franca of *bahasa Indonesia*, there was little to hold together the fragile unity of the archipelago. As Indonesia's only weekly news magazine for many years, *Tempo* was both a creator and signifier of national identity in the New Order. By deciding what would become "National" news, *Tempo* editors both consciously and unconsciously depicted the nation of Indonesia.

Each week, *Tempo* writers and editors hold a series of meetings at which they decide what will appear in the magazine, and few at *Tempo* will disagree with the assertion that the question of what will be included as National news is one of the most important and controversial of these decisions. Senior editors confirmed that in the past the repressive political atmosphere outside the magazine led to heated arguments within over what stories would be included, and my own observations of weekly planning meetings during 1999-2000 suggest that even in the post-banning era contents of the National section arouse debate. *Tempo* writers may whisper, doodle, or daydream throughout the discussion of what will appear in Law, Environment, or Books, but everyone pays attention to what will be included in National. Although I witnessed very few major arguments, participants in planning meetings often suggested ways of modifying a story's angle, or adding another dimension with a "box". Sometimes one of the senior editors would argue that a proposed National story was too limited in scope, or of only minor significance – in which case it

---

[3]   Benedict R. O'G. Anderson, *Imagined Communities* (London: Verso, 1983). See also George McT. Kahin, *Nationalism and Revolution in Indonesia* (Ithaca: Cornell University Press, 1952), and Daniel S. Lev and Ruth McVey, eds., *Making Indonesia: Essays on Modern Indonesia in Honor of George McT. Kahin* (Ithaca: Southeast Asia Program, Cornell University, 1996).

would be relegated to Events. Similarly, if a story was deemed to be of local interest only, it would be moved to the section on Regions. Regional correspondents who email in story ideas for the National section face an often skeptical Jakarta audience. Once, for example, when a correspondent sent in a suggestion from Riau that was determined to be unsuitably local, someone at the meeting called out "send it to the *Riau Pos!*"

During much of the history of the New Order, disputes within the government had to be covered with particular caution. The inclusion of a particular story within the National section draws attention to that event, and during the Soeharto years it was sometimes safer to bury an account of a particularly "hot" incident under one of the other rubrics in the back of the magazine. Despite the risks involved, each week *Tempo* editors and writers had to decide what would appear in the National section. The weekly snapshot of the nation of Indonesia was the result of a complex interplay between the editors' assessment of what had actually happened and what in their judgement could be safely included without putting the magazine at risk.

The content of the National section of *Tempo* magazine between its founding in 1971 and its banning in 1994 was influenced not only by the political context of the New Order, but also by reportorial routines and broader cultural frameworks.[4] The journalistic conventions that determine who and what will become news are situated in particular historical and cultural contexts. Behind the six questions basic to any news story – who, what, where, when, why and how – lies a "framework of interpretation" in which reporters and writers operate.[5] For example, which "whos" are newsworthy? What kinds of events even qualify as news? Where and when is news likely to occur? And most difficult of all to answer, how and why did something

4   For a full discussion of this approach, see James Carey, *Communication as Culture: Essays on Media and Society* (Boston: Unwin Hyman, 1988).
5   See Robert Manoff and Michael Schudson, eds., *Reading the News*, p. 5.

happen? Scholars taking a cultural approach to journalism have argued that in order to understand news, it is necessary first to understand the interpretive frameworks that give it meaning. These frameworks can include political and economic structures, social and occupational routines of news organizations, and the literary and cultural forms available in the society at large.[6]

During a two-month period in the spring of 2000, I conducted a content analysis of the National section of *Tempo*.[7] In this effort I was initially inspired by the work of American sociologist Herbert Gans, whose landmark study is required reading for anyone who seeks to understand how American journalists decide what's news. Gans examined a "a six-month sample of stories appearing in alternate months during 1967, 1971, and 1975" from *Time* and *Newsweek* magazines, CBS Evening News, and NBC Nightly News, and recorded both the actor and activity that dominated the individual story – or "who" and "what" each story was about.[8]

Like Gans, I also examined a sample of National news stories, but there the similarities end. My sample consisted of 330 magazines and 1291 stories extending over a twenty-nine year period. One edition was randomly selected from each month that *Tempo* was published between April, 1971 and March, 2000. A team of eight coders (seven students from the University of

---

[6]   Two well-known studies of news that emphasize political and economic frameworks are Martin A. Lee and Norman Solomon, *Unreliable Sources: A Guide to detecting Bias in the News Media* (New York: Carol Publishing Group, 1990), and S. Robert Lichter, Stanley Rothman, and Linda S. Lichter, *The Media Elite: American's New Powerbrokers* (New York: Adler and Adler, 1986). For a study based on the occupational routines of journalists see Gaye Tuchman, "Objectivity as Strategic Ritual: An Examination of Newsmen's Notions of Objectivity", *American Journal of Sociology* 77 (January 1972): 660-679, and for an example of literary or cultural analysis see Robert Darnton, "Writing News and Telling Stories", *Daedalus*, 104 (1975): 174-194.

[7]   I am grateful for the invaluable help of my research assistant Theresia Citraningtyas, without whom this content analysis could not have been completed.

[8]   Herbert Gans, *Deciding What's News: A Study of CBS Evening News, NBC Nightly News, Newsweek and Time* (New York: Pantheon, 1979), p. 6.

Indonesia, plus myself) coded each story in that edition's National section for "who", "what", and "where", along with the two most frequently quoted sources.[9] We also noted whether the story was an interview, a survey, or a profile. Stories that were interviews or profiles were deemed to have a "who" but no "what", whereas surveys were considered to have a "what" but no "who".

One of the difficulties of doing cross-cultural research is the problem of striking a balance between the act of "training" local assistants and the accidental reinforcing of the "truths" of an academic discipline that one comes to recognize as being dangerously culture-bound.[10] For example, most students of American journalism would agree that the main "who" of the story is the person who is quoted – or allowed to speak – the most.[11] The problems with this assumption became apparent during the three weeks of coder training, when I asked the coders to analyze a 1979 story about a speech that President Soeharto had made in Blitar, East Java.[12] The occasion of the speech was the dedication of a new memorial plaque that would be placed at the grave site of Indonesia's first president, Soekarno.

When I asked the coders to identify the "main who" of the story, the answer was unanimous: "Soekarno," they said. But how could this be, I asked? Soekarno was dead and buried. He wasn't saying anything, he wasn't doing anything. To me it was obvious that the "main who" was President Soeharto. Trying to explain, I told the coders that one means of identifying the "main who" is to

---

[9] My coders were Sylvia, Iin Purwanti, Siti Munawaroh, Henny Wati, Deibby Imelda Manahit, Grace Wangge, and Bayu Kristianto. Three were students in the English department, four were students in the Faculty of Medicine.

[10] For a disquieting discussion of ethical dilemmas in the fieldwork experience, see Clifford Geertz, *Available Light: Anthropological Reflections on Philosophical Topics* (Princeton: Princeton University Press, 2000), pp. 21-41.

[11] Sigel writes, "The people in the news are most often the sources of news. Presidents and those around them are the most prominent examples." Leon V. Sigel, "Sources Make the News", in Manoff and Schudson, *Reading the News*, p. 12.

[12] "Di Sini Proklamator Dimakamkan", *Tempo*, June 30, 1979.

see who gets quoted the most. There is a convention in journalism, I said, that the person who does the most talking is the most important.

At that point Citra, my assistant, interrupted. "But that's not true!" she said. "Not if you're Javanese. In Java, the people who do the most talking are weak. A really powerful person – like Soeharto – doesn't have to say anything at all."

Citra was right, of course, and we changed the code sheet. "Who" became *pelaku utama*, or "the main actor", which we defined as the person or persons who had set the story in motion.[13] We also identified *sumber 1* and *sumber 2*, or the first and second most quoted source. And finally, we identified whether or not p = s, or whether the main actor was also one of the two most frequently-quoted sources.[14]

There were other challenges. In designing the code book, I followed Herbert Gans' general division of "what" into government versus non-government activities. Yet we quickly realized that Gans' categories of government activity made little sense within the political context of the New Order, and would be of limited use in measuring the contents of *Tempo*'s National section. We therefore divided the activities of the Indonesian government into four general areas: (a) ideological, structural, and political, (b) military and diplomatic, (c) economic, and (d) public welfare.[15] We then divided each of these four categories

---

[13] We agreed that the *pelaku utama* could be a dead person, but only under highly unusual circumstances. If, for example, the story had been about Soekarno and his actions in uniting Indonesia and proclaiming independence – as the headline somewhat erroneously suggested – then he would have been the main actor. However to my knowledge we never saw another story in which this was the case.

[14] President Soeharto was determined to be the *pelaku utama*, or main actor, in seventy-two (or 5.7%) of the stories in my sample. He was either the first or second most-quoted source in only forty-eight stories.

[15] Gans' categories of government activity were (a) conflicts and disagreements, (b) decisions, proposals and ceremonies, and (c) personnel changes, including campaigning. Herbert Gans, *Deciding What's News*, p. 16. I am grateful to Joel Kuipers for his thoughts on developing my categories, and to Citra, Bambang Harymurti, Wicaksono, and Arif Zulkifli for their advice and suggestions.

into subcategories, which in several cases were deliberately designed to parallel the structure of Indonesian ministries [See Table 1].[16]

Most problematic were the subcategories under the general category of "Ideology, Structure, and Politics". Whereas many of the coders, for example, initially had no idea of what I meant by a "state ceremony", I also had to incorporate into the code book the subtleties of the New Order distinction between an "election" and a "change of government officials".[17] Even more difficult was the unexpected problem of where to put the activities of the DPR, or Parliament. Although I had at first categorized "routine acts of Parliament" under *pemerintah* or "government", several of *Tempo*'s desk editors told me I had made a mistake. "Routine acts of Parliament don't belong under 'government'," I was told. "They are 'non-government'."[18]

But this made no sense, I thought. Wasn't Parliament one of three branches of the government? Aren't members of the DPR paid with state money? Don't they pass laws, and aren't they considered to be *pejabat negara* or public officials? My informants were insistent. Although *pemerintah* is routinely translated into English as "government", Indonesians consider members of Parliament to be *wakil rakyat*, or representatives of the people.

---

[16] This explains the otherwise odd subcategory of "Art, Culture, Tourism", a grouping that makes sense only if one accepts the Soeharto government's definition of art and culture as something that can best be packaged and sold to tourists. See Melani Budianta, "Discourse of Cultural Identity in Indonesia during the 1997-1998 Monetary Crisis" *Inter-Asia Cultural Studies*, 1, (2000): 109-128 for a full discussion of this point.

[17] Clifford Geertz, *Negara: the Theatre State in Nineteenth-Century Bali* (Princeton, New Jersey: Princeton University Press, 1980). The selection of governors posed particular problems. Despite the trappings of an election – including a slate of candidates and a vote – these events were actually orchestrated by a small circle of political elites, and reduced to what McVey has called a "ritual affirming loyalty to the state." Ruth McVey, "Building Behemoth: Indonesian Constructions of the Nation–State", in *Making Indonesia*, p. 23.

[18] I am grateful to Wicaksono for initially pointing out this misunderstanding, and to Arif Zulkifli and Karaniya Dharmasaputra for further clarification of this point.

The DPR is thus not seen as part of the *pemerintah*, which translates more accurately as "administration".

Perhaps this incident should be viewed as a simple cautionary tale, a warning to the researcher who attempts to analyze news – or politics – without taking culture into account. Or perhaps it suggests that no single methodological tool is alone sufficient to unearth the framework of interpretation behind the news.

During the twenty-three year period before the banning in 1994, an overwhelming majority of the National stories in *Tempo* were either about the government or government activity [see Table 1]. Sixty-three percent of the 1123 stories examined for this period were either about government activities, parliamentary actions, or the activity of political parties that were closely related to the government.[19] Over 26% of the stories (n=293) were devoted to ideological, structural, or political aspects of the government. Of these subgroupings, the three biggest categories were "changes in government officials" (forty-six stories), "bannings" (forty stories), and "other announcements" (forty-four stories). Another 27% of the total number of National stories were devoted to activities relating either to the military or to government programs aimed at economic and social development. In this regard the contents of *Tempo*'s National section followed what is widely understood to be the pro-development agenda of the New Order.

The Soeharto government made a lot of announcements, and *Tempo* generally included them in the pages of the National section. When I asked Goenawan Mohamad about the presence of what could be called "non-news" in the National section – for example announcements of lists of gubernatorial candidates who appeared to be up for "election" but were actually going to be appointed, or

---

[19] If the activities of Parliament and of the political parties are removed from this total, then 56.01% of *Tempo*'s stories are about the government. In Herbert Gans' study of the American newsmagazines, about 51% of the "section columns" were devoted to government activities. Herbert Gans, *Deciding What's News,* p. 16.

stories about President Soeharto as "The Father of Development"–
he agreed that *Tempo* reported on these events as if they were the
substance of democracy rather than political spectacle. "The reporters
did focus more on the announcement, the statement, the decision,
not the process," he said. "Because there was no process, there was
no politics in the first place. If you had politics you would have a
real process of changing things where more people are involved."[20]
Of course, as Bambang Harymurti pointed out, many of the National
stories that appeared to focus on empty announcements might
actually offer hidden clues of conflict within the government, clues
that particularly knowledgeable readers could recognize. In this
regard National news in *Tempo* became part of an elaborate process
of negotiating and signaling among elites.[21]

Of the National stories that appeared in *Tempo* before the
banning, only about one-third (36.68%) were about non-
government activities. Of the stories related to activities outside
the government, the largest categories were either about conflict
(11.5%) or crime (8.6%).

Sixty-five stories or 5.79% of the total of National stories
before the banning were about political party activity. Determining
how to code these stories posed a problem similar to that of how
to categorize "routine acts of Parliament". Technically, the political
parties are independent of the state, and should therefore be coded
as "non-government". Yet the largest political organization, and
the one which beginning in 1971 won every election during the
New Order, was the government-created political organization
Golkar. And the Soeharto government repeatedly tried to engineer
other political party activity, with varying degrees of success.[22]

---

[20]   Interview with Goenawan Mohamad, June 20, 2000.
[21]   See Michael Schudson, "When? Deadlines, Datelines, and History", in *Reading
the News* for a discussion of how political elites use this signaling process as an
instrument of governance.
[22]   For an overview of government efforts to manipulate PDI, or the Indonesian Democratic
Party, see Arif Zulkifli, *PDI Di Mata Golongan Menengah Indonesia* (Jakarta: Pustaka
Utama Grafiti, 1996), and Robert Hefner, *Civil Islam*, pp. 180-184.

The most notorious example of this occurred in 1996, when the Soeharto regime conspired to oust Megawati Soekarnoputri as Chairperson of PDI, or the Indonesian Democratic Party. Because these stories cannot really be classified as either "government" or "non-government", I included them in a third grouping along with routine acts of Parliament (1.51%).

Nearly half (47.3%) of all stories that were published before the banning took place in Jakarta [See Table 2]. Two-thirds took place on the islands of Java, Madura, and Bali. Outside of Java, Madura and Bali, only provinces that contained very large cities or regional trouble spots commanded significant numbers of stories. These included North Sumatra (which contains capitol city Medan) with forty-two stories or 3.73%; East Timor, with nineteen stories or 1.69%; Aceh, with eighteen stories or 1.6%; Riau (the Sumatran province where the Caltex oil fields are located) with nineteen stories or 1.69%; and Irian Jaya (now West Papua), with seventeen stories or 1.51%.[23] In this sense, the portrait of Indonesia that emerged in the pages of *Tempo* was Java-centric. Its geography was consistent with the New Order concept of the nation: Java, Bali, parts of Sumatra, and tourist and resource-rich pockets of the outer islands.

Between 1971 and 1994, the great majority of "whos" in *Tempo's* National stories were public officials, former public officials, military commanders, and leaders of formal organizations who were known to the public. These "knowns" were three times more likely to appear as the "main actor", and four times more likely to appear as most-quoted sources than were the ordinary people whom American media sociologist Herbert Gans has characterized as "unknowns". Before the banning, President Soeharto was the most frequently appearing "main actor" in my sample, with sixty-eight appearances. As a source, he ranked number two – behind "anonymous".

---

[23]   Prior to the banning, *Tempo* had bureaus in Bandung, Yogyakarta, Surabaya, and Medan.

One of the most surprising things about the category of "who" was the number of stories that had no "main actor". There were forty-seven stories that were "supposed" to have a "main actor" (meaning that they were not surveys) in which the coder could identify no individual or group of individuals (such as members of parliament, generals, University of Indonesia students, etc.) as having caused the action.

This finding raises some intriguing questions. It is possible that despite the weeks of training (and intercoder reliability of between 80 and 90%) this was a coding error, and the coders were reluctant to assign "responsibility" for an occurrence. Yet after having examined many of these stories myself and confirming that there was indeed no "who", I believe that there may have been other explanations. Given the tight restrictions on the press and the ever-present threat of a banning, *Tempo* writers may have been reluctant to attribute responsibility (or blame) for an occurrence. Alternatively, Goenawan Mohamad suggested: "My theory is that we (*Tempo* people, but also maybe Indonesian journalists, or Indonesians living under a certain kind of regime) tend to be uncomfortable with 'subjecthood'. We tend to evade putting somebody as the subject, or the origin, of actions and situations….My sense is that this is an anxiety of 'doing'. The subject is made less exposed to an 'active situation'."[24]

Despite the high percentage of stories in which the main actor was a "known", even more striking was the number of stories about victims, in which *Tempo* journalists gave voice to ordinary people's struggle against the overwhelming power of the state. Victims were among the largest of the categories of actors in the National section of the magazine before the banning [See Table 3]. Of the 228 stories that were about ordinary people, sixty-two (27%) were about victims. The largest group of these individuals were victims of economic development. In many cases they had been victimized

---

[24]   Email correspondence from Goenawan Mohamad, April 9, 2000.

Political prisoners, Buru Island, no date [*Tempo*/Amarzan Loebis]

by government confiscation of their land. Other types of victims included political prisoners, victims of hate crimes, riots, state-sponsored violence, or natural disasters. Another group of individuals who could likewise be characterized as victims of the New Order were the "suspects" who made up an additional 5.1% of the total number of "main actors". Interestingly, the type of crime that appeared most frequently in *Tempo*'s National section was "subversion". Former Siliwangi Commander H.R. Dharsono, a defendant in one of the several trials resulting from the Tanjung Priok incident, was a typical "suspect" in the crime of subversion.[25]

Did the average reader notice *Tempo*'s emphasis on victims? It is difficult to say. But to my seven coders, students from the University of Indonesia in their early twenties, something was very clear. To these young people, none of whom had been regular readers of *Tempo* before the banning, what was most striking about the National stories was their obvious sympathy with "the little guy".[26]

---

[25]   *Tempo*, August 17, 1985.
[26]   The interview was conducted on June 2, 2000. I am grateful to *Tempo* reporter and George Washington University graduate student Ahmad Fuadi for transcribing the interview and providing me with an invaluable "glossary" of student slang.

When I conducted a three-hour focus group interview with my coders after the content analysis was completed, this is how they described what they had seen in the National section of *Tempo*:

> If there was a conflict between the government and ordinary people, [*Tempo*] told a lot more about the people's side.

> They showed the people's suffering. There were direct quotes from the people. Dramatic ones. And what's more, if they interviewed someone from the government, a mayor or whoever, they quoted only one. If the government provided an answer or an explanation it was more likely to be jargon.

> Quotes from the government weren't specific. For example they said they didn't have the authority to answer it. They denied it. "Oh, later I'll confirm it." Or maybe they based their answer on stability, or security. Or they said it had already been decided by the boss, they were just following procedures.

> Often in Tempo if there was a quote from a general there was a hidden message. Sometimes that general spoke in jargon, about national stability, or taking firm measures. If Tempo included a quote from a general, they didn't want readers to fall for what that general said, but actually implied something quite different.

What my coders saw as the "hidden message" of *Tempo* has also been noted by William Liddle, who described the "mission" of *Tempo* in the pre-banning period as having been explicitly political – "to defend those who can not defend themselves."[27] Goenawan Mohammad explained *Tempo*'s portrayal of ordinary people as victims in this way: "There is no government that can control totally the rest of the population, especially in Indonesia. So actually the government was all-powerful, but the people didn't succumb

---

[27] R. William Liddle, "Improvising Cultural Change", in *Leadership and Culture in Indonesian Politics* (Sydney: Allen and Unwin, 1996), p. 147.

totally to it. In an authoritarian bureaucratic state the government regime didn't try to enter your mind, they just try to control your behavior. They don't want to change you into a new man, but they want you to follow the directives of the government. In other words, the people still own this private area of themselves, of their lives, of their anger. They can speak of the government in private without being really scared."[28]

Indeed, as Amarzan Loebis' story suggests, even at Buru Island the detainees didn't completely succumb to government power.

When Amarzan approached Susanto Pudjomartono in 1979 with his offer to write a story on the release of the final wave of political prisoners from the penal colony, he was told to go ahead and write a one-page story. He did, and *Tempo* liked what he wrote.[29] After Susanto said that *Tempo* would publish his article in the National section, Amarzan asked about the honorarium. It was Rp. 60,000, a significant sum for the day. Usually contributors were paid a week after the magazine came out, but in Amarzan's case they agreed to make an exception. As Amarzan had explained to Susanto, he was in a difficult situation. "I was an ex-*tapol* [political detainee]," Amarzan told me. "I was a pariah."

A week or so later, Amarzan found a note under his door. It was from Susanto. *Tempo* wanted to hire him for a special project, *Apa & Siapa*, a book that resembled "Who's Who". Amarzan gladly took the job, and a year or two later, Goenawan invited him to take the writing test and join *Tempo*'s editorial staff. He passed the test, and became a permanent employee. His name was on the masthead, but only as "Amarzan."

"Where did you learn to write like this?" Amarzan remembered that Goenawan had asked. "At Buru," he answered. "I already knew how to write in the *Tempo* format because I had studied it at Buru."

---

[28]   Interview with Goenawan Mohamad, June 20, 2000.
[29]   *Tempo,* November 17, 1979.

Amarzan was still a young man when he was interned, and he knew that he had to prepare for a job on the outside. So he studied to become a *Tempo* journalist. Each week for nearly five years, a group of fourteen detainees had pooled their money – earned from selling onions, or oil pressed from the melaleuca tree – in order to buy a single copy of *Tempo* smuggled in by Bugis fisherman. The fishermen had bought the magazine in Surabaya. The prisoners carefully tore it apart, each taking a different section. When they were finished reading, they swapped.

The magazine had to be hidden, as reading materials were forbidden. Once one of their group was captured, and – because he wouldn't give up the names of the others – severely beaten. Shortly thereafter he died. Although the death of their friend forced the prisoners to stop buying the magazine, the hiatus was temporary. Amarzan recalls that he probably began reading *Tempo* in 1975, and continued until 1979, the year he was released.

Despite *Tempo* writers' use of certain rhetorical devices as a deliberate means of evading the censors, not all of *Tempo*'s narrative techniques were intentional. As James Carey has written, "there is truth in Marshall McLuhan's assertion that the one thing of which the fish is unaware is water, the very medium that forms its ambience and supports its existence. Similarly communication, through language and other symbolic forms, comprises the ambience of human existence."[30] News is also drama, with players, dramatic action, and an audience. Even the way we describe news, as "stories", reflects this dramatic component.[31]

Both the results of my content analysis and my focus group interviews suggest that during the years before the banning *Tempo* presented politics in Indonesia as a moral drama, a struggle between two equal and opposing forces: the government and the ordinary people. Although *Tempo* sided with the ordinary people in very

[30]   James Carey, *Communication as Culture: Essays on Media and Society*, p. 24.
[31]   Robert Darnton, "Writing News and Telling Stories," *Daedalus* 104 (1975): 174-194.

subtle ways, the government was not presented as being all bad – nor were the ordinary people presented as being unambiguously good. Just as there were a few true *ksatria* or warrior-nobles in the government, there were also criminals and rioters among the ordinary people. And the ordinary people were hardly passive or helpless. They demonstrated, they rioted, they went on strike, they burned one another's homes. They sent their complaints and representatives to Parliament. They had champions like the Legal Aid Institute (LBH), and they told their stories to *Tempo* journalists.

There are striking parallels between the way in which *Tempo* depicted the moral drama of the clash between these two powerful and deeply flawed forces and what has been called the "*wayang* tradition". This tradition, based in part on the great Hindu epics *Mahabharata* and *Ramayana*, has been explained in many places. What is most significant here is that the *wayang* tradition – like news – is a means of explaining reality. And like the struggle between the government and the ordinary people as depicted in *Tempo*, the *wayang* tradition can be described as "a stable world view based on conflict."[32]

According to Goenawan Mohamad, "the *Mahabharata* is a moral drama." In this way it resembles *Tempo*'s coverage of politics in the New Order. "The way I see it," he said, "it is the absence of politics. So the issue becomes moral. And that's also a danger. If politics exist, then negotiations exist. And negotiations cannot be morally pure. So there is a give and take."[33] Significantly, before the banning many of Goenawan Mohamad's own *Catatan Pinggir* (or Sidelines essays) mirrored the conflict between the government and the ordinary people that was presented in the National section. In *Catatan Pinggir* Goenawan frequently wrote about the struggle of individuals against the overwhelming power of the state. By telling the reader the stories of ordinary people, he transformed

---

[32]   Claire Holt, as quoted in Benedict R. O'G. Anderson, *Mythology and the Tolerance of the Javanese* 2nd edition, (Ithaca: Cornell Modern Indonesia Project, 1996), p. 16.
[33]   Interview with Goenawan Mohamad, June 20, 2000.

Barges carrying confiscated *becak* to be dumped in
Jakarta Bay, 1985 [*Tempo*/Ilham Sunharyo]

victims into heroes – or sometimes even into "saints". One of
Goenawan Mohamad's most famous essays, "The Death of
Sukardal", made explicit the government's victimization of a *becak*
or pedicab driver, a man who is crushed but not silenced by the
state's arbitrary power.[34] Sukardal was a pedicab driver whose only
means of livelihood was confiscated by the police in accordance
with a new regulation. After futilely attempting to stop the
authorities, Sukardal hanged himself in a final act of defiance,
leaving behind the words "If this is indeed a nation with justice,
then the security police must be investigated."

"He died, and he was not silent," wrote Goenawan. "And our
life, as a wise person once said, is made from the deaths of others
who do not remain silent."[35]

Although some have criticized *Catatan Pinggir* for its
ambiguity and disengaged stance,[36] "The Death of Sukardal"
suggests exactly the opposite. By commenting on the news in an

---

[34] *Tempo*, July 19, 1986. I am grateful to Wicaksono for suggesting that I pay particular
      attention to this essay.
[35] Quoted from the translation by Jennifer Lindsay, in Goenawan Mohamad, *Sidelines:
      Thought Pieces From Tempo Magazine*, (Jakarta: Lontar, 1994), pp. 111-3.
[36] See Ignas Kleden's foreword to Goenawan Mohamad, *Catatan Pinggir 2*, (Jakarta:
      Pustaka Utama Grafiti, 1996), pp. vii-xxi.

oblique way through the use of poetic language and metaphor, Goenawan challenged the authority of the state and reinforced the moral drama of conflict between the government and ordinary people that appeared elsewhere in the magazine.

For many years *Catatan Pinggir* was the most interactive part of *Tempo*, and the only part of the magazine that spoke directly to the reader. As Wicaksono remarked, perhaps *Catatan Pinggir* was like a "noisy spectator" – a perceptive and sometimes irritating skeptic in the audience who interrupts and bothers the *dalang* or puppet master. Or maybe, as desk editor Yusi A. Pareanom suggested, the voice of *Catatan Pinggir* was more like the *punakawan*, or wise clowns. Like the fool in *King Lear*, the *punakawan* alone have the courage to speak truth to power.[37]

As Benedict Anderson has observed, "in *wayang* of whatever sort, the *punakawan* appear both as comic characters *within the line* of the drama, embedded in its space and time, and as mouthpieces for satire and criticism directed straight at the audience, so to speak *at right angles* to the drama and outside its space and time."[38] This dual nature of the *punakawan*, a part of the *wayang* world but also its sly and powerful critic, resembles not only the voice of Goenawan's *Catatan Pinggir*, but the position of *Tempo* as well. A child of the New Order but also its subtle critic, *Tempo* operated both within and outside the moral drama of Indonesian political life.

Amarzan Loebis worked at *Tempo* until 1984 without attracting notice. Then one day a message came from Harmoko, the minister of information. The message was oral, nothing was committed to writing. "I know he's there," the message said. "I know he is working there. That's okay, I'll permit it, but his name can't be included."

---

37   Interestingly, Goenawan has written about the similarities between the *punakawan* and Lear's fool. "Send in the Clown," a manuscript in the author's possession.
38   Benedict R. O'G. Anderson, "Cartoons and Monuments", in *Language and Power*, p. 167-8.

Amarzan recalls that Goenawan came to him. "There's a message from Harmoko," Goenawan said. "If you don't want your name to be cut out from the masthead, I won't do it. I won't take it off." Amarzan says he told Goenawan to take his name off the masthead. "So I stayed at *Tempo*," he said, "but my name was no longer there."

A few years later, in 1986, the atmosphere on the outside grew more repressive. Another message came, this time from Soekarno, Director General of Press and Graphics. "*Tempo* is a political magazine, he said, and Amarzan can't stay there. Find a place for him in a non-political magazine."

So Amarzan moved to *Matra*, a men's magazine that was also owned by Grafiti Pers. He worked at *Matra* until 1988, when the New Order became even more "energetic" in persecuting ex-PKI. "Harmoko gave a speech about Lekra people at 'certain publications,' but he actually meant *Tempo*," Amarzan told me. "There were other people. So I left *Matra* magazine too."

Surprised, I asked how many other ex-Lekra people had been at *Tempo*. "Three," he said.[39]

Amarzan said it was an "open secret" at *Tempo* that he was a former political detainee, but that it didn't matter. "Competency was more important," he said. "If I wrote well, I got good evaluations; If I didn't write well, I didn't get good evaluations. At *Tempo* I was treated exactly the same as other people. There was no difference, there was no discrimination at all."

"It's difficult to imagine this happening at any institution other than *Tempo*," he added.

When I asked Amarzan why he thought that *Tempo* was like this, he said "because of Goenawan".

"His father was a freedom fighter," he said. "He came from the edge of Java, not the center of the Mataram [kingdom]. He always had critical attitudes. He always questioned. He always looked for answers."

---

[39] In addition to Amarzan Loebis, there was Martin Aleida and Teuku Manyaka Thayeb.

There are many paradoxes to *Tempo* magazine. *Tempo* was born into the cultural milieu of the New Order – and devoted a great deal of coverage to the government and its activities – but at the same time it also challenged it from within. What my coders identified as *Tempo*'s "hidden message" was one means of resisting government power; the magazine's hiring of former political detainees like Amarzan Loebis was another. Although *Tempo* published only a handful of stories on the Communist Party in its National section, that the magazine quietly employed three former members of Lekra, including one who had been at Buru, was an act of defiance.

There are many different kinds of opposition. As Arief Budiman once explained, "as intellectuals, we knew that something wrong was being done by the government. In Islam we have this kind of saying. If you see something bad happening, you have to stop it with your hands. If you cannot stop it with your hands, stop it with your mouth. If you cannot stop it with your mouth, stop it with your heart."[40]

"I think we don't want to always ask people to do something with their hands," Arief said. "Different people have different capacities. But at least we want people to stop with their heart. That means they are not betraying their conscience."

Not all "opposition" has to take the form of open defiance of the government. Opposition can also exist in the hearts of readers who see that something is wrong, but who may not be in a position to do anything about it. "*Tempo* is the expression of a kind of a meeting of minds of these middle class people," Arief said. "They may not dare to say anything, they dare not criticize the government. But by reading *Tempo*, they can. This is the voice of their heart also."

The mission of *Tempo* was justice, or, as Arief Budiman put it, "to supply [its readers] with the moral courage at least not to betray their conscience." That *Tempo* could continue to hold to this mission despite the constraints of the New Order was, as Amarzan put it, "miraculous".

---

[40]   Interview with Arief Budiman, December 6, 1999.

CHAPTER SEVEN

the readers

Tempo's readers are widely believed to be from the middle class.[1] But what does it mean to be "middle class" in Indonesia? This is a question that has confounded scholars for some time. According to classic Marxist analysis, class is tied to the position of different groups in the relations of production: owners vs. workers. But in the Indonesian context, as in many other developing countries, a history of colonial domination complicates things. Although Indonesia is clearly part of a global capitalist system, one of the more confusing legacies of colonialism has been what Tanter and Young refer to as the "missing bourgeoisie", and the substitution of a "militarized state" as the agent of capitalist development.[2]

Since 1981, Tempo's advertising department has reported survey results stating that the the overwhelming majority of its readers hold either "owner" or "management" level jobs in the public or private sectors, and "enjoy a high standard of income."[3]

---

[1] For example, when Salim Said recalled the founding of *Tempo*, he explained "the economy also started improving at this time, the so-called new middle class started to be formed, and they needed readings." Interview with Salim Said, April 1, 1998.

[2] In 1986, the Centre of Southeast Asian Studies at Monash University organized a conference on the Indonesian Middle Class, which resulted in a book on the same topic. See Richard Tanter and Kenneth Young, eds., *The Politics of Middle Class Indonesia* (Monash University: Centre of Southeast Asian Studies, 1990), p. 12.

[3] See *Tempo*'s advertising surveys from 1981, 1986, 1989, 1991, 1993, 1994, and 1998, available in the *Tempo* library. Additional survey data from 1985 is cited in

Although the percentages and categories vary from year to year, it is nevertheless significant that, throughout the 1980s, *Tempo* promoted itself as a vehicle for advertisers to reach "upper income individuals, officials, and decision makers."[4] By 1993, *Tempo*'s marketing literature explicitly mentioned social class, explaining "the editorial policy of *Tempo* is tuned to the requirements of Indonesia's burgeoning middle class."[5]

As Ariel Heryanto has noted, scholarly literature on the middle class has tended to be one of two possible persuasions.[6] The first emphasizes the essential conservatism of the middle class, and its "opportunism". A variant of this view examines patterns of consumption, essentially defining class in terms of monthly expenditures and consumer lifestyles. The second points to the middle class as the vanguard of change and sees within it the seeds of progressive reform. Although Ariel resolves this contradiction by pointing to the "pluralism" of the middle class – preferring, in fact, the term "middle classes", another way of looking at it is to see the middle class(es) as Janus-faced, sometimes acting out of self-interest, and sometimes rising to remarkable heights of sacrifice and heroism. This dualism is present not only in the contents of *Tempo*, but also in *Tempo*'s understanding and representation of its readers.

Daniel Dhakidae, "The State, The Rise of Capital and the Fall of Political Journalism: Political Economy of Indonesian News Industry", pp. 352-4.

[4] The most desirable category of reader came from "Class A or B", official groupings developed by the Biro Pusat Statistik, the Central Statistics Bureau, and based on monthly expenditures. In 2003 the monthly expenditures of "Class A" were five million rupiah or about $600/month.

[5] Interestingly, Indonesian census data shows that "professional and technical" and "managers and administrators" constituted only 2.6% of the population nation-wide in 1971, and 3.9% in 1990. In Jakarta they accounted for 6.03% of the population in 1971 and 8.39% in 1990. Cited in Richard Robison, "The Middle Class and the Bourgeoisie in Indonesia", in Richard Robison and David S. G. Goodman, eds., *The New Rich in Asia: Mobile Phones, McDonalds and Middle-class Revolution* (London and New York: Routledge, 1996), p. 84.

[6] See Ariel Heryanto, "Public Intellectuals, Media and Democratization: Cultural Politics of the Middle Classes in Indonesia", in Ariel Heryanto and Sumit K. Mandal, eds., *Challenging Authority* (London and New York: RoutledgeCurzon, 2003), pp. 24-59.

The bloody birth of the New Order in 1965 adds to the confusion and sense of unease in trying to define the Indonesian "middle class". Many scholars have argued persuasively that the New Order should be seen as the restoration of middle-class prerogative. For example, Tanter and Young have concluded that "whatever else the events of 1965 were about, they fundamentally involved the liquidation of the human and organizational basis of the most overt class-based political force in the country, and the foundation of a state pursuing profoundly different class interests."[7] The violent elimination of the PKI or Indonesian Communist Party has likewise led Michael van Langenberg to conclude that in the New Order state, the opposite of development and modernization is Gestapu, or the 30th of September Movement in which the Communist Party allegedly attempted to seize power. He writes, "[Gerakan September Tiga Puluh, or G30S/PKI] have been the keywords in emphasizing the birth of the New Order out of alleged communist treachery in the so-called attempted coup of 30 September, 1965, and the mass violence which followed. In the functioning of the New Order state-system, the terms are used to emphasize the preceding Old Order as a period of chaos, disorder, and mass violence – from which the Indonesian State, nation, and civil society have been rescued."[8]

Yet, as van Langenberg points out, in the official histories of the New Order, it is not the killings themselves that are remembered, but rather the role of the New Order as the restorer of stability and order. Periodic reminders of the ongoing threat of communist subversion, against which the citizenry had to be ever-vigilant, were central to the New Order's consolidation of power.

Few would argue with the assertion that the desire for order and stability are hallmarks of the middle class. But who benefitted

7   Richard Tanter and Kenneth Young, "Introduction" *The Politics of Middle Class Indonesia*, p. 7.
8   Michael van Langenberg, "The New Order State: Language, Ideology, Hegemony", in Arief Budiman, ed., *State and Civil Society in Indonesia* (Monash University: Center of Southeast Asian Studies, 1990), p. 126.

most from the economic policies of the New Order? Scholars
holding a wide range of political perspectives agree that whether
or not the middle class were the greatest beneficiaries of the New
Order economic policies, it was they who were its strongest
supporters. Richard Robison explains:

> Perhaps the major insight into the position and priorities of the
> middle classes has been offered by the dislocation, confusion
> and jostling for power that followed the overthrow of Soekarno
> in 1965 and the entrenchment of the New Order in the
> following decade. The student movements, largely upper middle
> class in that period, clearly indicated their primary concern that
> the social order should not be overtaken by radical and
> revolutionary change. They were virulently anti-communist
> movements with little attachment to the bureaucratic populism
> of the Partai Komunis Indonesia (PKI – Indonesian Communist
> Party) and might be best described as a mixture of social
> democrats and liberals. Many of these students, the so-called
> 1966 generation, now occupy senior positions in the New Order
> civilian hierarchy. Similarly, business and the small but
> influential body of intellectuals formerly associated with the
> defunct Indonesian Socialist Party (PSI) supported the military
> takeover, the replacement of Soekarno and the elimination of
> the PKI, although not necessarily the brutality with which the
> counterrevolution was prosecuted.[9]

The group that Robison describes here is identical with the signers
of the 1963 Cultural Manifesto and the students who were
associated with the independent newspaper *Harian Kami*. Arguing
that the middle class is not really a "class" at all, Robison has
suggested that it is instead a "complex set of entrepreneurial,
bureaucratic, and professional elements" who are "functionaries

---

[9]   Richard Robison, "The Middle Class and the Bourgeoisie in Indonesia", *The New Rich in Asia: Mobile Phones, McDonalds and Middle-class Revolution,* p. 85.

of the political, economic, social and ideological apparatus of capitalism."[10]

Daniel Lev doesn't disagree with the claim that the support of the middle class was crucial to the longevity of the New Order, but notes somewhat contradictorily that it was the "professional classes" who had only weak ties to the state who were also the era's most fervent reformers. He suggests that many of these professionals were either the scions of "downwardly mobile" *priyayi* families or "upwardly mobile" graduates of the university system that had flourished under Soekarno, and that many of them found employment in Indonesia's growing private sector.[11] In 1990, Lev predicted that these professionals would be the vanguard of carrying Indonesian politics beyond the New Order in issues ranging from promoting democracy and the rule of law to ending bureaucratic corruption and the abuse of power. Ariel Heryanto and Stanley Yoseph Adi have similarly argued that in Indonesia the "urban intelligensia" have moral authority and political power that far outweigh their relatively small numbers.[12]

Most scholars agree that it was the economic opportunities of the New Order period that allowed the professional classes both to flourish and to establish a solid economic base and social presence independent of the state. Journalism became a key occupation for many of these upwardly mobile university graduates, as well as for others who shared their values. Lev points out that the artists and literary figures who signed the Cultural Manifesto in 1963 were in the vanguard of this movement towards "social (or private) autonomy".[13] What Lev identifies as their "deep

---

10   Quoted in Richard Tanter and Kenneth Young, "Introduction", *The Politics of Middle Class Indonesia*, p. 10.

11   Daniel Lev, "Notes on the Middle Class and Change in Indonesia", in *The Politics of Middle Class Indonesia*, p. 29.

12   Ariel Heryanto and Stanley Yoseph Adi, "Industrialized Media in Democratizing Indonesia", in *Media Fortunes, Changing Times* (Singapore: ISEAS, 2002), pp. 51-2.

13   Daniel Lev, Ibid, p. 32. To put Lev's findings into an even broader context, several of the development theorists writing in the 1960s also saw an essential role for journalists in creating the conditions that would ripen nations for modernization

suspicions of the state" continued on into the New Order, and private groups such as KAMI and other student associations became the basis for the NGOs that were crucial to the formation of the ideology of the middle class.[14] Significantly, the group that Lev has identified as the vanguard of the new Indonesian middle class overlaps almost completely with the group of journalists and writers who founded *Tempo* in 1971. Three of the founders of *Tempo* (Goenawan Mohamad, Bur Rasuanto, and Usamah) were signers of the Cultural Manifesto. Goenawan, Christianto Wibisono, and Lukman Setiawan had worked for *Harian Kami*, and Fikri Jufri had written for *Pedoman*, which, like *Harian Kami*, was banned after the 1974 Malari incident. Nine other founding members of the editorial staff had been involved with the literary journal *Sastra*.[15]

In New Order Indonesia, the life of a journalist offered easy access to and knowledge of people in power, but was at least formally free of state control. Journalists working for private media had considerable autonomy, and many *Tempo* writers and editors told me that this independence was one of the more attractive things about being a journalist in the New Order. Arif Zulkifli, himself a *Tempo* writer, has grouped five different occupations into

and economic take-off. According to the classic work of Daniel Lerner, mass media assist in the development of the "mobile personality trait" of empathy, which enables individuals both to envision a different life and to strive towards it. Mass media were linked to strategies of economic development not only in that they allowed individuals in traditional societies to imagine more modern and democratic worlds, but also in that they could showcase the bounty of consumer goods offered by a fully developed capitalist economy. See Daniel Lerner, "The Passing of Traditional Societies", in J.T. Roberts and A. Hite, eds., *From Modernization to Globalization: Perspectives on Development and Social Change* (Malden: Blackwell Publications, 2000), pp. 119-133.

[14]   Daniel Lev, "Notes on the Middle Class and Change in Indonesia", in *The Politics of Middle Class Indonesia*, p. 33.

[15]   Acccording to Goenawan Mohamad, the nine others who had been involved with *Sastra* were Syu'bah Asa, Zen Umar Purba, Putu Widjaya, Isma Sawitri, Syahrir Wahab, Harun Musawa, D.S. Karma, Herry Komar, and Yusril Djalinus. Interview with Goenawan Mohamad, July 12, 1999.

what he calls the *golongan menengah* or "middle category": intellectuals, students, professions, newspaper editors, and those engaged in business and trade.[16] Significantly, he includes journalists in the category of intellectuals, along with researchers, professors, religious teachers, artists and cultural figures – perhaps out of agreement with the view that the defining characteristic of an intellectual is the distance he or she keeps from political power and the state bureaucracy.[17]

Of course the Indonesian middle class, whether it is made up of professionals, intellectuals, bureaucrats, or small manufacturers and retailers, cannot be viewed outside of the growth of the global capitalist economy. Between 1960 and 1991, Indonesian agricultural production declined from 53.9% of GDP to 19.5%, whereas manufacturing rose from 8.4% to 21.3% during the same period.[18] The middle class not only facilitated the growth of foreign investment and expansion of manufacturing and exports, it also constituted a growing market for consumer goods.

Howard Dick has put these consumer goods at the center of his work on the middle class, suggesting that the middle class is meaningful only in terms of "consumption categories", patterns of consumption that are significant in terms of how people think of themselves and relations with those around them. He writes, "through lifestyles people therefore manifest a kind of class consciousness in very practical ways. In this context, 'consciousness' does not refer to any identity of interests in political action that would be acknowledged by Marxists. The consciousness is rather an identification with a class of people pursuing a modern,

---

[16]   See Arif Zulkifli, *PDI Di Mata Golongan Menengah Indonesia* (Jakarta: Pustaka Utama Grafiti, 1996), p. 18.

[17]   See the 1993 "polemic" published in *Kompas* concerning the role of the intellectual in society cited in Arif Zulkifli, *PDI Di Mata Golongan Menengah Indonesia*, fn. 50, p. 30.

[18]   Richard Robison, "The Middle Class and the Bourgeoisie in Indonesia", *The New Rich in Asia: Mobile Phones, McDonalds and Middle-class Revolution*, p. 79.

westernized lifestyle that has, to a considerable extent, been based on role models fashioned and propagated by the national mass media, and especially television."[19]

One little-noted aspect of *Tempo* is the role it played in defining new middle-class lifestyles for its readers. From its very beginning, the pages of *Tempo* were filled with advertisements for a wide variety of consumer goods. For example Pan Am, Nu Derm Acne Cream, Honda motorcycles, Okasa Tonic, the Melani School of Dancing, Gamma Travel, and the Copacabana Casino were among the twenty-seven goods and services advertised in the October 1971 issue of *Tempo*. As the New Order years saw the flourishing of high-rise apartment buildings, housing "estates", and shopping malls, along with the increased use of credit cards, electronic goods, and luxury cars, these changing patterns of consumption were also reflected in the pages of *Tempo*.

It may, in fact, be advertising and changing patterns of consumption that link the work of the "modernization" theorists with the actual formation of a middle class in Indonesia. The consumer goods advertised in *Tempo* were a critical piece of what development specialists and Indonesian technocrats alike saw as the network of market relations that would ensure development along capitalist lines. Widespread consumption of goods and services were key to this vision; no less an authority than Walt Rostow himself had concluded that the fourth stage of economic development was the era of "high mass consumption".[20] Yet the

---

[19]   Howard Dick, "Further Reflections on the Middle Class", *The Politics of Middle Class Indonesia*, p. 65. Dick's "consumption categories" are remarkably similar to the "consumption communities" described by American historian Daniel Boorstin in Daniel Boorstin, *The Americans: The Democratic Experience* (New York, Vintage Books, 1974), pp. 89-163.

[20]   The modernization theorists had to work against the alternative model of economic development espoused by the Soviet Union; even W.W. Rostow, creator of the now-famous "five stages of economic growth" had to finesse the question of how the Soviet Union had managed to modernize while by-passing several of these stages. See W.W. Rostow, *The Stages of Economic Growth*, 2nd edition (London: Cambridge University Press, 1971).

Victim of a "mysterious shooting", Pondok Kelapa, East Jakarta, 1984 [*Tempo*]

images created by advertisers and spread through the pages of magazines like *Tempo* were hardly monolithic. If anything, they suggested the pluralism of middle class aspirations.

As the two case studies below will show, the Indonesian middle class(es) are plural, fluid and sometimes contradictory. Examination of the case of the "mysterious shootings" in 1983 suggests that while the middle class yearns for stability and the elimination of crime, it can also be ill at ease with social order that comes at the cost of the breakdown of the rule of law. An analysis of advertising in *Tempo* suggests the other face of the middle class, one interested in acquisition and social advancement through consumption. Not only did *Tempo* cater to both sides of the middle class, but this Janus-faced view of its readers was present within the organization of *Tempo* itself.

One way to measure the desire for social order to is examine how disorder or crime (*kriminalitas*) is represented.[21] The *Petrus* or killings that were carried out by "mysterious gunmen" (*penembak*

---

[21]   Herbert Gans has argued that one of the "enduring values" of news is the desire for "social order", which can be seen in the number of stories that report on either the breakdown or violation of social order. Herbert Gans, *Deciding What's News*

misterius) that occurred in Indonesia between 1983 and 1988 provide a fascinating glimpse into the concerns of the middle and professional classes. In fact, the mysterious shootings were never particularly mysterious, and the details of the killings have always been reasonably well known.[22] In March 1983, the Yogyakarta army garrison commander began an operation called *Operasi Pemberantasan Kejahatan*, or "Operation Combat Crime". Its goal was to eliminate *gali*, or petty criminals, gang members, and "recidivists" known to the authorities. The *gali* were ordered to report to garrison headquarters, where they were told to register, provide information on friends and family members, and pledge to refrain from engaging in criminal activities. As David Bourchier writes, "Those who did not turn up to be registered, or did not keep their appointments with the garrison, were hunted down and killed by squads of military men."[23] It's estimated that six hundred *gali* were shot in Yogyakarta alone. In April, Lt. Gen. Yogie Suardi Memet announced that Yogya's "crime prevention" operation would be applied in other areas. "The goal is good, to create an atmosphere of calm among the public," he said. "We now see that the public feels safe."[24] As the general predicted, within a few months the killings had spread to other cities. Estimates of the total number of deaths range from the Indonesian Legal Aid Institute's estimate of 4000 to near 10,000.[25]

(New York: Pantheon, 1979), p. 42. For a discussion of the relationship between "criminiality" and Soeharto's New Order government, see James Siegel, *A New Criminal Type in Jakarta: Counter-Revolution Today*, (Durham: Duke University Press, 1998).

[22] For a complete account of *Petrus*, see David Bourchier, "Crime, Law and State Authority in Indonesia," *State and Civil Society in Indonesia*, pp. 176-212.

[23] David Bourchier, "Crime, Law and State Authority in Indonesia", *State and Civil Society in Indonesia*, p. 186.

[24] *Tempo*, May 21, 1983.

[25] David Bourchier, "Crime, Law and State Authority in Indonesia", *State and Civil Society in Indonesia*, p. 186. Bourchier bases the higher number on estimates made by a Dutch journalist from data supplied to him by the police, as well as Armed Forces Commander Benny Moerdani's own statement that many deaths went unreported.

The way in which the mysterious shootings took place was nearly always the same. The suspected *gali* was met by four or five "heavily built" men, who would either shoot him upon sight or bundle him into a jeep or Toyota and take him to a deserted place, where he would be killed and his body dumped. The *gali* were always shot at close range, and with .45 or .38 caliber pistols. Their corpses were usually dumped in public places, including rivers, roadsides, shopping centers, or other well-traveled spots in which they were sure to be found. Discovery of the bodies was well publicized in media reports. It was clear that the "discovery" of the corpse was intended to be part of the operation.

In August, 1983, *Tempo* did a cover story on the mysterious shootings.[26] National editor Susanto Pudjomartono wrote the story. As Susanto said, from the beginning "everybody knew" that Benny Moerdani, the Commander-in-Chief of the Armed Forces, was behind the killings. "We never named openly this as an intelligence operation," Susanto said. "But if you read between the lines, you will get it."[27]

Indeed, the focus of *Tempo*'s story was not to discover who was behind the shootings, but rather to show the effects, both positive and negative. In fact, *Tempo* made it clear that this was a government operation, answering its own rhetorical question "who actually are the gunmen?" with "many point to the security apparatus."

Despite the New Order imperative of reporting on government activities favorably, *Tempo*'s story was generally balanced, including quotes from sources who were critical of the shootings, stories of prison inmates who were terrified of being shot upon their release

---

26   *Tempo*, August 6, 1983.

27   Interview with Susanto Pudjomartono, Feb 18, 2000. David Bourchier writes that *Petrus* was not merely an acronym of *penembak misterius*, mysterious gunmen," but also "a deft allusion to Catholicism (Petrus=Peter) and therefore to Moerdani, a Roman Catholic." David Bourchier, "Crime, Law and State Authority in Indonesia", *State and Civil Society in Indonesia*, p. 188.

from prison, and a harrowing account of a man named Suwito who had been picked up by five men, shot three times, and left for dead – all the while insisting that he was innocent of any crime. Nevertheless, a greater portion of the story's space was devoted to quotations from those who supported the extra-legal killings.[28] One obvious reason for *Tempo*'s stance towards the mysterious shootings can be found in the statement of former head of Special Operations (Opsus) General Ali Moertopo: *Petrus* was most certainly a "security operation".

Yet there are other possible explanations for *Tempo*'s coverage of the killings. The public tended to support the *Petrus* campaign, a disconcerting fact that can be seen in the results of a public opinion poll that were published in the same story:

> Maybe the high crime rate in Jakarta makes citizens of the capitol have attitudes that are more "harsh". This is apparent in the results of a *Tempo* survey being prepared for upcoming Independence Day. This poll reached around 1500 respondents from various regions and levels of society. Preliminary results are in from 139 respondents from Yogyakarta, Surabaya, Medan, Bandung, and Jakarta. In response to the question who is it proper to shoot? the answers were: big time corruptors (25.64%), drug dealers (24.91%) and robbers (20.51%). Yet when counted alone, respondents from Jakarta pointed to robbers (28.41%) drug dealers (23.86%) and extortionists (18.8%). Big time corruptors only obtained 14.77% votes.

---

[28] Of the twenty-four paragraphs that quoted a source on the advisability of the *Petrus* campaign, fourteen quoted sources who were in favor, and ten quoted sources who were ranged from being somewhat critical to outright opposed. The sources quoted in favor of *Petrus* included MPR/DPR (Parliament and People Consultative Assembly) head Amir Machmud, the Rector of Jakarta Institut Ilmu Al Quran Prof. K.H. Ibrahim Hossein, and Central Java Governor M. Ismail. Those opposed included Adnan Buyung Nasution, the head of the Indonesian Legal Aid Institute, former Vice President Adam Malik, Bishop Dr. Leo Soekoto, and criminal sociologist Prof. Dr. Soerjono Soekanto.

The preliminary responses to this poll also showed that 64.75% of the respondents approve of the mysterious shootings, but with a note: only those who "have truly been proved to commit a crime" should be shot to death. It isn't clear if this proof has to be done via a legal forum or not.

Although Bourchier suggests that by July 1983 public support of the killings had begun to wane, this is not borne out by *Tempo*'s survey. If anything, *Tempo* appeared to agree with those surveyed who felt that the shootings were justifiable provided that there was some sort of "legal forum" first. In the words of former Vice President Adam Malik, who was quoted in the story: "We have courts. If need arises, we can capture [criminals] in the morning, bring them to trial in the afternoon, and shoot them in the evening. This means that the death results from a legal decision, and that we are acting on a legal basis."

Significantly, *Tempo*'s coverage of the mysterious shootings can be seen as supporting two ideas that were – at least in the case of *Petrus* – somewhat at odds: the desire for a reduction in crime, and the desire for rule of law. The way in which *Tempo* framed the story supports the view expressed by the head of the West Java Council of Ulamas E.Z. Muttaqien: "When criminals are wiped out, the public feels relief. But this feeling of satisfaction now will turn into fear if these acts of vigilantism continue." Why? Because continuation of the mysterious shootings might result in "chaos." As *Tempo* concluded:

> Whether or not one agrees with the manner in which it's being carried out, certainly it remains to be seen how far the audacity of the people to confront the robbers and extortionists who approach them will go. And certainly: how long the shootings can continue without causing new feelings of uneasiness.

In August 1983, perhaps sensitive to the sympathetic accounts of victims in this and other media stories, the government decided to ban all further reporting on the killings.[29]

Under the New Order the Department of Information (Deppen) not only monitored the content of news stories, it also took an active role in regulating advertising. Some of the rules were "corporatist", designed to equalize the distribution of ads among stronger and weaker media. Advertising was restricted to 35% of the total column space. Page limitations varied. Until 1986 the limit for daily newspapers was twelve pages, but by 1994 it was twenty.[30] It was widely believed that there were ways of getting around these limitations – "if you were willing to bribe Deppen officials".[31]

In 1999, I examined a sample of over one thousand advertisements published in *Tempo*. Beginning with 1971, I coded each of the ads in twenty-seven magazines, one from each year that *Tempo* was published. I used a random number table to select the month, and then chose which week to examine by cycling from week one through to week four (or five). For each product advertised, I noted the type of product, the name of the product, and whether or not the advertisement had English-language copy.[32] Initially I tried to note the country of origin of the product, but it quickly became clear that this was impossible to determine, as the company listed in the text was usually the importer rather than

---

[29]   David Bourchier, "Crime, Law and State Authority in Indonesia," *State and Civil Society in Indonesia* p. 192.

[30]   David Hill, *The Press In New Order Indonesia*, p. 47. See also fn. 46, p. 58.

[31]   Email correspondence, Bambang Harymurti, March 30, 2003.

[32]   *Tempo*'s account managers are responsible for the following eight industries: telecommunication and digital, education, automotive, pharmacy, consumer goods, cigarettes, banking, and electronic goods. Interview with Tito Edi Prabowo, July 30, 2003. In most cases, my categories can be seen as subdivisions of *Tempo*'s categories. For example I've divided what *Tempo* calls "consumer goods" into "food and beverages" and "toiletries and drug care". I've likewise divided *Tempo*'s category of "education" into "courses and seminars" and "media and books". Some of *Tempo*'s current categories, such as telecommunication, did not exist during the years prior to the banning.

the manufacturer. The result was a portrait of what was advertised in *Tempo*, and how this changed over time.

The three biggest categories of products advertised were drugs and vitamins, media and books, and products aimed at businesses. (The latter included office equipment such as photocopiers, supplies and furniture, and shipping services.) When I calculated the three largest categories of products advertised each year, I found that "products aimed at businesses" made it into the top three groupings 74% of the time, "drugs and vitamins" 62%, and "media and books" 59% of the time. Other categories that dominated advertising in *Tempo* were "travel and leisure" (37%) and "cigarettes" (22%).

It is interesting to see how the largest groupings of advertisements change over time. Table 4 shows a gradual but steady increase in the percentage of advertisements for high end goods such as "financial services", "automotive", "electronic goods", and "jewelry, watches, and glasses", along with a relative decrease in the percentage of ads for cheaper products such "food and beverages" and "beauty products and toiletries". The percentage of advertisements for "courses and seminars" increases too, perhaps suggesting the importance for education and self-improvement among the middle classes.

What accounts for these changes? Is it possible that as *Tempo* became more profitable it began to reject advertisements for certain low-end products? To answer these questions, I spoke with Mahtum Mastoem, the man widely credited with creating *Tempo*'s advertising and marketing image. Mahtum joined *Tempo* in 1971.[33] Like Harjoko Trisnadi, Mahtum had previously worked at *Jaya* magazine. After a year of working at *Tempo* as a writer, Mahtum joined the business section in 1972. Eventually rising to become the head of marketing, he stayed with the magazine until its banning. Although Mahtum joined with *Gatra* in 1994, he continued to work for *Matra* magazine, a glossy men's magazine

---

[33] Interview with Mahtum, January 8, 2004.

also owned by Grafiti Pers. Nobody knows more about advertising in *Tempo* than Mahtum.

Today Mahtum works for the Indonesian Newspaper Publishers' Association (SPS). I met him at the SPS office on the 6th floor of the Press Council Building, a nondescript government building that housed much of the press bureaucracy of the New Order. Mahtum was praying when I arrived, so I had several minutes to examine the yellowing SPS posters taped to the drab cinder block walls of the waiting room. The posters proclaimed the importance of freedom of the press. It occurred to me that although the SPS had waited until the safety of the post-Soeharto era to become an outspoken champion of press freedom, it was better to be late than never.

At a few minutes after one, Mahtum arrived and showed me into a plain room furnished with several chairs, a sofa, and a vase of plastic flowers. He is a friendly man, with an easy smile and the gregariousness of an ad man. His skin is light-colored, his face open and boyish, and although he is in his mid-fifties, he looks much younger. Mahtum spoke with enthusiasm of *Tempo*, and he loves to talk about advertising. "We at *Tempo* were all autodidacts," he said. "Myself also, I didn't graduate from college, only high school. My school was at *Tempo*."

I asked him about the very early days of *Tempo*, and its marketing plan. "There was no one who ever thought about the middle class," he said. "We only wanted to make a product like *Time* magazine. Maybe it was simple, but we never thought about the readers. Because of that, until 1976 or 78, *Tempo*'s circulation was very small. Maybe only 25,000 or 40,000. Then we were introduced to LPPM (Management Training Institute). It was a kind of brainwashing," he laughs. "We learned about management. And after we learned management, our circulation soared to 100,000. We, including Goenawan, had great confidence in management."

I told Mahtum of my meeting with Tito Edi Prabowo, a young

account manager in *Tempo*'s advertising department. "Oh yes, I know him. He is one of my boys," he said, smiling broadly.

Tito had told me that the changes in the types of products advertised in *Tempo* were the result of macro factors, such as changes in the economy, and that *Tempo* does not deliberately choose to pursue advertising from one type of industry over another. To *Tempo*, a full-page display ad for Cartier watches is no more desirable than an ad for Poly Color hair dye.

I asked Mahtum if he agreed with Tito that the increase in the number of advertisements for luxury goods in *Tempo* was the result of changes in the market, rather than the magazine's desire to go after these particular advertisers. "Both," he said. "*Tempo*'s segment was most fitting with expensive goods. *Tempo*'s readers were middle to upper class readers, so there were lots of ads for cars, watches, lifestyle."

"When I was in charge of advertising in *Tempo*," he said, "I felt that *Tempo* had to make trends in advertising. It was a trendsetter. So I didn't want to accept ads for patent medicines, for example. Ads that used a P.O. box I wouldn't accept."

"Advertisements that weren't good, I'd send them back and say improve them first," Mahtum added. "They not only had to be informative, they also had to be artistic."

"For example, there was once an ad for tires, and a picture of a woman wearing a bikini," he said. "So I asked, which is being displayed, the tires or the woman? Don't treat our readers as if they are stupid. I looked for ads that made people smart."

Although it is tempting to explain the prevalence of certain types of ads as reflecting the preferences of middle class readers, there are other factors that must be taken into account as well. Barter, for example. In the early days of *Tempo*, when it was too expensive to pay regular airline fares to send reporters overseas, *Tempo* frequently "bartered" with airline companies. Former *Tempo* writer Salim Said recalled how in the very early days, *Tempo* journalists always flew Cathay Pacific, which was a big advertiser.

"I remember that I went to Bangkok via Hong Kong because I had to fly Cathay Pacific," he said. "There's no direct flight to Bangkok, so I flew first to Hong Kong and then to Bangkok. A flight that's regularly four hours took the whole day."[34] Tito likewise pointed out that today, "handphone" companies have barter-type arrangements with *Tempo*, exchanging cell phones for free or reduced-rate advertising.

What about the high percentage of ads for "courses and seminars"? This could be an example of *kerjasama*, or cooperation. For example, if the University of Indonesia was organizing a seminar, members of the committee could ask *Tempo* to be a sponsor of that seminar in exchange for a free ad. Many of the ads in my sample for "courses and seminars" were not full-page display ads, but rather the smaller cheaper ones taking up only part of a page. Likewise, many of the "media and books" advertisements were for books and periodicals published by Grafiti Pers, the owner of *Tempo*.

Advertising can and cannot reveal many things. It is a form of symbolic communication, but its intent is clear: to induce readers to buy goods and services. The people who produce advertising have an obvious goal in mind, and they draw upon whatever images and symbols they feel will best achieve that goal. Media scholar Michael Schudson has suggested that "advertising may shape our sense of values even under conditions where it does not greatly corrupt our buying habits."[35] In other words, even when a particular ad does not induce us to buy something, it may still promote certain attitudes and lifestyles. In many cases, the most important of these values is consumption itself, along with the corollary notion that we can find happiness through the acquisition of material goods.

In his well-known history of American advertising, Roland Marchand suggested that far from reproducing an image of reality,

[34]   Interview with Salim Said, April 1, 1998.
[35]   Michael Schudson, *Advertising, the Uneasy Persuasion: Its Dubious Impact on American Society* (New York: Basic Books, 1984), p. 210.

advertising draws upon familiar symbols to create an idealized view of reality, or reality as it should be.[36] He remarked upon the similarity of early advertising images to the 19th century parlor game of *tableaux vivant* or "living pictures", a popular home entertainment in which costumed guests would re-enact well-known scenes from famous paintings, popular literature, or the Bible. The scenes were "slices of life", powerful and pleasurable because of their familiarity. Marchand has argued that the scenes depicted in advertisements can also be seen as *social tableaux*, drawing upon scenes and symbols that are "sufficiently stereotypical to bring immediate audience recognition."[37] In advertisements from the 1920s, for example, certain symbols – the fireplace, father reading his newspaper, mother perched on the arm of his chair, two small children playing on the hearth – evoked the family circle. Similarly, whereas the telephone, desk, and office block invoked the masculine world of "business", the mirror, pearls, and the "French" maid invoked glamor and femininity.

The concept of *tableaux* and depictions of individuals as incarnations of larger social types are not alien to Indonesians. Benedict Anderson has suggested that the mythology of *wayang* also provides the young Javanese "with a wide choice of models for his own personality."[38] Whether it be the cool wisdom and essential fairness of Yudhistira or the strength and simple honesty of the warrior Bima, the Hindu-Javanese version of the *Mahabharata* depicts characters that are a variety of social types. Their social traits are immediately recognizable. Like the characters populating the scenes depicted in advertising, these personality types are reassuring in their familiarity; there is pleasure in finding immediate recognition.

---

[36] Roland Marchand, *Advertising the American Dream: making way for modernity, 1920-1940* (Berkeley: University of California Press, 1985).

[37] Roland Marchand, *Advertising the American Dream*, p. 166.

[38] Benedict R. O'G. Anderson, *Mythology and the Tolerance of the Javanese*, (Cornell University: Cornell Modern Indonesia Project, Southeast Asia Program, 1996), p. 40.

Michael Schudson has suggested that the symbols, scenes, and story lines found in advertising can be seen as "capitalist realism", comparable with the socialist realist art of the 1930s:

> Advertising, like socialist realist art, simplifies and typifies. It does not claim to picture reality as it is, but reality as it should be – life and lives worth emulating. It is always photography or drama or discourse with a message – rarely picturing individuals, it shows people only as incarnations of larger social categories. It always assumes that there is progress. It is thoroughly optimistic, providing for any troubles that it identifies a solution in a particular product or style of life. It focuses, of course, on the new, and if it shows some sign of respect for tradition, this is only to help in the assimilation of some new commercial creation.[39]

Mahtum is a man who has spent his entire career in advertising, but one who has never studied its history. He said that in the early days of *Tempo*, he and his colleagues marketed the magazine "by nature," knowing nothing of market segments or theories of marketing. Nevertheless, he is interested in advertising theory, and enthusiastically agrees with the notion that the products advertized in *Tempo* may have helped to create the "dreams" of the middle class. It was how readers dreamed of "changing their lifestyles," he said. According to Mahtum, reading the ads was like watching the Indonesian television dramas known as *sinetron*.

What picture of life as it should be lived emerges out of the pages of *Tempo*? Close textual analysis of a sample of advertisements may offer some clues.[40] In August 2003, five faculty members

---

[39]   Michael Schudson, *Advertising, The Uneasy Persuasion*, p. 215.

[40]   When doing my content analysis of advertising, I noted each ad that could be seen as a social tableau, meaning that it involved characters as well as some suggestion of setting and plot. Later I went through this list and selected a sample of fifteen ads. I was especially interested in the small number of ads that showed men and women together, and the even smaller number of advertisements that showed images of Indonesians together with foreigners.

from the English department at the University of Indonesia met with me in an informal focus group to discuss the symbols present in a sample of fifteen ads. The group included Melani Budianta and Manneke Budiman, both noted cultural critics and scholars.[41]

A well-dressed Indonesian couple is enjoying breakfast together. Graceful palm fronds in the background suggest the spacious patio of a large and elegant home. The husband, wearing an immaculately pressed shirt and tie, is finishing up his coffee before he leaves for work. His wife is smartly dressed in a feminine bow blouse with her hair done up in a bun. Her jewelry is simple – a gold wedding ring and pearl earrings. She gazes fondly at him, with a happy smile on her face. A jar of Nescafé instant coffee sits on their table, next to a breakfast of soft-boiled eggs, toast, and sliced cheese. Pretty cloth napkins, white china, and a floral table cloth suggest the well-appointed table of an upper-middle class household.

The text in the advertisement explains her happy smile. Her husband is enjoying "to the last drop" the tasty cup of coffee she has prepared for him. It is so easy, and can be made right at the table, with the flavor he can enjoy. Unlike traditional Indonesian coffee powder, Nescafé dissolves without leaving even a trace in the bottom of the cup. Bold letters in the text make the point explicit, you can enjoy Nescafé "until it is completely gone".

This tableau appeared in the June 12, 1982 issue of *Tempo* magazine. Although the Indonesian-language text doesn't use the word, the scene depicted is "modern". The couple's clothing, their table setting, and most importantly the food they are eating for breakfast – strikingly different from the traditional Indonesian breakfast based on rice – all suggest a particularly Western version of modernity. The jar of Nescafé, placed strategically in the center

---

[41]   The group also included Lilawati Kurnia, Meuthiati Ranthy Anggraini and Avianty Agusman. I also discussed these ads with *Tempo* editors Hermien Kleiden and Isma Sawitri.

of the table, also represents a break with tradition. The advantage of Nescafé is that it is fast, easy, and you can fix it yourself. But most significantly, it is "good to the last drop", which in this context means that unlike traditional coffee powder, Nescafé won't leave a thick residue in the bottom of your cup. The expression *sampai habis bersih* literally means until it is clean gone.

Although the advertisement associates Nescafé with modernity, it is important to note that the modernity depicted is one of modern consumer goods, not of changing social roles. Both the scene and the text make it clear that it is the wife who has selected and prepared the coffee. In the cozy domestic scene depicted, the husband is the one who will soon be leaving for the office. Although the wife is well-dressed, there is nothing about her appearance that would suggest she is a working woman. Subtle visual cues suggest the husband is the breadwinner in the family. Similarly, although the wife has made the coffee herself, this does not mean that the family is without a *pembantu*, or maid. Obviously the couple has enough money to employ a cook – and, according to my focus group, most definitely has one, although she can't be seen. How do they know this? "Because they are rich," they concluded.

The sample of advertisements I examined showed very few instances of "working women". One exception is an advertisement for Girard-Perregaux watches. A beautiful European woman sits at a concert piano, alone on a darkened stage. The light shines off her white face and arms. On one slim wrist we see a watch. The copy tells us that a "successful woman who has reached the peak of her career" is a woman who chooses Girard Perregaux.[42] A career woman? Maybe. But hardly a working woman with an ordinary job. A small photo above the main illustration refines her image

---

[42]   *Tempo*, May 24, 1980. Interestingly, the advertisement uses the word *wanita*, which has the feminine nuances of the word "lady". In this regard it can be distinguished from *perempuan*, which means "woman" in the same sense as it is generally used by Western feminists.

further. We see the same woman sharing a glass of champagne with a man in evening clothes. The two are alone. As one informant suggested, "the woman's 'career pinnacle' is not only her work, but also that she has the man. It's very connected with the man." It is clear that "she is not purely on her own."

The advertising copy emphasizes the "eternal" beauty of the watch, its "diamonds", and that it appears in "collections". The watch is as classic and eternal as the music she plays.

Roland Marchand has suggested that advertisers are "apostles of modernity". Yet exactly what form this modernity takes varies from culture to culture, and in *Tempo* the evidence is contradictory. One of the most striking things about the advertising in *Tempo* is the way in which foreign – especially Western – products and ideals are portrayed. Western products are not just associated with modernness, as in the Nescafe ad, but also with wealth, quality, and the good life. One rough index of the appeal of foreignness is the percentage of advertisements with copy written in English. The trend is upward, except for a somewhat surprising dip in the 1980s:

Percentage of Ads in English

1971-1974:	15.7%
1975-1979:	15.0%
1980-1984:	10.6%
1985-1989:	8.78%
1990-1994:	29%
1998-1999:	30%

Mahtum explained the prevalence of English in advertisements as a marker of lifestyle. "It has nothing to do with the language they use in the home," he said. "It's lifestyle. And advertising people were happy to use English in ads from a psychological aspect for marketing – especially in ads for cars. The headlines would be in English, but the content in Indonesian. Credits cards too. It's very psychological."

According to Mahtum, the small dip in the use of English in the 1980s was related to the Indonesian government's campaign to use more Indonesian. "It was a kind of Indonesianization program," he said, "to develop nationalism, language. It was done from time to time by various ministries, but it wasn't too successful. It began to be violated in the 1990s, when globalization began."

It is not just language that reveals foreignness. Many of the appeals, both visual and textual, associate luxury and an affluent lifestyle with goods and surroundings that are "Western". An Arrow shirt advertisement from June 14, 1975, for example, associates the Brigade shirt "from the French Collection" of Arrow [English in the original] with sexiness, masculinity, and the admiring gaze of beautiful women. The scene is the woods, a picnic on the grass. An attractive man and woman – both foreigners – are lying on something. Is it a blanket? The man's jacket? It is hard to say. She is wearing a soft floral dress, her long wavy hair cascading over her shoulders. The symbols of wealth are unmistakable. A glass of wine, her expensive watch and pendant, his Arrow shirt and tie. No rings are visible, and they don't appear to be married. Most significant of all is her gaze. He is looking dreamily into her eyes, but she is staring directly at his chest. The text explains it: "Allow her to see the shape of your body." She is "piercing" his clothes with her eyes. "Why not?" the copy coyly suggests, "if the shape of your body is worthy of admiration."

"When an ordinary shirt won't do, Brigade, the latest French model Arrow shirt, will show in a refined way the shape of your body that deserves her admiration....With the style of the revolution from France – Brigade, by Arrow, from the French collection."

What is being sold here is Frenchness. One of my informants explained:

It's definitely not Indonesia. Nothing like this happens in Indonesia! It's not normal to wear these kind of formal clothes, drink wine, and lie on the ground. There are lots of ants. And it's hot. Drinking wine, that only happens in restaurants. For a romantic conversation like this, people wouldn't be outdoors. The only people who sit on the grass and eat are poor people sitting on newspapers, for example in Monas [the National Monument] park. Not people from this social class. This is very private; you can't see any other people.

"What is being sold is a dream," another added. "These people are rich, that's the important part. They are not normal workers. Not professors! Who has an opportunity to do something like this?"

The dream of being rich appears in many ads. In an advertisement for Citizen Watches it is explicit: wear the watch and "feel like a millionaire."[43] The scene is two people at the beach: a laughing dark-haired woman in a bikini leans into a handsome, bare-chested man in bathing trunks. He holds a shell in one hand, a small knife and a large pearl in the other. Who are they? "The man is foreign, the woman is 'Indo', or mixed," said one of the members of my group. "Like Sophia Latjuba, [a movie actress and model famous for posing in bathing suits in men's magazines.]" she added. The man looks proud and happy. And why shouldn't he? He's found a pearl, he has a beautiful girlfriend, and he's wearing a Citizen watch. The copy reads "Sun, sea, breezes…the feeling of free time, far from the business of the world, without inhibitions. Find something unexpected, as beautiful as their time together. As beautiful as a Citizen watch."

"What makes him feel like a millionaire?" I asked.

My informants all agree. "Not because of the watch, but because of the activities. It's the adventure, the feeling of success."

One aspect of this ad that is strikingly similar to many others in *Tempo* is its orientation towards male readers. Although I had

---

43   *Tempo*, October 25, 1975.

initially selected ads on the basis of whether or not they portrayed human figures, upon closer scrutiny, all of the ads in my sample targeted men. In some ways this is unsurprising. According to *Tempo*'s own marketing data, at any given time the vast majority of *Tempo*'s readers were male. The table below suggests the numbers for the years in which data are available:[44]

Percentage of Male Readers

1986:	76%
1989:	86.34%
1991:	86.34%
1993:	86.34%
1994:	84.48%
2002:	68%

Mahtum agreed that most of *Tempo*'s ads seemed to be targeting men, and said that he had personally become aware of this in the mid-1980s. First, he said, the majority of *Tempo*'s readers were men. "Of the women who read it," he said, "most went along with their husbands only. Maybe it was only 1, 2, or 5% who truly bought it."

"And second," he said, "because of that, *Tempo* was almost identical with a men's magazine. And because the news was mostly written from the perspective of men, women seldom wanted to read the stories."

Given the preponderance of male readers of *Tempo*, it is interesting to see how "maleness" is depicted in the magazine. As in the United States, one of the best indicators of attributes of masculinity can be found in cigarette ads. An advertisement for Bentoel Besar (Big Bentoel) cigarettes shows a *wayang kulit* or shadow puppet image of Bima, one of the five Pendawa brothers

---

[44]   The earliest marketing package I was able to find was dated 1980, and in it *Tempo* simply stated that a majority of its readers were male.

from the *Mahabharata*.[45] Bima is the third of the brothers, and is known for his physical strength, his huge club, and his long fingernail, all of which have obvious sexual connotations. He is the strongest, and "the most masculine". Large letters below the image say "Big Bentoel, the taste of masculinity."

Alongside the shadow puppet is a list of characteristics, presumably of both Bima and the smoker of Bentoel Besar – "the big one," as Manneke Budiman pointed out. "Size does matter," he laughed. The characteristics include "independent in thought, strong in faith, humane, intelligent, innocent, not a hypocrite, [and] willing to sacrifice himself for truth and justice." As Melani Budianta suggested, there is a significant contrast between the words and the image. "The sexuality of the picture is not written in the words," she said. "The words are all spiritual, and very 'New Order'." The ad plays with both the lofty and sexual aspects of masculinity.

Another interesting aspect of the advertisement is what it suggests about social class. Bima is usually considered to be *kasar*, or un-refined, a characteristic that most middle-class Indonesians would probably not choose to describe themselves. Again, according to Melani Budianta, Bima is not usually associated with a sophisticated class, but rather with an unsophisticated one. In this regard he is similar to the Marlboro Man, who is also associated with nature and working outdoors.

By contrast, a 1975 ad for 555 International – also a "longer cigarette" – is full of markers of the upper class.[46] The English-language text reads "International length cigarettes should taste as good as they look." The stylized model plane, the glass and decanter of brandy all suggest the "distinction" of 555 International cigarettes. The airplane alludes to flying first class, as do the words "international", "distinguished", and "style".

---

45   *Tempo*, May 17, 1980.
46   *Tempo*, September 13, 1975.

A 1982 advertisement for the Jayakarta Grill at the Hotel Sari Pacific is one of the few in which foreigners are interacting with people who are clearly Indonesian. The scene is an elegant restaurant, in which a handsome young Indonesian couple is dining with a foreign couple. The waiter shows the bottle of wine to the foreign man, while the Indonesian couple smile approvingly. The text reads, "Jayakarta Grill is the best in Jakarta for you who wish to taste the varieties of European foods."[47] Which couple is the host? Although my informants did not immediately agree, after some discussion the consensus was that the ad is aimed at the Indonesian businessman who may be in the position of having to invite foreign guests out for a meal. The Indonesian language text states that at the Jayakarta Grill he can be sure that his "favorites" will be served, along with "famous" wines and "impeccable" service. Most important of all, his guests will be pleased.

Things "international" are generally associated with wealth, luxury, the "executive" class. This is particularly obvious in advertisements for automobiles, which frequently show well-dressed Indonesians stiffly posed around their cars – often in settings that do not appear to be in Indonesia at all. Although Tito from *Tempo*'s marketing department pointed out that frequently producers of advertising combine two or more photographs to create these anachronistic settings, when I showed examples of these ads to my focus group they concluded that most readers would assume the characters depicted were Indonesians living overseas. For example, a 1982 ad for a Honda Accord, "the Executive Choice," shows an Indonesian couple dressed for a party, standing alongside a white sedan.[48] They are Indonesian, or "Asian at least." She wears a wrap dress, fine jewelry, and, according to my focus group, has just come from the salon. Her right hand clasps her husband's arm, her left hand holds a small purse. She

---

[47]   *Tempo*, June 12, 1982.
[48]   *Tempo*, June 12, 1982.

leans into the car. Behind them is a house that could easily be in any American suburb. Light from a porch reflects off the bare branches of the trees, the grassy lawn, and the paved driveway. It is autumn.

"The impression is overseas," said one of the members of my group. "Indonesians will think this is a picture of Indonesians overseas. This is their house in Perth, or wherever."

Yet not all the ads in *Tempo* extol the desirability of things from overseas. 555 International cigarettes may "proudly" announce their "fine Virginia flavour", but other cigarette ads in *Tempo* boast of the taste of authentic – or more literally "native" tobacco. A 1982 advertisement for Mascot cigarettes asks "What's the use of smoking if not for the enjoyment of authentic tobacco flavor?"[49] The smoker depicted is a young Indonesian man wearing a denim shirt. There's no watch, no wedding band, no jewelry. As one informant said, "Ordinariness comes out of this man." And this is exactly the point: the tobacco is local, the taste is real, and the cigarettes are as authentic and as natural as he is. "This is why the choice of smokers turns to Mascot, to enjoy the real taste and satisfying aroma of authentic tobacco."

Another ad in which the man is even more ordinary is a Brylcreme ad from 1976.[50] The ad depicts a boxer, a young man with thick black hair that looks as substantial as the boxing gloves he wears. "You're always superior and admired," the text reads. "Brylcreem makes your scalp fresh and clean…your hair soft and easily controlled." Although the ad urges readers to stop using "old-fashioned" and "thickening" cremes, there is something very old-fashioned about the appearance of this ad. In the lower corner is an image of the same man, the boxer, wearing a short-sleeved polka-dot shirt. A smiling woman in a sleeveless dress touches his hair, and they seem to be embracing playfully. There is nothing romantic

---

49   *Tempo*, June 12, 1982.
50   *Tempo*, March 13, 1976

about the picture, in fact they look more like brother and sister than lovers. Their clothes could be from the 1950s. "They look like friends. He's finished boxing, and she's congratulating him after the match. She's amazed that his hair still looks perfect."

"Compared with the other ads, this one is corny [*kampungan*]," Melani Budianta explained. In the 1970s, boxing was not done by Indonesian celebrities, but rather by poor people. "They are poor, and sometimes they die." Although it is not clear that the couple depicted are from the working class, everyone agrees that if this advertisement was intended to influence middle class readers, it would have failed.

One thing that is clear from analyzing these ads is that if we take as a starting point the idea that companies advertised in *Tempo* because they wanted to reach the "middle class", there is no one definition of what the middle class is. As Tito pointed out, *Tempo* doesn't pick and choose among advertisers, but accepts all ads that don't violate the advertising law or "code of ethics". Moreover, some companies, like those that produce flu medicine, place their ads in all types of media.

If we look to advertising in *Tempo* for increased understanding of the middle class, the message we get is contradictory. Some of the advertisements put being "Western" in the forefront, others celebrate the "original" or local. Likewise some products are placed in settings that are evocative of the "new rich" (*orang kaya baru*) but others depict scenes that can be seen more clearly as lower middle or even working class. As Manneke Budiman said, "Maybe half of the readers are truly middle class, maybe half are from the lower middle class who are probably never going to buy a Kijang [automobile]. But what is advertised here can be seen as their dream. From a financial aspect, you can't possibly buy this. But if I want to construct myself as middle class, I might use this model. There isn't an agreement or conspiracy between the magazine and the advertisers, but the image of the middle class they want to show isn't opposed. It's the same road."

Perhaps another way of reconciling the apparent conflict is to point out the pluralism of the middle classes in Indonesia. In terms of monthly expenditures, some *Tempo* readers are indeed "new rich", and others – like the university lecturers and professors I interviewed – are perhaps better categorized as lower middle class. But expenditures are only one facet of middle class identity. Other less tangible factors are education and even aspirations. For these reasons, Ariel Heryanto has suggested that an alternative to the term "middle class" might be "urban intelligentsia", although as Joel Kuipers has noted, the problem with this category is that it is a self-definition.[51] But perhaps this is significant in terms of *Tempo*'s readership.

Tempo's advertising and marketing departments may conceive of the "ideal" *Tempo* reader as a twenty-six to forty year-old man with high monthly expenditures putting him in "class A or B" of the Central Bureau of Statistics. This reader clearly exists. But this is not the reader that *Tempo* writers have in mind when they write, nor is it the one reflected in the content of the magazine – which is often quite critical of the consumerism depicted in the advertisements. When I asked a group of *Tempo* writers to tell me who they imagine when they think about their readers, they described Indonesians much as themselves: relatively young (aged twenty to forty) and well-educated.[52] Each writer I spoke with mentioned students and activists. Although several writers did mention people in business and office holders (including cabinet ministers), they were quick to add that they also imagined small business people and *karyawan* (or employees). Significantly, the most important attribute of the "imagined reader" was his or her

---

[51] Ariel Heryanto and Stanley Yoseph Adi, "The Industrialization of the Media in Democratizing Indonesia," *Media Fortunes, Changing Times*, p. 51. I am grateful to Joel Kuipers for first suggesting that I consider representations of social class in *Tempo*, and for discussing my findings with me.

[52] The writers and editors who responded to my informal survey were Purwani Diyah Prabandari, Edy Budiyarso, Arif Zulkifli, Nugroho Dewanto, Rommy Fibri, and Karaniya Dharmasaputra. Each of these writers joined *Tempo* after 1998.

interest in current economic, political, and social conditions in Indonesia. Several writers explicitly mentioned members of the academic community; researchers and lecturers like those in my focus group, all of whom said they read *Tempo* for Goenawan Mohamad's *Catatan Pinggir* essays, as well as the news coverage, reviews, features, and investigative pieces.[53] Although several writers referred to their readers' monthly expenditures, all but one put these expenditures well below the approximately $600/month of "Class A".

Perhaps the problem in defining Indonesia's "middle class" has been the tendency of scholars and commentators to focus on one single defining characteristic, be it opportunism and self-interested desire for social stability and personal advancement, or progressivism and commitment to democratic reform. *Tempo* readers embody all these traits and more. To the marketing department, some of whom perhaps secretly long for the stability and economic prosperity of the New Order period, it is the readers who hold "professional and managerial" jobs and high monthly income and expenditures that matter. But to the editors and writers who are the heart and soul of the magazine, it is the middle class readers who yearn for a better and more democratic Indonesia who are *Tempo's* real target audience. It is perhaps not surprising that this should be the case. Since the founding of the magazine, *Tempo's* writers and editors have, like their readers, also embodied the complex and sometimes contradictory traits of those Indonesians who make up the nation's "middle class".

"In the beginning, the New Order had the support of a large part of society," said historian Onghokham, adding that Soekarno's Guided Democracy was "a complete disaster" for the middle class.[54] "The middle class doesn't care about politics, or the consolidation of the political parties," he said, "but they do get upset about

---

[53]   When I asked Goenawan Mohamad who he thought of when he wrote *Catatan Pinggir*, he said that he wrote for his friends, or for people like himself. Interview, December 23, 2003.

[54]   Interview with Onghokham, October 8, 1999.

corruption." Sometimes, as the *Petrus* case suggests, they also get upset about crime. Many *Tempo* readers, perhaps like those surveyed in the August 1983 poll, favored stability over "rule of law", but with a certain degree of discomfort. Sometimes opportunistic and concerned with their own advancement, the Indonesian middle classes (like those of Western nations) were generally more interested in their own lives than they were in political activism. But there were contradictory impulses too, and the middle classes were also capable of great heroism and self-sacrifice. One indication of this sacrifice would come in 1994 when *Tempo* was banned by the Soeharto government. And perhaps not surprisingly, the leaders of that movement would come from within *Tempo* itself.

CHAPTER EIGHT

the exodus

On the afternoon of Saturday July 11, 1987, thirty-two employees resigned from *Tempo*.

Although such a walk-out was not unprecedented in Indonesian journalism, it was unprecedented at *Tempo*, which was widely considered to be one of the best employers in the business.[1]

The group planned to establish a new weekly news magazine called *Editor*. Their aim was to compete head to head with *Tempo*, and by the time they walked out on the 11th of July, they had already established the company as a legal entity, found financial backing, and obtained a SIUPP, or permit to publish. Those who left *Tempo* came from a wide range of positions, with the most senior being Syu'bah Asa, who had been with the magazine since its founding. The group of reporters, writers, and editors was joined by several employees from *Tempo*'s production department, as well as eight from elsewhere within the Grafiti Pers publishing group – bringing

---

[1] The always wily Minister of Information Harmoko was sanguine about the exodus, pointing out that it was "natural" and the "basic right" of the employees. "Don't forget, *Tempo* [itself] was the splinter of *Ekspres*." *Suara Pembaruan*, July 20, 1987, quoted in Daniel Dhakidae, "The State, The Rise of Capital, and the Fall of Political Journalism", p. 399. Dhakidae suggests that Harmoko may have had a material interest in *Editor* magazine, perhaps owning shares either under a pseudonym or in the name of a relative. See fn. 48, p. 403.

the total that day to forty. The walk-out came as a complete surprise to *Tempo*'s chief editor Goenawan Mohamad, although according to others it had been an open secret in the newsroom for months.[2]

When *Tempo* was established in 1971, nearly all of the founders were poets, writers, and intellectuals. Few had any real grounding in journalism. By the mid-1980s, Goenawan Mohamad and other senior editors had deliberately "modernized" *Tempo*'s practice of journalism. This included the introduction of a widely imitated code of ethics, in-house training, and an elaborate system of deciding what would become news. Alongside the more professional model of journalism also came a more rational system of management. *Tempo* was one of the first Indonesian publications to develop a transparent system of management and promotion. Other changes included the decision to recruit reporters from top universities and the development of journalism as a life-long career.

Neither transition was an easy one. Exploration of what became known as "the *Editor* exodus" reveals widespread dissatisfaction with the changing practice of journalism in *Tempo*. Significantly, a key component of the split was what was perceived by those who left as the new "industrial" style of management. Other issues were important too, including money, shares, and a growing feeling that there had been a loss of *keakraban* or closeness between managers and writers. As one of the leaders of the *Editor* group explained to a reporter, "the press is no longer an institution of struggle, it is now an industry."[3]

---

[2]   Toriq Hadad told me that as a cub reporter in *Tempo*'s Jakarta bureau, he had known of the plot for at least three months. Interview, December 29, 2003. For a complete account of the *Editor* exodus, see "Kasak-Kasuk Sebelum Bobol", *Jakarta-Jakarta*, July 24 - August 6, 1987.

[3]   Quoted in "Kasak-Kasuk Sebelum Bobol", *Jakarta-Jakarta*, July 24-August 6, 1987. Although I personally interviewed many of those involved in the exodus, memories do fade. Thus, whenever possible, I used details and quotations from works that were published at the time, rather than reconstructing the incident from interviews that were conducted after an interval of nearly fifteen years. This translation and all others are mine, unless otherwise noted.

Saur Hutabarat, one of leaders of the exodus, said that his dissatisfaction with *Tempo* began in 1986, over a year before the walkout actually took place.[4] In an interview with the magazine *Jakarta-Jakarta*, Saur described the Tuesday in which an appeals court had reduced the sentence of retired General H.R. Dharsono from ten years to seven. H.R. Dharsono had been convicted of conspiracy in the Tanjung Priok incident several years earlier, and the reduction in his sentence was significant news. Although *Tempo*'s deadline had already passed, Saur nevertheless went to the prison in Salemba to report the story. According to Saur, chief editor Goenawan Mohamad agreed that the story should be included, but assistant chief editor Fikri Jufri did not. Saur recalled that Fikri gave him a sharp reprimand, saying that with the inclusion of the story, *Tempo* would be late in getting to the printer, and therefore late in circulating. This would be bad for business.

"It's not an issue of being offended," Saur was quoted as saying, "it is an issue of idealism. Indeed, from the side of business, the lateness would be felt. But we can't sacrifice news only because of speed."

According to Saur, *Tempo*'s management no longer viewed the employees as the company's most valuable asset, and he was not the only one who felt this way. Others also believed that *Tempo* was losing its "humanity". For example Syu'bah Asa, the author of the highly regarded series of articles on renewal in Islamic thought, said that in controversies the management always took the side of the bosses, never that of the employees. This was especially painful for Syu'bah, who was one of the magazine's founders. He told a reporter from *Jakarta-Jakarta*, if we complained to Goenawan, Fikri, Harun Musawa, or Yusril Djalinus, the answer was always the same. "The door is open. If you want to leave, leave."

---

[4]   This and many of the details that follow are taken from "Kasak-Kasuk Sebelum Bobol", *Jakarta-Jakarta*, July 24-August 6, 1987.

"There was no longer open management at *Tempo*," he added.

For others, a more important issue was a desire for "pluralism" in media and an end to *Tempo*'s monopoly. Bambang Harymurti, who had attended some of the meetings of the *Editor* group, later said that like many of the younger reporters he felt that it was bad for *Tempo* to monopolize the market for news. "There was some talk about pluralism in journalism," he said, "because *Tempo* was so dominant, and it was not good for the society."[5]

"We agreed that there was a need for there to be another weekly news magazine," Bambang said. "But then there were other people who wanted to join in order to kill *Tempo* and replace it with a new magazine. And that's where the line divided us." He said that he and managing editor Bambang Bujono believed that if the *Editor* group were actually to succeed in "replacing" *Tempo*, they would be no better than their erstwhile rival.

Nevertheless "we were friendly to their cause," he added. "We understood why all this grievance."

Recruiting for the new magazine began in May, 1987. The new recruits consisted mostly of workers who had not yet become permanent employees and who felt dissatisfied with *Tempo*'s management system. Saur Hutabarat, as the head of *Tempo*'s Jakarta Bureau, supervised the reporters who worked in *Tempo*'s main office, and was thus in a good position to recruit young people with the most potential – as well as the most reason to be dissatisfied.

When he was asked "why steal people from within?" he explained "we have no assets. Our only asset is our professionalism. It is what we can sell to our investors. Therefore we choose the best people to convince our investors....We want to do it fast."[6]

5   Interview with Bambang Harymurti, March 28, 1998.
6   Quoted in "Kasak-Kasuk Sebelum Bobol", *Jakarta-Jakarta,* July 24-August 6, 1987. According to Daniel Dhakidae, the capital for *Editor* came from the Panin Bank Group, which included banking, insurance, real estate, textiles, shipping, and control of twenty-one large companies with assets of 360 billion rupiah in 1988. Dhakidae, "The State, The Rise of Capital, and the Fall of Political Journalism", fn. 46, p. 403.

Saur's group thought the management must have been deaf not to hear the rumors. Everyone who knew of the plan was nervous and fidgety.

On the 10th of July there was so much tension that a group of journalists who had already decided that they weren't leaving *Tempo* held an impromptu meeting. About forty journalists met to chat with Harun Musawa, one of the founders of *Tempo*, in the editorial meeting room on the seventh floor. After a while Fikri Jufri dropped by, and the atmosphere grew even more tense. Not suspecting what was going on, Eddy Herwanto and Syu'bah Asa, two of the organizers of the exodus, walked into the room. They had been looking for Fikri on the eighth floor, when they came upon the meeting by accident. Suddenly they were facing a "court" of their colleagues. Fikri asked Syu'bah if it was true that he was going to leave, and he answered, "what if it's not?" Fikri said he needed an answer, and Eddy said that yes, he and a number of *Tempo* writers were going to leave.

"We are all going to come to say farewell tomorrow," Eddy said. The plan was to pay off their debts to the cooperative and to the company. Their wages had been paid through the 11th, but they were willing to work until the 14th, to finish the cover story.

Fikri refused their offer. There was no reason for them to come back to work, he said, as *Tempo*'s editors had already changed the cover story. It wasn't going to be on the rupiah, as planned, but rather on computer crimes. According to Syu'bah, Fikri's comment was short. "It doesn't matter," he said. "We are ready."

One reason they were ready was because of the efforts of a handful of writers and editors including Bambang Harymurti and Bambang Bujono who had known of the exodus and had planned ahead. "Even if they don't want to kill *Tempo*, they want at least to make it ineffective during their early publishing time so they can get a bridgehead," Bambang Harymurti said. "But people like me and Bambang Bujono think that's not fair. We have to make sure that *Tempo* will still [survive]."[7]

---

[7]   Interview with Bambang Harymurti, March 28, 1998. One interesting question

On the morning of Saturday, July 11, the entire *Editor* group came to the office to pay off their debts to the employees' cooperative and bid farewell to their colleagues. It was an emotional time. Toriq Hadad, who was at that time a reporter in the Jakarta bureau, said "I truly cried, many of my close friends left. I couldn't stand it, I went home. My good friends. Ahmad Lukman, he was a good friend. Mustaf Ayami he was from the same region as me. We could speak Javanese together."[8]

Goenawan was in the United States at the time of the exodus, but he cut short his trip and immediately returned to Indonesia. "They kept me in the dark," he later recalled. "I was shocked. I couldn't sleep for three days."[9]

But what did the exodus mean? Was it merely an internal feud at *Tempo*, or did it have broader significance within the Indonesian press industry? For Daniel Dhakidae, one of Indonesia's most highly regarded intellectuals and media analysts, the meaning was clear. The *Editor* exodus was part of a long-simmering struggle between labor and capital, a struggle that had been submerged under the New Order rhetoric of development, professionalism, and the "family" principle. Dhakidae argued that the real problem was the development of the press industry, and the "alienation of the worker-journalists" who had no choice but sell their labor in an open market. He wrote:

> What belonged to them – the expertise, the naked technique of
> knowledge transmission – had been transformed into something

---

is how did *Editor* manage to get its SIUPP, or Permit to Publish, so quickly and to short-circuit a process that ordinarily took months if not years? In all likelihood it was because the largest shareholder of P.T. Indodharma Utama Media was Bambang Prakoso Rachmadi, the son-in-law of Sudharmono, Golkar Chair and State Secretariat minister. Bobby Arief Rudianto Soekarno, the son of Soekarno, Director General of Press and Graphics at the Department of Information was another shareholder. See Dhakidae, "The State, The Rise of Capital, and the Fall of Political Journalism", fn. 48, p. 143.

8   Interview with Toriq Hadad, July 11, 2002.
9   Interview with Goenawan Mohamad, December 30, 2003.

beyond their control: business expansion, the new products, new publications as the result of diversification....The consequence was the clash between two kinds of unequal freedoms when the management said: "The door is open. If you wish to quit you can go." The journalists' claim for freedom to write was answered by a different, stronger, and depressing freedom: the 'freedom' to sell their expertise of knowledge transmission to another company. At this stage the logic of 'living in the greater family of the press' where a journalist is not a worker but a *karyawan* [employee] was severely compromised.[10]

Daniel Dhakidae's reference to the difference between workers (*buruh*) and employees (*karyawan*) is significant in the history of labor in the New Order. The word worker was used during the Soekarno years, especially by the Indonesian Communist Party (PKI) and its satellite organizations. After 1965 the term had the taint of PKI and was thus anathema to General Soeharto's New Order, which preferred the more neutral word employee. Everyone who worked in a company – from the office boys and drivers to the directors – could be considered employees. It was a classless term, outside of the relations of production.

The distinction between worker and employee was especially sensitive in the press industry because it was connected with two other important issues: the perception of journalists as media "professionals" who were independent of social class, and what was considered to be the critical role of the press in sustaining New Order economic development.

The "integralist" philosophy of the New Order, which rejected both Communist and liberal notions of the struggle between capital and labor, was deeply hostile to labor unions.[11] Preferring instead

[10]   Dhakidae, "The State, The Rise of Capital, and the Fall of Political Journalism", pp. 402-3.
[11]   For a good overview of the "integralistic" theory of the state and its relationship to labor unions and economic development, see David Reeve, "The Corporatist State: The Case of Golkar", in Arief Budiman, ed., *State and Civil Society in Indonesia*, esp. pp. 157-163.

the family metaphor, it promoted corporatist associations that emphasize the shared interest of all members of society in promoting development and prosperity. One such association was the PWI or Indonesian Journalists' Association. In the early 1970s, all other journalists' associations were disbanded, and the PWI was declared to be *satu-satunya wadah*, the "one and only body" representing the interests of journalists. As Daniel Dhakidae concluded, the relationship between a journalist and newspaper company was thus not a relation of production, but rather "a relation between members of a family."[12]

In the case of journalists, the family principle was also linked to the New Order's understanding of journalistic professionalism. Journalists were understood to be professionals, not workers, and to be endowed with both superior social status and dignity.[13] Moreover, under the Pancasila press system, they were expected to be engaged in the struggle for the common good of economic development, and to be above association with a particular social class or group. Minister of Information Ali Moertopo expressed this view in a 1978 address at the Journalist Training Center when he said:

> A journalist belongs to a profession of the members of society who struggle on the basis of idealism. Journalists do not struggle for their own group as a labor union, but for the interest of the whole society....A worker struggles for his own interest to create a conflict between labor and capitalists, and thus a class struggle; if a journalist struggles for only a certain sector of the society he is not a journalist."[14]

---

[12] Dhakidae, "The State, The Rise of Capital, and the Fall of Political Journalism", p. 390.

[13] As has been previously noted, in his 1996 study of the Indonesian Democratic Party (PDI) and the middle class, Arif Zulkifly grouped journalists in the category of "intellectuals", along with researchers, professors, religious teachers, artists, and cultural figures. Arif Zulkifli, *PDI di Mata Golongan Menengah Indonesia*, p. 18.

Was the *Editor* exodus then a manifestation of employee dissatisfaction with the owner/capitalists and the constraints of the pro-development, pro-business Pancasila press? According to the Minister of Manpower, Admiral Soedomo, who was a somewhat surprising champion of labor unions within the press industry, the *Editor* group left *Tempo* because of "the lack of a mutual labor agreement between the *karyawan* [employees] and the management...A mutual labor agreement will elaborate in detail everything pertaining to the right and responsibility of a firm and the *karyawan*."[15] Some of the statements of the leaders of the *Editor* group likewise suggested that, at bottom, the case was a labor dispute. Syu'bah Asa and Eddy Herwanto, for example, claimed that *Tempo*'s management no longer seemed to be very concerned with the employees as human beings.[16]

There was also a sense that *Tempo* had somehow slipped from the heroism of its earlier days of "struggle" and become more "industrial". There is a familiar dichotomy in the history of the Indonesian press that pits the *pers perjuangan*, or press of struggle, against the industrial press, or *pers industrial*. As Ariel Heryanto and others have noted, Indonesian press history rests on a powerful myth of an idealized past in which journalism was part of the national struggle for independence.[17] In this dichotomy, the *pers perjuangan* is believed to have more integrity, be more independent,

---

14 Quoted in *Warta Berita*, May 15, 1978, translated by Daniel Dhakidae, in Dhakidae, "The State, The Rise of Capital, and the Fall of Political Journalism", p. 393.

15 *Berita Yudha*, July 23, 1987, quoted in Dhakidae, "The State, The Rise of Capital, and the Fall of Political Journalism", p. 398.

16 Full statements of their views can be found in "Kasak-Kasuk Sebelum Bobol", *Jakarta-Jakarta*, July 24-August 6, 1987.

17 Ariel Heryanto and Stanley Yoseph Adi, "Industrialized Media in Democratizing Indonesia", in Russell H. K. Heng, ed., *Media Fortunes Changing Times* (Singapore: Institute of Southeast Asian Studies), 2002, esp. pp. 52-3.

and to be more engaged in a struggle for the common good than the "industrial" press. Heroes of the *pers perjuangan* include both Mochtar Lubis and Rosihan Anwar who, as the editors of *Indonesia Raya* and *Pedoman*, survived bannings by both the Soekarno and Soeharto regimes.[18] In contrast, the industrial press was viewed as being concerned only with making money. Unlike the crusading *pers perjuangan*, the industrial press was also believed to be willing to compromise with the state in order to stay in business.

Certainly much of the rhetoric of the *Editor* group reflected the invidious distinction between this idealized past and the more pragmatic business orientation of the present. Saur Hutabarat claimed that "business was pushing aside freedom of thought." And according to Syu'bah Asa, in matters that were controversial, "*Tempo*'s management always sided with the owners."[19] Indeed, the view that *Tempo* had become concerned only with profit-making spread well beyond the *Editor* group. Martin Aleida, the first person I interviewed about *Tempo*, told me that he had left the magazine in 1985 because it had lost its idealism and strayed far from its original mission. But was this true?

One thing that had clearly happened since the founding of *Tempo* was that the magazine had become very prosperous indeed. Circulation was high, upwards of 160,000, and advertisers were said to be "lining up" to place their ads in Indonesia's one and only weekly news magazine. One important indicator of *Tempo*'s

---

18   In a survey of sixty-five Indonesian journalists conducted between 1996 and 1998, Angela Romano asked respondents to nominate journalists and editors whom they saw as role models. The three most frequently nominated were Mochtar Lubis (41.5%), Goenawan Mohamad (27.7%) and Rosihan Anwar (26.2%). Although Romano does not use the term *perjuangan*, or struggle, the characteristics her respondents say they admire in these three editors include bravery in opposing authorities, integrity, and watchdog skills – all of which are fundamental to the concept of *pers perjuangan*. Romano, *Politics and the Press*, p. 63.

19   "Kasak-Kusuk Sebelum Bobol", *Jakarta-Jakarta*, July 24-August 6, 1987.

prosperity was the 1986 move to the new Wisma Puncak building on Jl. Rasuna Said in Kuningan, a rapidly developing business artery that was part of Jakarta's "golden triangle". Grafiti Pers owned 50% of the nine-story building; the other 50% was owned by P.T. Puncak Daya Realty, a property developer.

The move to the new building sparked much discussion, and not a few complaints.[20] First, the editorial and production offices would be separated, with production on the seventh floor and editorial offices on the eighth. Second, although the location was "strategic" and "in the center of the heart of the city", the upscale environment would be quite different from the old and somewhat seedy neighborhood of Senen. *Tempo*'s office had previously been located in one of Jakarta's biggest markets, Proyek Senen, a project that had been developed by the city in cooperation with the Jaya Development group. The sprawling market complex sold everything from razor blades and soap to cheap tee-shirts and clothes. As Toriq Hadad remembered, "if it rained and our shirt got wet, we could just go out and buy a new one!"[21]

Kuningan would be different. As *Tempo*'s generally irreverent in-house magazine *Grafiti* pointed out, "if in Senen we can easily go out for food and choose from a wide range of places that are all close by, it's not going to be like that in Kuningan. There aren't any food stalls around Wisma Puncak." The article added that for those who had "thick wallets," it would still be easy to find food, as there were plenty of international restaurants in the area. "But don't grumble yet," it concluded, "there are plans to build a canteen on the ground floor."

Once the move was completed and the new building opened, *Tempo* celebrated with a *selamatan*, or dedication ceremony and blessing. *Grafiti* magazine recorded the event in detail. "At the end of last July," the story began, "*Tempo* magazine turned over a

20   *Grafiti*, April/May, 1986.
21   Interview with Toriq Hadad, December 29, 2003.

Ciputra [right] offering yellow rice to Goenawan Mohamad [third from right] at the dedication of *Tempo*'s new building in Jl. Rasuna Said, 1986. From left, Eric Samola, Fikri Jufri, Lukman Setiawan, and Haryoko Trisnadi [*Tempo*/Ali Said]

new leaf. From the danger and hullabaloo of Senen market, *Tempo* evacuated to the elite neighborhood of Kuningan that has the face of dollars [*berwajah dolar*]"[22]

Five hundred people attended the ceremony, which was held on the still-empty sixth floor of the new building. The dedication began with greetings from Goenawan Mohamad, publisher Eric Samola, and Ciputra. After H. Musthafa Helmy led in the reading of a prayer, Ciputra marked the occasion by cutting the traditional yellow rice cone. Reporters and writers milled around tables overflowing with rice, side dishes, and spit-roasted goat. A huge display of flowers from the developer spelled out the word "succes [*sic*]."

During the dedication ceremony, each of the speakers expressed the hope that *Tempo*'s traditional closeness and open management style wouldn't be lost in the move to the new upscale neighborhood. Yet of the three speeches that were given that day, the one that would be remembered was Ciputra's – although perhaps not for reasons the developer had intended.

---

[22]   *Grafiti*, August/September 1986.

Ciputra began by pointing out how unusual Grafiti Pers was as a company. "In private companies," he said, "like those owned by William Soeryadjaya, or Liem Sioe Liong, or even our own private company, it's the family that holds the highest position. If we look at the state-owned enterprises, it is those who run politics and power who are the most important factor. But at *Tempo*, what we see is that it is the founders and shareholders – including the employees – who hold power, and have the right to pick representatives and make changes, even among those who lead the company.

"*Tempo* combines capitalism with materialism," he said, "and the shareholders of *Tempo* have already become capitalists in a small way. They are already semi-bourgeois. Whether or not Mr. Goenawan agrees with this, I say that he has already become bourgeois."

"Now this is what makes us happy," Ciputra continued. "We remember *Tempo* fifteen years ago, if they saw a pedicab [*becak*] collide with a car, *a priori Tempo* defended the pedicab. Even if the car was right, if the pedicab was wrong. Because *Tempo* wanted to defend the weak."

Ciputra speaking at the dedication of the new *Tempo* building, Jl. Rasuna Said, 1986 [*Tempo*, Ali Said]

"Now *Tempo* doesn't *a priori* defend only the weak," he said, "but it also defends the truth."

"And if capitalism is right," Ciputra added, "it should also be defended."

While conducting research in Jakarta, I heard Ciputra's speech referred to at least half a dozen times. Although the point he seemed to be making was relatively straight-forward, that *Tempo* was now willing to defend "the truth" even if it meant defending the wealthy and powerful, this is not the way that his speech is remembered.

The first I ever heard of Ciputra's speech was in 2000, when I gave a talk on the results of my content analysis of *Tempo*'s National section at a meeting of the editorial staff. Of my findings, the one that sparked the most controversy was my discovery that after returning to publication in 1998, *Tempo*'s National section focused far less frequently on "victims" than it had before the banning. During the discussion, chief editor Bambang Harymurti recalled how Ciputra had once said that *Tempo*'s editors had always sided with victims until they themselves owned cars.[23]

When I showed my findings to Goenawan at about the same time, he likewise commented that Ciputra had once said "you guys always defended the weak. But once you got cars, now you defend the rich."

"We were not very happy with that," Goenawan added, "and we had a guilty feeling all the time. Because it was cynical. But sometimes it was true."[24]

Regardless of what Ciputra had actually said at the dedication of the new building, what people heard and remembered was that once *Tempo* had become wealthy, it had changed. Perhaps it had even slipped from its original mission of defending those who

---

[23]   The discussion didn't end with the meeting, and in fact led to the circulation of several rounds of internal emails that called for introspection on the part of *Tempo* editors and writers.

[24]   Interview with Goenawan Mohamad, June 20, 2000.

cannot defend themselves. This change was the cause of both concern and consternation.

When I later asked Goenawan Mohamad about my interpretation of what had been heard in Ciputra's speech, he vigorously disagreed. "No," he said, "it was an inside joke! Ciputra was teasing me because he thought that *Tempo* was always siding with the weak, and now you have this new building, how can you do it?" Even when I showed Goenawan the full text of the speech and the accompanying article in *Grafiti*, he continued to disagree. "I never told them, 'please defend the weak,'" he said. "I just told them that when you have two sides and that one is not having access to expression, you have to give them more space."[25]

Perhaps one reason that Ciputra's comment seemed to strike a nerve is that much of the rhetoric during the *Editor* exodus and its aftermath focused on the rising wealth of *Tempo*'s owner-shareholders, and what was perceived to be the unequal distribution of the shares. Nearly everyone agrees that a major cause of the *Editor* walk-out was the issue of who owned the shares and who was profiting from the rapid expansion of Grafiti Pers – especially after its 1982 acquisition of the *Jawa Pos* newspaper. The dissidents believed that as the company grew bigger, those with vested interests accumulated more power. As Fikri Jufri later recalled, the *Editor* group wanted to run their own magazine, and to return to the "original idea" of *Tempo*. "That is good," he said. "I give them all my support. But if you want to leave a company by taking people, and clandestine, I don't think it's right."[26]

> Goenawan always said to me, "Fikri please don't be pushy, because if you say something, you have such big power, you have to be strict with your power. Use your power less." And so we limit ourselves. But we did have different salaries, yes. I'm a founder,

25   Interview with Goenawan Mohamad, December 30, 2003.
26   Interview with Fikri Jufri, March 11, 1998.

and I'm a director, and I'm in charge as the second in command....Maybe when we grew outside of *Tempo* [magazine] that was the beginning of the dissatisfaction. Because why is it always the same persons who are getting this and this? It's not about money, but about position, about power. Why is it always Goenawan and Fikri [who profit]?....And when we take over the *Jawa Pos*, and its Goenawan again and Fikri. That envy comes because we began small...like one for all and all for one, and suddenly it's different. Why does Fikri Jufri get a bigger car? Maybe we made mistakes. Maybe we made mistakes because we are mortal.

There were not ideological differences, he concluded, "but differences in the class system maybe." Ironically, Fikri Jufri's characterization of the dispute as having been about differences in the "class system" was similar to the views of many of those who left *Tempo* – as well as to some of those who stayed. One former *Tempo* journalist who was a senior editor during the 1980s explained that it wasn't unusual for an organization that developed from very small beginnings into a company that was both rich and influential to have these kinds of problems. "I think that until the early 1980s we at *Tempo* were on the same level," he said. "But then *Tempo*'s profits went up. And that brings a distinction between the owner the shareholders and the non-shareholders."

> In the early years of *Tempo*, the shares were meaningless, but suddenly after ten years or so they were very, very profitable. And year by year the shareholders enjoy bigger profits than the non-shareholders. And before long we get to envy.
>
> And it happened that not all the owners have the same level of skill. And then the promotions were given to the shareholders, not because of their skill, but because they were shareholders. And this was Goenawan and Fikri's decision. And some of us began to think that Goenawan has changed.
>
> Although Goenawan was a bit shy of his new wealth, it was

different with Fikri. Fikri is very extroverted. I remember one day he came in with gold, one hundred grams, I think, and he showed it. "Look, I have gold now!" he said. "And luxury cars."

It's different with GM. He just drove a Kijang, not a BMW. But even people who used to be Goenawan's close friends accused him of being a "shy cat capitalist" [*kapitalis malu-malu kucing*] because although he did not show off with his new wealth, he's still very rich. This happened in the early 1980s. So as it happened, at the micro level there is a bigger gap between the haves and the have nots. So I can understand if [some people] were very bitter."[27]

Virtually all sides involved in the *Editor* dispute agree that the shares were an issue. Syu'bah Asa was quoted as saying that those who owned priority shares [Goenawan, Fikri, Harjoko Trisnadi, Lukman Setiawan and Eric Samola] also held key positions at *Tempo*. "Regardless of whether the work of a director sparkles or is terrible, he isn't going to be changed. Until death he isn't going to be changed."[28]

A bigger concern than the question of who actually owned the shares seems to have been the question of unfairness, and why it was that some people had become so rich while others had not. Several *Tempo* people told me that it wasn't even the dividends that were the problem but rather the *tantiem*, a percentage of the profits that was paid out to the directors before the dividends were calculated. The board of directors decides who gets the *tantiem*, and of course the directors are chosen by the shareholders. In the case of *Tempo*, the majority shareholders were also the directors. The *tantiem* is part of the basic law of businesses that regulates limited companies in Indonesia and dates back to the colonial era. All limited companies pay out *tantiem*. Yet at *Tempo* it sparked controversy in part because nobody other than the directors knew exactly how large the *tantiem* was. According to Toriq Hadad, much of the controversy came down to a question

---

[27] Confidential interview, March 9, 1998.
[28] *Jakarta-Jakarta*, July 24-August 6, 1987.

of "openness". As he said, "we didn't know what the profit was. The employees were left out."[29]

Although everyone at *Tempo* acknowledges the right of the founders of the company to own shares and make a profit, there still seems to have been a profound ambivalence about capitalism and the way it works. Whereas no one challenged the assumption that it was Goenawan, Fikri, and the other founders of *Tempo* who had created the magazine and assumed all the risks of the new enterprise, what rankled was the idea that the founders continued to reap dividends from their shares while others who had worked at the same company for many years did not. Even Goenawan now says that giving the directors shares in the company was "a mistake". Why?

The work of historians and scholars of the political economy of Indonesia may shed some light on these apparent contradictions. Like other post-colonial societies, Indonesia attained independence only after a great struggle to throw off the yoke of economic exploitation. The Dutch means of domination was of course capitalism, and much of the rhetoric of the early Republic was strongly opposed to capitalism as an economic system. For example the radical nationalism of Soekarno's Indonesian Nationalist Party was "strongly influenced by Marxism and...sharply alienated from Netherlands Indies colonial society."[30] The corporatist streak in Indonesian political thinking thus has as much to do with the rejection of capitalism as it does with Javanese notions of harmony.

The work of anthropologists suggests that on a more individual level, many Malay peoples have a cultural aversion to talking about

29   Interview with Toriq Hadad, December 29, 2003.
30   Herbert Feith and Lance Castles, *Indonesian Political Thinking, 1945-1965* (Ithaca: Cornell University Press, 1970), p. 152. In a discussion of "distinctively Indonesian thinking," Feith and Castle write "this holistic perspective showed itself, also, in a marked preference for collectivist forms of social organization, [and] a dislike of the profit motive and *enrichissez-vous*..." p. 18.

money. Many Javanese consider it unseemly to be too concerned with money and the accumulation of wealth, especially for men.[31] This was one reason why Indonesians of Chinese descent were deemed essential to the functioning of the economy – they, unlike their Malay counterparts, were assumed to be both competent with money and unashamed of their pursuit of wealth. The derisive description of Goenawan Mohamad as a "shy cat capitalist" epitomizes the notion that excessive wealth should be a cause of embarrassment. Indonesians of Chinese descent are assumed to be an exception to this rule, which also helps to explain why they are likely to be targets of envy and even hate.

One of the great ironies of the "critique" of *Tempo* for being too capitalist is that the *Editor* group set up their new magazine in a fashion almost identical to that of *Tempo* – also giving shares to the founding owners of the magazine. Moreover, if we examine *Tempo* as a capitalist organization, we find upon closer inspection that it was a very peculiar one indeed.

Goenawan once told me that at *Tempo* his slogan was "socialism on the inside, capitalism on the outside" (*sosialisme ke dalam, kapitalisme ke luar*). What he says he meant by this was "to make no nonsense in generating profit in our business," but at the same time to try to create a more "egalitarian way" of enjoying that profit.[32]

Around the time of the assassination of Anwar Sadat in 1981, Goenawan went to Israel, where he had an opportunity to visit a *kibbutz*. He remembers having been impressed with the collective eating and the sharing (which he said they had always done at *Tempo*), but he also noticed how wealthy the community was. "The *kibbutz* was very rich," he said, "but the people were happy.

---

[31]   For a good summary of this literature, see Robert W. Hefner, "Introduction", in Robert Hefner, ed., *Market Cultures: Society and Morality in the New Asian Capitalisms* (Westview Press, 1998), esp. pp. 23-24.
[32]   Email correspondence, April 24, 1998.

And I tried to think about that. You could be very capitalistic, but internally you could be egalitarian."

Goenawan actually tried to institute several egalitarian plans. One was to pour as much money back into the company as possible. Another was to make sure that profits were paid out in the form of wages to those who worked at *Tempo*, rather than as dividends to the shareholders or as taxes to the government. In the mid-1980s, when the *Editor* exodus occurred, *Tempo* employees were getting eighteen months of salary each year.[33] There were also bonuses, like the gift of a car once a reporter successfully "graduated" from a program of in-house training and became a member of the editorial staff. After ten years of working for *Tempo*, there was the gift of a house.[34]

But even these programs caused controversy. Or, as Goenawan put it, "of course you couldn't be a *kibbutz*." When *Tempo* inaugurated the car policy, he explained, "I had a regulation, you have to have one level of car. Everyone, a jeep. But people started to complain. 'I work harder and I have a better job than he does, and I should have a better car.'"[35]

One thing that makes the story of ownership and shares at *Tempo* particularly complicated is that *Tempo*'s Yayasan Karyawan, or employees' foundation, collectively owned 20% of the shares of *Tempo*. By the mid-1980s, this was not unusual in Indonesian

---

[33]   *Jakarta-Jakarta*, July 24-August 6, 1987, also interview with Fikri Jufri, March 11, 1998. The rationale behind increasing the number of months of salary rather than the base salary itself was that if times got hard, the number of extra months could be cut but the base salary would remain the same.

[34]   According to Bambang Harymurti, it was actually the gift of a house "allowance", equal to twenty months' worth of salary. When I asked him if this was enough money to buy a house, he laughed and said, "well, it depends on how big your salary is and what kind of a house. But it's enough for your down payment." Interview, January 8, 2004.

[35]   Interview with Goenawan Mohamad, December 30, 2003. Or, as *New York Tribune* editor Horace Greeley had written nearly 150 years earlier of the American utopian community Brook Farm, envy was like the snake in the Garden of Eden. Horace Greeley to Charles A. Dana, August 24, 1842, James Harrison Wilson Collection, Library of Congress. Quoted in Janet E. Steele, *The Sun Shines for All*, p.15.

news organizations; in 1984, in fact, the 20% rule became institutionalized as part of the Basic Press Law.[36] This regulation was a significant prop in helping to bolster the government's claim that journalists could not be "workers" because they were actually "owners". Yet, as Angela Romano has shown, most news organizations – if they even set aside the 20% of the shares in the first place – did not pay out dividends to employees *as individuals*. This was not the case at *Tempo*. Each year, dividends were calculated on the basis of a complicated formula that took into account the total number of employees, the total number of months worked, and the number of months an individual had worked at the magazine. And the dividend was paid out as actual money.

So if the working conditions at *Tempo* were so good, and the employees so well paid, what then was the real cause of the 1987 *Editor* exodus?

One important factor seems to have been the division between those who continued to see themselves as artists and those who defined themselves as "professionals". And more than a problem of self-definition, there were also changes at *Tempo* that reflected Goenawan's desire to create a modern, efficient institution.

In 1981, *Tempo* began sending its managers to the Lembaga Pendidikan Perkembangan Manajemen [LPPM], a not-for-profit institute that taught management techniques primarily to business people.[37] LPPM had been established in 1967 as a "modernizing" institute. Goenawan recalls that the programs usually lasted for three months, and included training in decision making and budgeting, as well as "financial management for non-financial managers".

Nearly thirty years later, Goenawan still lights up when he talks about LPPM. "It was crucial," he said. "And I introduced that every manager had to go there." Take budgeting, for example.

---

[36]   According to Goenawan, the Department of Information followed the model of *Tempo* in implementing this regulation. Interview, December 30, 2003.

[37]   Yusril Djalinus, email correspondence, February 24, 2004.

"Budgeting was done from the bottom up," he said.. "You ask each department to draw up a budget, and then you consolidate it and then the financial manager discusses it. And then after that, everyone who drew up the budget is mandated to spend the budget without consulting the financial director, but reporting only to his or her immediate superior. Like the head of the library would spend money according to his budget, and only report it once a month to me."[38]

Goenawan says at that time no other Indonesian media institution was studying management in this way – which may indeed have been part of the problem. According to *Tempo*'s current chief editor Bambang Harymurti, Goenawan had fallen in love with management.

"The problem," Bambang said, "was that people like Goenawan Mohamad and other senior editors who were in a honeymoon period think that well, being journalist is easy – I did it, but this management is tough. And of course it's hard for those young people to argue against the senior." Bambang explained that he personally felt that in a news organization it was the editorial side that should be supreme, not the management side. "I was always angry at the fact that if you were a fresh university graduate at that time and you go to *Tempo* and work on the editorial side, you find out that you're better off working on the management side."[39]

Grafiti magazine, *Tempo*'s in-house publication, actually foreshadowed some of this tension. One year before the *Editor* exodus, *Grafiti* published a six-page interview with Goenawan Mohamad entitled "GM Answers" [*GM Menjawab*] in which Goenawan responded to questions raised by *Tempo*'s staff. One of a handful of serious questions raised the issue of management: "After your success in leading *Tempo* for the past fifteen years, I

38   Interview with Goenawan Mohamad, December 30, 2003.
39   Interview with Bambang Harymurti, March 28, 1998.

want to know: which is more difficult, being a journalist, or being a manager?" Goenawan's answer was revealing: "Probably being a manager. You have to take into account lots of concerns: moral as well as material, individual as well as social, cultural as well as structural. And a lot of issues that don't make sense." The questioner? Bambang Harymurti.[40]

For some of *Tempo*'s senior writers, who had been at *Tempo* since the more relaxed earlier days, the new rules were at best annoying and at worst insulting. In the old days, there hadn't been any rules. In fact, there hadn't even been any meetings. Susanto Pudjomartono, who was for many years the editor of *Tempo*'s National section, recalled how planning was done in 1977 when he was first hired:

> *Tempo* was founded in 1971, and the organization was a mess at the time. There was no planning for the next week's issue. Usually after this week's issue was published or printed, then Goenawan or Fikri invited a few of us, five or six, to lunch. At that time our office was in Senen shopping center, the third floor of the shopping center, and there are literally hundreds of *warung* or restaurants, and usually we pick our favorite restaurant, because we know all the employees there, we know everybody, and so we will talk about next week cover story. And then upon returning to the office we will inform everybody, oh next week's cover story is that and that, and she will write that and that and it's up to you!

Susanto, with a degree in Mass Communication from Gadjah Mada University, was himself comfortable with the new management techniques, and in fact became *Tempo*'s first director of education and training. But for others the transition to a more rational system of management was quite difficult. The two *Tempo*

---

[40]   *Grafiti*, February/March 1986.

writers for whom the transition was perhaps the most irksome were Syu'bah Asa and Salim Said. Although their cases were quite different, they had one important characteristic in common: they had both been with the magazine since its founding in 1971.

Syu'bah Asa is a stocky man with a round face, an Afro-style corona of light brown hair and wire-rimmed glasses. Although Syu'bah's professional relationship with Goenawan dates back to 1970 and *Ekspres* magazine, he has actually known Goenawan since 1964, when he read one of the young poet's articles in H.B. Jassin's literary magazine *Sastra*, and invited him to come to Yogyakarta to give a talk. They became close, having in common not only a shared struggle against Communism, but also mutual friends such as the poet and playwright W.S. Rendra. Although Syu'bah Asa studied at IAIN [Institute Agama Islam Negeri], and is often referred to as "one of the Muslims at *Tempo*" – meaning that he is believed to be someone who can represent the views of the Islamic community – he and Goenawan nevertheless became close friends. Of Goenawan, who is almost always described as being secular in orientation, Syubah says that "he is also religious in his sense."[41]

Yet by the mid-1980s, there were changes at *Tempo*, changes that made Syu'bah increasingly unhappy. He says that he felt oppressed by the new emphasis on "efficiency", "management", and the desire to be "modern". Being a writer was no longer valued, he said, compared with what could be called "managerial." What was important was "how to be modern."

"Before," he said, "we worked in Senen, in a two-storey building that shook when the wind blew. There were only thirty-six people working there. When a writer from *Time* magazine came to visit, he said that this was impossible – that in America thirty-six people couldn't possibly make a weekly magazine like this. But this is the Indonesian style. Only a few people working, but

41   Interview with Syu'bah Asa, August 2, 2000.

working from morning til night, sometimes without shirts, smoking, shouting, making all kinds of jokes, and producing a magazine with beautiful language."

By 1986, Syu'bah's lovely memories of *Tempo* as a community of equals were faint indeed, having long been replaced by a management system that he described as "rigid". The scale of work was no longer human, he said, describing an incident in which he had taken some of his vacation time to research and write two stories on *pesantren*, or Muslim boarding schools, for a cover story on Abdurrahman Wahid, who was at that time "just getting started" on the political career that would take eventually him to the presidential palace. More than fifteen years later, it still annoyed Syu'bah that he hadn't been reimbursed for his efforts. "Paper procedures," he sniffed. "I hadn't filled out a form in advance saying where I was going, what dates, how could I be reached, and detailing the payments. If we only had bills as proof, receipts, it wasn't enough." The system was inhumane, he said. "Comrades had become employees."

"Goenawan was a pioneer," Syu'bah concluded. "Lots of people, myself included, always wanted to value what was old. We were more traditional, perhaps, compared with him. He was never afraid to change or move. Goenawan was always in front."

Salim Said had a similar story. An expert on both Indonesian cinema and the Indonesian military, Salim is small and intense. When I met him at the Taman Ismail Marzuki complex in 1988, he was the head of the Jakarta Arts Council. He is passionate on the subject of Goenawan Mohamad.

Like Syu'bah, Salim had also known Goenawan since they were very young. "We were friends," he said, "sharing one small bed when we were poor, before both of us got married."[42] Salim even helped Goenawan apply for the licence for *Tempo*. "I was one of the founders in a literal sense," he explained. "I was the one

---

[42]   Interview with Salim Said, April 1, 1998.

with my own scooter running around the city applying for the license to publish in 1970." During the early years of *Tempo*, one of Salim Said's first responsibilities was to head up the education and training program for new hires. "We did not recruit journalists," he said, "we recruited people fresh from university. And we trained them."

So what went wrong? Why did Salim Said leave *Tempo* in 1987? The problem began after he was accepted into the doctoral program at Ohio University. He asked permission to go to Ohio, but promised that he would return to *Tempo* once he finished his Ph.D. "And it was agreed," he said. "So I felt assured."

> But when I returned home, I found that my name was not on the file anymore. Because according to the law, according to the organization, you cannot leave the country, the magazine, the head office, for one year. They say you are welcome, but you need to start again. They gave me my rank when the magazine was first published, back sixteen years. And the editor, he's a nice person, but I think he made a wrong mistake. Because he worshiped the organization. He admired it as an artist. He admired the organization he created or they created, the way he admired a good poem. There is no more discussing it. Go back to the law.

Salim Said is not alone in comparing the building of *Tempo* to the creation of a poem, but his anger and sense of betrayal is perhaps unparalleled. Yet there is also important substance to his criticism. Although Salim Said doesn't use the term "modern", like Syu'bah Asa he describes a system that had become increasingly rational and – according to some – increasingly bureaucratic. "When I returned home in January 1986 from the U.S.," he said, "I found the office completely changed. The human interrelations between the leaders and those newly recruited people who came to *Tempo* by admiring *Tempo* when they were still in university…I saw the differences between our ideas in the beginning, and I felt uneasy with that. And I started to become a person who irritated other people. And that slowly brought me to the position where I decided to get out."

Goenawan's long-time and perhaps best friend Arief Budiman also noted the new "bureaucratic" tendencies of *Tempo* in the 1980s, and described how their own friendship had suffered.

> When you have a big organization you become very busy and you have to select your guests, other things. Now this is also why Salim [is angry with] Goenawan, because he felt he has the privilege, knowing Goenawan from early on. And when Goenawan was very poor, he was the one who provides everything for him....I had that feeling also, I was very close to him once. But when I came to the office I felt uncomfortable. He was very busy, especially because he was already an important person. So that's bureaucracy.[43]

Of course one man's bureaucracy is another's rational system of management, and Goenawan Mohamad is proud of the changes he brought to *Tempo*, changes that were widely imitated by other Indonesian news organizations. I asked Goenawan about a 1986 interview he did in *Grafiti* magazine in which he sounded defensive about the new system of management. "Maybe I am," he said, "but I tried to explain, because I don't think many people understand. People who are not used to this, it is a kind of new ethic."

Goenawan explained that when he started out in *Tempo*, he asked H.G. Rorimpandey, one of the founders of the newspaper *Sinar Harapan*, what aspect of the magazine he should watch most closely. The answer? "Organization."[44]

---

43   Interview with Arief Budiman, December 6, 1999.
44   Interview with Goenawan Mohamad, December 30, 2003.

"And he was right," Goenawan said, "because when I saw *Sinar Harapan*, I didn't want *Tempo* to be like that. Conflicts all the time. Factionalism. Manado and Batak, and then they used no system, no system whatsoever! [They] would spend money, travel....I remember there was an advertising manager at *Sinar Harapan*, with a house with a swimming pool, and nobody checked."

"I learned from mistakes at *Sinar Harapan*," he said. "So I had a very very strong organization. Because I thought that if we didn't do it, we would collapse. Especially with the big egos."

And what about Salim Said's complaint? "It's a difficult problem," Goenawan said. "My whole life is planning fairness."

According to Goenawan, it was Yusril Djalinus, the architect of *Tempo*'s system of career planning, who always insisted on applying the standards fairly. "When Salim Said went to the U.S.," Goenawan explained, "we sent him money, a kind of salary. It was unprecedented. But Yusril said that if we did it, we'd have to institutionalize so to make things fair, and then it's easier to handle. And he was right. So Salim Said got special treatment."

"I remember, I learned that from [*Kompas* editor] Jakob Oetomo's mistake. There was no rule at *Kompas*, just his rule....you had this extra salary, hidden from everybody else. Yusril said don't do that. Because once you did it, there is no secret. And then, it's not fair. Special treatment. Of course when you did a thing like this, you couldn't be very quick in rewarding people who were very very bright. And that is another problem."

Under Goenawan's leadership, one of *Tempo*'s most significant achievements was the development of a system of career planning that has continued more or less unchanged to this day. A career at *Tempo* begins with a probationary period, which – if all goes well – is followed by several years of work as a reporter. After passing a program of additional training and special assignments, a reporter is then promoted to the editorial staff, meaning that he or she has become a writer. After working for several years as a writer, the candidate is then invited to undergo further training and tests in order to become a desk editor. The next stage is managing editor, a position of considerable responsibility that includes supervising several desk editors. *Tempo*'s chief editor, executive editor, and assistant executive editor are chosen from among the ranks of managing editors. Senior staff are invited to become "senior editors", a position that confers both status and the freedom to develop one's own story ideas. Each stage is divided by periods called *magang*, or internships, in which a candidate must complete a program of special assignments designed to prove his or her fitness for the next level. For example in order to progress to the editorial staff, a reporter must complete *Magang-1*, or M-1, a program in which he or she researches and writes a total of forty stories in four different compartments.[45]

With its strict procedures for recruitment and promotion as well as its emphasis on discipline, fairness, and training, the organization of *Tempo* bears a striking resemblance to another "modern" institution: the Indonesian military. "Because there was no real competition, career planning [at *Tempo*] had to be observed very religiously," Goenawan explained, adding that he couldn't promote anyone without having them go through this series of tests. According to Goenawan, the alternative to rational career planning was paternalism, the system of management commonly found in other Indonesian mass media. An important result of *Tempo*'s highly-structured system was that its very predictability allowed for more egalitarianism. Goenawan recalled that Jakob Oetomo, the former editor of *Kompas*, had once commented "in *Kompas* we have fathers, In *Tempo* you have only brothers."[46] At *Kompas*, Jakob Oetomo was called *Pak Jakob*, or "father". At *Tempo*, Goenawan was *Mas Goen*, or "brother".[47]

---

45 Interview with Setiyardi, December 29, 2003. Setiyardi reminded me that in the "old days," passing M-1 meant that you got a car. For his generation, the group hired after 1998, there was not enough money for cars.

46 Interview with Goenawan Mohamad, December 30, 2003.

47 When I had previously asked about this, several friends pointed out that it is particularly Javanese to refer to someone as *Mas* rather than *Pak*. It is true that the term is Javanese, but it is the sentiment behind it – an emphasis on closeness rather than deference – that is especially significant in this context.

As a person who brought order and rationality to a traditionally disorganized industry, Goenawan bears some similarities to Jakarta's popular former Governor General Ali Sadikin. Ali Sadikin was Governor of Jakarta between 1966-1977, and although he was appointed by President Soekarno, his modernizing vision was in keeping with the spirit of the New Order. As Mochtar Lubis wrote, when "Bang Ali" [brother Ali] took over as governor of Jakarta, the city was a mess. Traffic was terrible, city streets were full of holes, entire neighborhoods flooded when it rained. "City residents faced crises in nearly all areas of their lives – housing, work, transportation, business, telephone connections, education, and more."[48]   According to Mochtar, it was Ali Sadikin's "military training as a Marine" that had taught him the importance of discipline. Jakarta was also lucky, Mochtar added, because in addition to his "sense of discipline, his firm heart and his hard head, [Ali Sadikin] also had a feeling of social solidarity, and an equally large sense of humanity. His heart was easily touched by those who were weak and helpless, as well as by the poor and subjugated." Like Ali Sadikin, Goenawan Mohamad combined strict discipline with a communitarian spirit and concern for the weak.

In addition to *Tempo*'s program of career planning, there were other aspects of the magazine's organization that made it particularly "modern". One was the annual SWOT meetings. SWOT was an acronym for "Strengths, Weaknesses, Opportunities, and Threats" that, according to Goenawan, Erik Samola had "borrowed" from the Jaya Development Group. The SWOT meetings were off-site retreats, in which people from various divisions met to talk over problems and make plans for the future. Sometimes SWOT meetings were held in hotels – itself a treat for young reporters and writers – or, after Grafiti Pers built its "villa" Wisma *Tempo* Sirnagalih, in the hills of West Java, in Puncak. Usually involving

---

48   Mochtar Lubis, "Kata Pengantar", in Ramadhan K.H., *Bang Ali Demi Jakarta*, pp. 8-9.

a bus ride as well as an over-night stay, the SWOT meetings allowed plenty of time for recreation as well as talk.

One of the most significant but least-recognized aspects of *Tempo*'s history has been its role in the development and institutionalization of professional values in Indonesian journalism. *Tempo* developed one of the industry's first codes of ethics, as well as a very strict policy towards the acceptance of "envelopes" or bribes.[49] Goenawan himself created the system of "*layak Tempo*", a means by which potential stories are evaluated for suitability. Criteria include the "hotness" of the newspeg, the story's magnitude, its relevance to Indonesia, its angle, and its degree of drama. Goenawan says that he developed the system as a result of his training at LPPM – and that before the system was instituted, it sometimes took a full day to decide which stories should be included in the magazine. Several people told me that by the time *Tempo* was banned in 1994 the system had become so internalized that if there was any controversy at all over the appropriateness of a story, someone would simply call out "magnitude" and the conflict would be resolved.

Another institution that *Tempo* created in the 1970s was the "coordinator of reporters" or "K.R." Developed by Yusril Djalinus, the K. R. was responsible for reporters working both in and outside of Jakarta. Each of the bureau chiefs, including the assistant for foreign correspondents and the head of the Jakarta bureau (who controlled up to thirty reporters), reported to the coordinator of reporters. In its carefully organized hierarchy, the K.R. was a system of spatial organization and control not unlike the "territorial organization" developed by the Indonesian military.[50]

So why did the group of thirty-two writers and reporters leave *Tempo*? By now it should be clear that there is no single answer.

---

[49] Atmakusumah has pointed out that *Indonesia Raya* editor Mochtar Lubis was the first Indonesian editor to develop an "anti-envelope" policy.
[50] See Harold Crouch, *The Army And Politics In Indonesia*, esp. pp. 222-3 for a discussion of the territorial organization of the army.

Some, like Syu'bah Asa and Salim Said, missed the feeling of informality and closeness that had characterized the magazine in its early days, and resented the new regulations and "paper procedures", with their emphasis on efficiency, management, and the "desire to be modern", For others, the problem seems to have been money, and the contradiction between what Bambang Harymurti called *Tempo*'s "ideological training of egalitarianism" and the economic power of its owner-directors.[51]

Yet significantly, this conflict was not so much a dispute between capital and labor as it was an unintended consequence of the overwhelming power of the state. The Department of Information's endless list of rules controlling and regulating the press created an artificial monopoly for *Tempo*, a situation which exacerbated tensions already present within the magazine. Although the *Editor* group used the rhetoric of "pluralism in media," what many of them really wanted was more opportunity for self-advancement. Eighteen months of salary plus the promise of cars and housing allowances weren't always enough to satisfy the ambitions of the immensely talented stock of *Tempo* writers. As Toriq Hadad explained, in 1987, in the Economics and Business section alone there were already three employees who were fully capable of becoming managing editor.[52] Or, as several writers told me, *Tempo* already had a chief editor, and there was no place for his would-be replacements to advance.

The lack of a place to advance at *Tempo* for those who had arrived subsequent to the magazine's founding bears striking parallels to what archeologist Peter Bellwood has called "founder rank enhancement" among Austronesian peoples.[53] Bellwood

---

[51]   Interview with Bambang Harymurti, January 8, 2004.
[52]   Interview with Toriq Hadad, December 29, 2003.
[53]   Peter Bellwood, "Hierarchy, Founder Ideology, and Austronesian Expansion", in James J. Fox and Clifford Sather, eds., *Origins, Ancestry, and Alliance* (Canberra: Australian National University, 1996), pp. 18-9. I am grateful to Joel Kuipers for sharing this article with me.

describes this process as one in which "junior founders moving into relative or absolute isolation (such as a new island, previously inhabited or not) could establish senior lines, aggrandize their resources, and attempt to ensure methods of genealogical inheritance which would retain privileges for their descendants." Bellwood suggests that in societies in which founders are revered by their descendants, "separation" gave founders of new communities opportunities they wouldn't have enjoyed in their previous homes. Perhaps for the *Editor* group, the desire to establish a new magazine – and to give themselves the status and privileges of founders – was the ultimate push to leave *Tempo*.[54]

Whether or not the magazine had strayed from its original "mission" by the time of the 1987 *Editor* exodus, *Tempo* had clearly changed since its founding. Its new building in Kuningan, and the fear that the magazine no longer "*a priori*" defended the weak were just two indications of its new-found riches. Despite Goenawan Mohamad's attempts to practice "socialism on the inside", *Tempo* had become part of the establishment. But the question remained, would this be enough to protect the magazine from its enemies on the outside?

---

[54]   Supriyono, who was a reporter at *Tiras* (the successor to *Editor*) in the late 1990s, told me that when he worked at the magazine, the founders were all still there and were "legendary". Interview, April 29, 2004.

the ghost

"It was as if the regular army had joined the guerrillas."
– Aristides Katoppo, May 4, 1998

The banning of *Tempo* launched a covert war within the New Order. It changed many lives, and inspired heroism and sacrifice from people who had never before thought of themselves as "activists". It led to the creation of an independent journalists' association that shook up Indonesia's somnambulant press industry, and gave new impetus to a pro-democracy movement that continues to have an impact to this day. Yet perhaps the greatest transformation occurred within Goenawan Mohamad himself. For years, Goenawan had been forced to compromise with government authorities in order to keep his magazine alive – but the banning of *Tempo* changed all that. After June 21, 1994, there would be no more compromises, no more ambiguity. Within a matter of months, regime insiders were reportedly referring to Goenawan Mohamad as "the most dangerous man in Indonesia."[1]

---

[1]   Major General Sjafrie Sjamsoeddin of the Jakarta military command is reported to have made this comment to Major General Zacky Anwar Makarim, who repeated it to his niece, Rayya Makarim. Rayya is a screenwriter and friend of Goenawan Mohamad's. Although I was unable to verify the truth of the story, so many young activists and journalists repeated it to me that by the late 1990s it had clearly taken on a life of its own.

The rough outline of the story of *Tempo*'s banning is well known. On June 11, 1994, *Tempo* published a cover story on a dispute within the government over an agreement to buy thirty-nine used war ships from the former East Germany. The story focused on the issue of the purchase price, as well as on the conflict between Minister of Research and Technology B.J. Habibie and Minister of Finance Ma'rie Muhammad. Some military officials – especially in the Navy – also objected to the purchase of the ships, seeing Habibie's move as a usurpation of their authority.[2] A few days after the story was published, President Soeharto made a speech at the dedication of a naval facility in Teluk Ratai, Lampung, in which he criticized the press for fanning controversy and jeopardizing national stability. Shortly thereafter *Tempo*, along with the magazine *Editor* and the tabloid *Detik*, was banned.[3]

The letter that came from the Department of Information on June 21, 1994 gave no explicit reason for the withdrawal of the magazine's SIUPP, or permit to run a press business, stating only that *Tempo* had disturbed national stability while failing to safeguard the Pancasila press.[4] The vagueness was characteristic of the Department of Information during the New Order. In effect, the Minister of Information was accountable to no one other than President Soeharto himself. Moreover, the fact that the Department of Information could use its authority to withdraw a newspaper or magazine's SIUPP amounted to a *de facto* banning. Critics had

---

[2]   These and other details can be found in Coen Husain Pontoh, "Konflik Tak Kunjang Padam", *Pantau*, August 2001.

[3]   Arief Budiman and Olle Törnquist conclude that it was an "open secret" that the banning resulted from *Tempo*'s insinuation that there was corruption involved in the purchase of the ships. Arief Budiman and Olle Törnquist, *Aktor Demokrasi: Catatan Tentang Gerakan Perlawanan di Indonesia* (Jakarta: Institut Studi Arus Informasi, 2001), p. 126.

[4]   Alumni Majalah Tempo, *Buku Putih Tempo: Pembredelan Itu*, pp. 12-13.

long observed that bannings not only violated constitutional guarantees of a free press, but were also prohibited by the Basic Press Law of 1966, which stated explicitly that the press would not be subject to censorship or bannings. As Goenawan Mohamad himself had written several years earlier, when a SIUPP was cancelled, "the accused is not given the right of self-defense, let alone in an open forum. Supposedly, there is a Press Council hearing (headed by the Minister of Information, with members appointed by the government) that makes the decision to cancel the SIUPP. But if there is indeed such a session, it is closed."[5]

It was also not clear who was actually responsible for the banning of *Tempo*. Some said it was Minister of Information Harmoko, others said it was B.J. Habibie, and still others said it had to have been Soeharto himself.[6] Tensions within the magazine that paralleled political conflict on the outside make the question of why the magazine was banned a tendentious one even today.[7]

After *Tempo* was banned for the first time in 1982, its editors developed a policy of "lobbying" various factions within the government. Although this lobbying was done in part to monitor news, it was also intended to facilitate communication with the political elite. While Goenawan Mohamad was chief editor of *Tempo*, no one particular faction was believed to dominate the magazine. According to many observers, however, this perception of neutrality began to change in the early 1990s, especially after

---

[5]   See Goenawan Mohamad, "SIUPP", *Tempo* June 22, 1991.

[6]   Bambang Harymurti believes that Harmoko was the *dalang* or mastermind behind the banning. Interview, June 1, 2000. B.J. Habibie reportedly told several individuals that he hadn't intended to have *Tempo* banned, but that he had instead wanted to sue the magazine. See the interview with Adnan Buyung Nasution cited in Arief Budiman and Olle Törnquist, *Aktor Demokrasi*, p. 129. Yet even if this is true, as the authors point out, Habibie made it clear that he himself wasn't going to do anything about the banning.

[7]   For theories of the banning, see Duncan McCargo, "Killing the Messenger," The 1994 Press Bannings and the Demise of Indonesia's New Order," *Press/Politics* 1:4 (Winter 1999): pp. 29-45.

Goenawan indicated that he wished to retire from his position, and more and more of his daily responsibilities fell to Fikri Jufri.[8] As Bambang Harymurti explained, "the problem is that if this is part of a strategy, then the one on the top should be not on anybody's side. Goenawan was that kind of person. But Fikri was not. So that's what swayed the balance."[9]

To make matters worse, Goenawan Mohamad's announcement in 1993 that he wished to step down as *Tempo*'s chief editor led to a kind of "succession crisis", in that none of the other senior editors had the full support of the rest of the editorial staff. Goenawan's own choice was Washington bureau chief Bambang Harymurti, but in 1993 Bambang was considered to be too junior to lead the magazine. In the plan finally agreed upon by the board of directors, Fikri Jufri was to be appointed chief editor for two years, followed by Yusril Djalinus. After two more years, Bambang Harymurti would replace Yusril. This three-tiered arrangement was unofficial because any formal agreement required the approval of the Minister of Information.[10]

Thus, on the day that *Tempo* was banned, Fikri Jufri was acting chief editor, although Goenawan Mohamad was still legally in charge of the magazine. Fikri Jufri's name had been filed with the Department of Information some months earlier, but there had been a bureaucratic delay. According to longtime press observer Daniel Dhakidae, "the rumor was that the Department of Information, specifically Harmoko, just didn't like Fikri Jufri."[11]

These disputes over personnel within the organization of *Tempo* in the early 1990s were significant because they paralleled what Bambang Harymurti described as a "change of mandarins" that was simultaneously occurring outside the magazine. Acting

---

8   Interview with Salim Said, April 1, 1998. I heard this view repeatedly, including from many *Tempo* alumni.
9   Interview with Bambang Harymurti, March 28, 1998.
10   Interview with Bambang Harymurti, June 1, 2000.
11   Interview with Daniel Dhakidae, February 26, 1998.

chief editor Fikri Jufri was believed to be close to the old mandarins, whereas managing editors Amran Nasution, Herry Komar, and Karni Ilyas were considered to be friendly with the new ones.[12]

This "change of mandarins" has been well documented by Robert Hefner, who bluntly characterized it as Soeharto's "dangerous new policy on Islam." Hefner described the "final phase" of this policy as "based on the idea that the president could best neutralize the growing pro-democracy movement by mobilizing conservative Muslims to his side."[13] Symbolic of this change of policy was Soeharto's willingness to smile upon the creation of ICMI, the Association of Indonesian Muslim Intellectuals that was established in 1990. Headed by Minister of Research and Technology B.J. Habibie, ICMI's very existence signaled a shift towards political Islam. Although ICMI's membership included widely-respected Muslim intellectuals and political activists, Hefner has argued that among these sub-groupings, it was the bureaucratic elite that was the most politically significant:

> Inasmuch as this group was concerned about reform at all, then, the type they had in mind was best expressed in the Indonesianized English phrase popularized by ICMI, *proporsionalisme*. *Proporsionalisme* in government and the economy was to become one of ICMI's most lasting contributions to Indonesian political discourse. For elite Muslims like Habibie, the slogan had an alluring ideological appeal. It clothed their rivalry with secular nationalists for the spoils of state in the garb of a populist struggle for Muslim civil rights.[14]

---

12 Interview with Bambang Harymurti, March 28, 1998.
13 Robert Hefner, *Civil Islam*, p. 167.
14 Robert Hefner, *Civil Islam*, p. 140.

ICMI's chief rivals for the "spoils of state" were Christians and Indonesians of Chinese descent, both considered by conservative Muslims to hold disproportionate power in the New Order political constellation. Loosely grouped together under the term "nationalists", the anti-ICMI group "included secular nationalists; Golkar traditionalists; military nationalists; Christians, Buddhists, and Hindus; secular modernizers; opponents of Habibie's industrial policies; and, most of all, democratic Muslims uneasy with what Abdurrahman Wahid and others regarded as the 'reconfessionalization' of Indonesian society."[15] In the eyes of many supporters of B.J. Habibie, this anti-ICMI group also included *Tempo* magazine.[16]

It is a well-known fact of President Soeharto's leadership style that he frequently played one political faction off against another. Soeharto's creation of and support for what Hefner termed "regimist Muslims" was partly in response to what the president saw as the rising power of the Indonesian armed forces (ABRI) under General Benny Moerdani. In 1988, Soeharto removed Benny Moerdani from the post of ABRI commander-in-chief, and reassigned him to the less important post of Minister of Security and Defense. In 1993, he was removed from this position as well. As Robert Hefner wrote, "most Indonesian observers regarded the president's ICMI initiative…as an effort to balance the president's loss of support among the military with a new base among Muslims."[17] It is within this context that the rumors that Fikri Jufri was "too close to Benny Moerdani" can best be understood. Former *Tempo* managing editor Agus Basri, who shared this perception, explained it this way:

---

[15]   Robert Hefner, *Civil Islam*, p. 142.
[16]   Goenawan Mohamad recalls that after *Tempo* was banned, ICMI intellectual Adi Sarsono was quoted as saying "don't be so naive to defend *Tempo*. " According to Goenawan, "he presumed that *Tempo* was the instrument of Benny Moerdani. And if Muslims defended *Tempo*, then they would defend Benny Moerdani." Interview with Goenawan Mohamad, July 11, 2002.
[17]   Robert Hefner, *Civil Islam*, p. 159.

Under Goenawan's leadership, *Tempo* was neutral. When it was held by Fikri, there was a bias. Benny was always good. You can see that when Benny had a wedding for his daughter, it becomes the cover story. When Benny makes a book, it becomes a cover story. Benny is always in the Pokok dan Tokoh [People] section. It sure looks like Fikri is Benny's man. However at that time Benny was already being sidelined….So Harmoko asks me what is it with Fikri? The point is that Benny is always good, but Habibie is always bad.[18]

Fikri Jufri categorically denies these accusations. "*Tempo* was banned because of a plot," he said. "Habibie comes to Soeharto," he said, as part of a plot to kill *Tempo* "because *Tempo* is an enemy." Nothing infuriates Fikri Jufri more than the persistent rumor that the magazine was banned because of his closeness to Benny Moerdani. According to Fikri, this is "a total lie…Benny never came to our office," he said. "He doesn't even know where our office is! He has nothing to do with us."[19]

As Hefner made clear, Benny Moerdani's opponents – the "Islamic wing" of the military (which included generals Feisal Tanjung, Hartono, Syarwan Hamid and Prabowo) – were not supporters of the variety of Islam embraced by Nahdlatul Ulama or Muhammadiyah, but were rather "animated as much by personal political ambition as any ideological conviction." According to Bambang Harymurti, in 1994 there was already in place a "team" of supporters of B.J. Habibie who were preparing the way for the leader of ICMI to succeed Soeharto as president. It was in their best interest to get Fikri Jufri out of the way.

In the months prior to the banning, there were at least four offers to "topple" acting *Tempo* editor Fikri Jufri. The first offer went to Ciputra, who as a businessman of Chinese descent may

---

[18]   Interview with Agus Basri, July 26, 2000.
[19]   Interview with Fikri Jufri, March 11, 1998.

have been considered vulnerable and therefore more likely to succumb to political pressure. According to Ciputra's long-time friend and associate Harjoko Trisnadi, General Feisal Tanjung had informed the developer during a golf game that "*Tempo* was going to be closed" unless they got rid of Fikri. Ciputra relayed the message to Goenawan, who responded "why should I do this based on a rumor? It's not certain."[20] Although Ciputra may well have been tempted, according to Harjoko he was not about to cross Goenawan.

There were other offers to topple Fikri. Harmoko approached Agus Basri, and Bambang Harymurti and Karni Ilyas received offers as well.[21] Each offer was reported to Goenawan, and each was refused. Yet as Karni Ilyas reportedly asked Goenawan, why jeopardize the magazine just to save one man? Maybe it was better to sacrifice one person than to lose the entire ship. Goenawan said he told Karni that sacrificing even one person was too many.[22]

Thus when *Tempo* decided to do a cover story on the controversial purchase of the thirty-nine war ships in June 1994, even some writers within *Tempo* believed that editor Fikri Jufri was biased against Habibie. For example, managing editor Agus Basri – a critic of Fikri's, and the author of a cover story on Habibie and ICMI that had been published some weeks earlier – said that the articles on the East German ships "had a certain meaning". He recalled the atmosphere in the office when a report came in stating that one of the ships had been struck by a wave and nearly

---

[20]   Interview with Harjoko Trisnadi, June 28, 2000.

[21]   It was Akbar Tanjung who made the offer to Bambang Harymurti. Interview with Bambang Harymurti, June 1, 2000, and interview with Agus Basri, July, 26, 2000. *Tempo*'s own "White Book" describes a meeting that took place two months before *Tempo* was banned in which "a *Tempo* bureau chief was called to a minister's home and given notice that unless Fikri Jufri was removed from the position of chief editor, *Tempo* would be shut down by the government." Interestingly, both Agus Basri and Bambang Harymurti believe that they were the bureau chief in question. Alumni Majalah Tempo, *Buku Putih Tempo*, p. 105.

[22]   Interview with Goenawan Mohamad, June 20, 2000.

sunk during the journey from Germany to Indonesia. "Fikri was there," he said. "When the news came in about the ship sinking, Fikri called out '*Alhamdulillah*!' [Praise be to God]. Isma Sawitri was editing at the time, and was perhaps influenced by him. And indeed, Isma didn't like Habibie either."

Agus added that economics editor Max Wangkar, who wrote the story, also had a problem with Habibie. "He [Max] is a Christian," Agus explained. "He graduated from a school of theology in Maluku."[23] With "analysis" like this, it was clear that the atmosphere within the magazine had become poisonous indeed. Despite Agus' assessment of the situation, at this point neither he nor any of Fikri's other critics within *Tempo* were openly willing to let Harmoko – or anyone else outside the magazine – call the shots. This would change after the banning.

Later, Goenawan Mohamad said that during the entire week of June 21 he had had a sort of premonition that something bad was about to happen. Goenawan was at Jakarta's Soekarno-Hatta airport when he heard the news that *Tempo* had been banned. On his way to Central Java, where he was going to visit the grave of his father, he immediately returned to *Tempo*'s office in Kuningan.

At the office, everything was in turmoil. Fikri Jufri called an impromptu press conference, and the newsroom erupted into cheers when he told a television reporter "it's a violation of the Basic Press Law." Fikri challenged the statement of the Director General of Press and Graphics that *Tempo* had received six written warnings, three stern warnings, and thirty-three oral warnings from the Department of Information. "From where is he counting," Fikri demanded, "since *Tempo* began to publish?"[24]

A stream of faxes poured into the newsroom. People said it was as if someone had died, with friends and family making the obligatory

---

23   Interview with Agus Basri, July 26, 2000.
24   "Pemerintah Batalkan SIUPP '*Tempo*', '*Editor*' dan '*Detik*'", *Kompas*, June 22, 1994.

visits during the twenty-four-hour period of mourning before a burial. In Yogyakarta, art students wrapped *Tempo*'s bureau in white paper, the traditional color of mourning. Yogya bureau chief Rustam F. Mandayun later recalled that although the wrapping made it difficult to work – the windows had to be kept shut and it was very hot – no one tried to removed the shroud.

In the elite circle of Jakarta's senior editors, there was recognition as well as sadness. Aristides Katoppo, whose own newspaper *Sinar Harapan* had been banned in 1986, warned Goenawan not to act too hastily; he knew all too well that if *Tempo* were to return to publication there would have to be sacrificial lambs. Atmakusumah, the former managing editor of *Indonesia Raya* – who had been personally banned from working in Indonesian media since his paper was shut down in 1974 – likewise knew the sorrow and frustration that comes with a press banning. It was not only the loss of one's livelihood, but also the knowledge that the Indonesian people had lost another independent source of information.[25]

But among the younger journalists there was not just sorrow, there was anger. When the government-sponsored Indonesian Journalists' Association (PWI) issued a statement saying that it could "understand" the decision to ban the three magazines, this anger erupted. On June 22, as Minister Harmoko appealed for "introspection" from all sides, hundreds of journalists and activists took to the street, marching to the Department of Information and demanding that the ban against the three publications be revoked. When their demands to meet with officials were turned down, organizers staged an even bigger protest for the next day.[26]

---

[25] Atmakusumah learned that he had been banned from working in the Indonesian media directly from the Director General of Television, Film and Radio. At the time he was working as the senior press assistant at the United States Information Service in Jakarta. Interview with Atmakusumah, June 21, 2003.

[26] "Hundreds protest against press bans", *The Jakarta Post*, June 23, 1994. Many observers have pointed out that the English language *Jakarta Post* was often more *berani* or courageous in its coverage of such events than was the Indonesian language press, perhaps because of its limited and elite readership.

Riot police clash with demonstrators protesting the banning of
Tempo, *Detik*, and *Editor*, 1994. [Donny Metri]

Andreas Harsono, the former editor of *Pantau* magazine and a
founder of ISAI (Institute for the Study of the Free Flow of
Information) remembers that for the two weeks after the banning
there were meetings nearly every night – many in his own house.[27]
Whereas the PWI urged that the government quickly issue new
permits to publish so that the journalists who had been affected
by the bannings would be able to work again, it was well
understood that this would constitute a government hijacking of
the three publications.[28]

The most violent demonstration occurred on Monday, June
27, when riot police broke up a group of peaceful demonstrators
who were marching towards the Department of Information.[29]
Many of the demonstrators were badly injured, including the
painter Semsar Siahaan, whose leg was broken. Others suffered
bruises and head injuries. About thirty-two people were arrested.
One of those arrested was the poet and dramatist W.S. Rendra.

The brutality of the attack on the demonstrators had a
profound effect on Goenawan Mohamad. "Goenawan was

---

27   Interview with Andreas Harsono, July 16, 1998.
28   "SPS Imbau, 3 Media yang Dibatalkan SIUPP-nya Bisa Diterbitkan Kembali",
      Kompas, June 23, 1994.
29   "Police Club Protestors in Jakarta", *International Herald Tribune*, June 28, 1994.

shocked," said Arief Budiman, his best friend since their student days. "And I think in a sense there is a guilty feeling. Because before, I think he looked at all this activism of students as being *hura-hura* [commotion]....I think he was very moved when he saw it was the students and these young people who struggled to defend him when the others ran away."[30]

Whether it was shock or guilt or amazement at the sacrifice his defenders were willing to make, Goenawan knew he had to fight the banning. "When I saw my friends being beaten," he said, "and when I saw students being beaten, that was when I decided the path I was going to take."[31]

"It was dramatically different," Arief concluded. "Goenawan became very bitter against the government. Before he was more compromising. [Afterwards] he will oppose the government, whatever the cost."

While demonstrations protesting the banning were taking place in the streets of Jakarta and elsewhere, there were also furious behind the scenes maneuvers – both on the part of *Tempo* and on the part of government officials. Five days after the banning, Goenawan Mohamad learned of an offer to "save" *Tempo*. It came from Colonel Prabowo Subianto, the son-in-law of President Soeharto. The offer grew out of a meeting that developed in the same way that many things happen in Indonesia – by coincidence. It began at the five-star Jakarta Hilton, where Goenawan and his wife were attending a wedding. Many of their other friends were there, including Fikri Jufri and Susanto Pudjomartono, who was then chief editor of *The Jakarta Post*. After the reception they decided to stay for dinner in the Taman Sari Restaurant. On the way out, they ran into publisher Eric Samola, who had been attending a meeting in the Lagoon Tower, a different part of the

---

[30]   Interview with Arief Budiman, December 6, 1999.
[31]   Interview with Goenawan Mohamad, April 17, 1998.

hotel. The meeting had been called by Hashim Djojohadikusumo at the behest of his brother, Colonel Prabowo Subianto. Involved with the hard-line Indonesian Committee for Solidarity with the Muslim World (KISDI), Prabowo "was well-known for his hatred of the Catholic General Benny Moerdani."[32] Hashim had invited Samola, director Harjoko Trisnadi, and assistant director Mahtum Mastoem to hear the colonel's offer.

After the accidental encounter in the lobby of the Hilton, the group agreed to call a midnight meeting at Goenawan Mohamad's house. With the exception of Fikri Jufri, all of the directors of Grafiti Pers were present at this second meeting. "We pretended to go home, and then we called each other," Goenawan explained. "We didn't want to make Fikri panicky."[33]

There was good reason to be panicky. During the five days that had elapsed since *Tempo* was banned, the board of directors had been waiting for the government to make its move. Ordinarily when newspapers were banned in Indonesia, the Department of Information issued a new SIUPP to a reconstituted publication – usually with a different chief editor and reconfigured ownership. Often the paper was forced to accept a different name. As Aristides Katoppo, the editor of *Sinar Harapan*, explained, "it's a different version of the so-called mysterious killings. Same thing. There is no mystery, but it creates, intimidates the process. And so that is part of the intent, especially if, as in this case, it also involves the military."[34]

The directors of Grafiti Pers were well aware of the precedents. Aristides Katoppo said that he had personally sought out Goenawan to share his own experience with the 1986 banning of his newspaper

---

[32] Prabowo had been active in organizing civilian vigilantes in East Timor against the pro-independence movement, and after 1989 was one of the architects of the violence against Acehnese rebels. For these and other details of Prabowo's activities as a backer of the "regimist Muslim campaign against the pro-democracy movement," see Robert Hefner, *Civil Islam*, pp. 201-2.

[33] Interview with Goenawan Mohamad, July 11, 2002.

[34] Interview with Aristides Katoppo, May 4, 1998.

Sinar Harapan. He explained that the essential questions were how do you get a new license, and what kinds of sacrifices do you make? In his own case, Aristides said, "my intention was to keep the means of expression, the newspaper, alive. I was sufficiently realistic and pragmatic to know that I had to pay a price. The price was that heads would roll. It was my head."

And then there was the issue of the name. As Indonesians of Chinese descent had discovered at the very beginning of the New Order, there was no faster or more humiliating way to lose your identity than to be forced to change your name. It was a lesson that the Soeharto government had learned well. Again, according to Aristides:

> They asked us to give five different names. Okay, the first name is *Sinar Harapan* [Ray of Hope], the second name is *Sinar Harapan*, the third name is *Sinar Harapan*, the fourth and fifth – *Sinar Harapan*. That's five no's. Well, we try again. *Suara Harapan* [Voice of Hope]. I tried to have the initials S. H. in it. Again, no, there may be no *Sinar* [Ray] in it and no *Harapan* [Hope]. So at one stage finally we reached the name *Suara Pembaruan* [Voice of Renewal].

Measured against the standard of what had happened to *Sinar Harapan*, Hashim's offer to the directors of Grafiti Pers could even be seen as "generous". As Goenawan recalled, "*Tempo* could be published again under the same name, whereas normally they wouldn't under the new law. But there were two conditions. First they would have the right to decide the people on the editorial board, and second they would have the first option to buy the shares when *Tempo* was going to sell."

"They understood nothing about the press law," he concluded. "They wanted to control *Tempo*."

Hashim had given them a deadline of 8:00 in the morning, and at 4 AM they sent back their answer. The decision was unanimous:

they would refuse the offer. Was there much discussion? "No," said Goenawan. "It was clear I was very strong. By then I realized that we had to fight this government." But why had Eric Samola, Ciputra's representative on the board, agreed to refuse the offer? Goenawan still doesn't know the answer to that question. "It was surprising," he said. "To me he was a hero that night."[35]

Prabowo did not give up so easily. According to Goenawan, after the meeting with Hashim failed to produce results, Prabowo then tried a different approach: a secret offer to *Tempo* director Yusril Djalinus. The idea was that Yusril would replace Fikri Jufri as chief editor of the new magazine. "You see Yusril was not visible," Goenawan explained. "He is the man who organized the whole thing. The organization man. He created the system. But he was invisible, behind the scenes, and so they thought he would be available because he was not perceived to be ideological. Yusril was never an activist. So that's why he was invited by Prabowo. Prabowo thought that it would be very easy to buy Yusril." But Yusril refused to be bought. "He's a man of integrity," said Goenawan.[36]

Amran Nasution, the former national editor of *Tempo* and someone who was close to Prabowo, was the midwife of this second attempt to take over the magazine.[37] According to Agus Basri, in the middle of these negotiations Prabowo called Amran and cancelled the whole thing. Why? "Because President Soeharto wouldn't permit it. Later it was believed that the president's family was going to get involved. They would take charge of *Tempo*."

For whatever the reason, it was clear that the government's tactics had changed. The matter was now in the hands of Bob Hasan, a close friend of President Soeharto.[38] Many Indonesians

---

[35] Interview with Goenawan Mohamad, June 20, 2000.

[36] Interview with Goenawan Mohamad, October 10, 1998. Yusril is also a man of great modesty. Although he was unfailingly helpful to me with regard to many other matters, he was very reluctant to answer questions about this particular incident.

[37] Interview with Agus Basri, July 26, 2000.

[38] Quoted in Alumni Majalah Tempo, *Buku Putih Tempo*, p. 125.

derisively referred to Bob Hasan as *raja hutan*, or "king of the forest" because of his monopoly over the plywood concession. It is likely that one factor in the president's decision was the upcoming APEC [Asia-Pacific Economic Cooperation] conference, which was scheduled to be held in Jakarta in November. In testimony before Parliament on June 29, 1994, Minister of Information Harmoko had said that he would give new SIUPPs to the journalists and non-editorial employees of *Tempo*, *Detik*, and *Editor*.[39] Many people believed that it would be embarrassing for the Soeharto government not to have resolved the issue of the bannings before the APEC meeting began. Rumor had it that the president was concerned enough to hire an American consulting firm to handle the public relations for the meeting.

It was at this point that Goenawan Mohamad developed a new strategy. *Tempo* would appoint two teams of negotiators. One, the board of directors' team, was charged with finding a new investor. It consisted of Herry Komar, Mahtum Mastoem, and Lukman Setiawan. The second team, "team five", represented the employees and was made up of Bambang Bujono, Isma Sawitri, Toriq Hadad, Yopie Hidayat, and Bambang Harymurti. The employees' team had been democratically elected, and was charged with trying to get a license for a new magazine with a different name.

Because Goenawan believed it was inevitable that *Tempo* would be taken over, he used the two teams to buy as much time as possible. His plan was to prolong the negotiations until November, so that they would run into the APEC meeting and thus embarrass Soeharto. "Because once you fail," he explained, "you cannot protract the negotiations. And the theory was that in November they had to publish something, so there was this protracted war of negotiations so that no magazine would emerge. This is why we decided to pay everybody full salary."[40] Grafiti Pers paid full salaries to 350 employees between June, 1994 and the end of October,

---

[39]   Alumni Majalah Tempo, *Mengapa Kami Menggugat.* p. 28.
[40]   Interview with Goenawan Mohamad, June 20, 2000.

and then additional "severance pay". For those who had been with the magazine for more than ten years, the amount totaled twenty million rupiah ($9,000) plus bonuses.[41]

When asked how the matter got in the hands of Bob Hasan, Goenawan was quick to reply. "By Soeharto," he said. Goenawan believes that Habibie went to Soeharto for advice on how to solve the *Tempo* problem, "maybe because Ciputra had pushed him." Ciputra went to Habibie because he was afraid that he would lose his business, and then Habibie forced Ciputra to negotiate with Bob Hasan. "To me it was a betrayal [for Ciputra] to negotiate with [Bob Hasan] independent of us," Goenawan said. "And a month later you have this *Gatra*. Even the name *Gatra* was given by Soeharto."[42] According to Goenawan, the government's plan was that everyone should enter the new magazine. "So that they could tell the world that it was banned, but bad elements were kicked out. It's *Tempo*. That's their theory."[43]

Harjoko Trisnadi confirmed Goenawan's account, although he emphasized that Ciputra went to Bob Hasan as a representative of Yayasan Jaya Raya – the former owner of *Tempo*. "Ciputra felt that he had been present at the founding of *Tempo*," Harjoko said, "that he had provided capital for *Tempo*, and that he had suffered a loss. He therefore felt he had a right to obtain a new SIUPP."[44]

---

[41] "Sharing out the '*Tempo*' family fortune", *The Jakarta Post*, June 18, 1995. According to Bambang Harymurti, the people who joined *Gatra* received a double bonus because they received compensation from *Tempo* in addition to their new salaries. "For the people who didn't join *Gatra* it was really frustrating," he said. Interview with Bambang Harymurti, March 28, 1998.

[42] Interview with Goenawan Mohamad, April 17, 1998.

[43] Interview with Goenawan Mohamad, June 20, 2000.

[44] Interview with Harjoko Trisnadi, June 28, 2000. Harjoko went on to explain that ultimately Bob Hasan double-crossed Ciputra. "At the time of publication, there were only two shareholders, Bob Hasan and Ciputra. Ciputra represented the Jaya Raya Foundation as the former owner of *Tempo*. And in fact, actually at the very beginning of the company, Ciputra's shares were bigger than Bob Hasan's. But afterwards because the role of Bob Hasan was very strong, little by little Ciputra's shares were reduced for various reasons. And Ciputra could do nothing about it. Finally he had only 20%."

In July, the board of director's team also reached an agreement with Bob Hasan. A meeting of all *Tempo* employees was then called at the *Tempo* offices in Kuningan, and about three hundred people participated. The atmosphere was heated, and the discussion emotional. When the group finally took a vote, about 70% decided to join the new magazine.[45] As *Gatra*'s new chief editor Herry Komar later told *The Jakarta Post*, "we need to reassess the meaning of idealism."[46]

For each former *Tempo* employee the decision of whether to join with *Gatra* was personal, and in many cases, wrenching. Some argued that idealism only went so far if you had no platform from which to express your views. As Agus Basri said he told Toriq Hadad, "if you don't join *Gatra*, what can you possibly do? When Soeharto falls, it will be I who will bring him down."[47] Others joined for financial or other pragmatic reasons. Perhaps they felt that they had already hit a "glass ceiling" at *Tempo*, and that *Gatra* would open new opportunities for professional advancement.

Despite accusations from some *Tempo* alumni that *Gatra* was "living off the corpses of others" and counter-accusations that those who refused to join *Gatra* were "putting on airs" by claiming to be more idealistic and democratic than everyone else, most ex-*Tempo* employees were surprisingly forgiving of their friends who had made a different choice.[48] Of the directors of P.T. Pikatan,

---

[45] Goenawan Mohamad freed all non-editorial staff to go to the new magazine. Bambang Harymurti explained that the future of the non-editorial staff had been Goenawan's nightmare. "They were overpaid according to the market at that time," he said, "and they had nothing to do with what had happened. So *Gatra* was a good place to release that responsibility, and to make your enemy pay for your struggle." Interview with Bambang Harymurti, October 11, 1998.

[46] "After a year, where have they all gone?", *The Jakarta Post*, June 18, 1995.

[47] Interview with Agus Basri, July 26, 2000.

[48] For example, Choirul was one of the non-editorial staff who did not join *Gatra*. At the time of the banning, he was paid about one million rupiah a month, which he said was plenty to live on, even enough to buy a new book each month for his small daughter. But when the directors' team presented the plan for the new magazine, Choirul said that he couldn't join an organization headed by Bob Hasan. His wife (a teacher) and their extended families agreed with his decision. Despite

Goenawan's company, only Harjoko Trisnadi went to *Gatra*. Goenawan said that Harjoko once told him that he joined *Gatra* because Ciputra had pressured him. "If you are ethnic Chinese you live in fear," Goenawan said.[49]

In the end, forty former journalists and a number of non-editorial employees – including five office boys – decided not to join the new magazine. Shortly thereafter they established their own company, P.T. Reksa Mitra Berjaya (RMB), in a rented house in Tebet, South Jakarta. By January 1995, there were 110 shareholders in the cooperative firm.[50] Grafiti Pers paid for the house and sold them all the equipment they needed "on credit and at a very good discount" before the remainder was sold at public auction. As Bambang Bujono, who would later become the chief editor of *D & R* magazine explained, "one side went to *Gatra* and compromised with government, and one side – we're the diaspora. It's like the Palestinians, we're the diaspora."

Each of the members of P.T. RMB agreed to donate between 25 and 40% of his or her earnings to the association, although some contributed far more.[51] One of their first jobs was to work as "fixers" for American television reporters during the November APEC conference. Other activities included publishing daily bulletins for the Jakarta Stock Exchange, and designing covers for *SWA*, the economic magazine that was partially owned by Grafiti Pers.

---

the financial loss, Choirul said that he personally never saw the people who joined *Gatra* as enemies. In his view, they had to live with their own burden of guilt, and it was not up to him to judge others for making the decisions they did. Interview, July 22, 2000. For criticism of the *Gatra* group, see "Jika Kelak *Tempo* Terbit Lagi", *Tiras*, December 7, 1995.

[49] Interview with Goenawan Mohamad, July 11, 2002.

[50] Bambang Harymurti explained that 110 was the number of *Tempo* employees from all over Indonesia who refused to join *Gatra* – and many of those who found full-time employment elsewhere also joined Tebet. "Everyone was on the payroll, but they were only paid a token amount. For them it was more a symbol of solidarity than a financial aid." Email correspondence, August 3, 2002.

[51] Bambang Harymurti, for example, donated his entire monthly billing of six and a half million rupiah to P.T. RMB. His monthly "salary" from the Tebet group was Rp. 2 million. Interview, March 28, 1998.

By far the biggest contract for P.T. RMB came from Surya Paloh's P.T. Surya Persindo Group, the publisher of *Media Indonesia* newspaper. Surya Paloh had offered to hire the ex-*Tempo* journalists to produce a Sunday edition of the paper. He did this because, as Bambang Harymurti put it, he had once "been in the same boat."

> He wanted to help out. For instance he wanted to make sure that Goenawan would not be blacklisted by providing space for him to write on the cultural…less political side. To keep Goenawan alive as a writer, because he was worried that the government is very smart at making you a non-existent person. I think that *Media Indonesia* was one of the first Indonesian media that printed his articles.[52]

But the involvement of the Tebet group with Surya Paloh was not without controversy. Surya Paloh was born in Aceh, the son of a police officer. In the 1960s, he was the founder and chair of the Medan branch of KAPPI, the anti-Soekarno, anti-Communist youth organization. He became a Golkar activist in the 1970s, and after the 1977 election was appointed to the MPR (People's Consultative Assembly). After making a fortune in the catering business, he turned to publishing – establishing the daily paper *Prioritas* in 1985. Despite Surya Paloh's connections with prominent political and business leaders, including Soeharto's son Bambang Trihatmojo, the Department of Information revoked *Prioritas*'s permit to publish in 1987.[53] In November, 1992, Surya Paloh wrote to the Supreme Court requesting a judicial review of the ministerial regulations that enabled the Department of Information to withdraw a publication's SIUPP. The Court ultimately rejected Surya Paloh's request, claiming

---

[52] Interview with Bambang Harymurti, March 28, 1998.
[53] These and other details of the Media Indonesia/Surya Persindo Group can be found in David Hill, *The Press in New Order Indonesia*, pp. 91-97.

that "appropriate procedures had not been followed," but his challenge forced such procedures to be established. Surya Paloh had thus paved the way for *Tempo*'s lawsuit against the Department of Information in 1994.[54]

The concern of many in the Tebet group was that Surya Paloh was too close to "Cendana", or President Soeharto's family, because of his business connections with Bambang Trihatmojo's Bimantara group.[55] To assuage these fears, Surya Paloh himself called Goenawan Mohamad and invited the ex-*Tempo* group to work for *Media Indonesia*.

"He called me, and said he was interested in *Tempo* journalists," Goenawan remembered, "because he wanted to make his newspaper good. I said the only person who should take it is Bambang, and then I can support it."

"He's rather crazy but charmingly crazy," Goenawan added. "And of course he liked me because I defended his position when he went to the court, challenging Harmoko."[56]

Because of these concerns, the Tebet group initially set up a complicated contractual arrangement with Surya Paloh. Although the ex-*Tempo* journalists wanted the deal to be "company to company", Surya Paloh wanted "persons." So they devised a middle ground. The first twenty people were hired as individuals, but as Bambang Harymurti explained, "their friends in Tebet knew that this was just a scheme in order to get a job. And because of that we were given a personal account by *Media Indonesia*. Everyone gave the password to the [Tebet] treasurer, so they would never accept the money directly from *Media Indonesia*. The treasurer would take it out and put it in the big fund and then distribute it."[57]

---

[54]   David Hill, *The Press in New Order Indonesia*, p. 51.
[55]   David Hill describes media industry speculation that Bimantara was an investor in Surya Persindo in *The Press in New Order Indonesia*, pp. 101-103.
[56]   Interview with Goenawan Mohamad, April 17, 1998.
[57]   Interview with Bambang Harymurti, October 11, 1998.

By September, Surya Paloh had grown tired of this arrangement and wanted full-time employees. Bambang said, "he gave me an ultimatum, either you take the job as executive editor, or we cut off this contract. And at that time *Media Indonesia* was the biggest source of income we had." The Tebet group put it to a vote, and decided to accept a compromise, which was that Bambang Harymurti and two others would take full-time jobs at *Media Indonesia*, thereby enabling the rest of the Tebet group to retain their status as independent contractors. Bambang recalls that he told his friends, "if I accept the position, I am a professional too. It doesn't mean that I will just sit there, I have to do a job. So that's what happened."[58]

"Surya taught me a lot," Bambang added. "He taught me how always to be a moving target. And he taught me that if somebody wants to shoot you, make sure they are afraid that if they miss, they will shoot somebody powerful by mistake."[59]

One of Surya Paloh's more audacious acts was his offer to hire journalists who had joined AJI, the Alliance of Independent Journalists. AJI was founded on August 7, 1994 as a direct result of the banning of *Tempo*. Part journalists' association and part "independent media union", AJI would eventually come to play a major role in the development of a free and independent press in Indonesia. But in 1994 it was outlawed because it violated the ministerial declaration that said there would be only one journalists' association in Indonesia. That organization was PWI, and membership in it was compulsory. Founding member Andreas Harsono explained the relationship between the banning of *Tempo* and the creation of AJI:

> We were angry. Really angry. And I suppose that we all became
> more angry after the PWI issued a statement saying that it could

---

58   Interview with Bambang Harymurti, March 28, 1998.
59   Interview with Bambang Harymurti, October 11, 1998.

understand the banning. We said what kind of organization is this? So we went to the PWI, it was a few days after that statement, and we give them a deadline until the 4th of August. On the 4th of August we went there again, had our protest, and they didn't want to confront the mission statement, and we set up AJI on August 7.

Tempo owned a villa in near the small town of Sirnagalih, in the hills of West Java near Puncak Pass. The group of journalists who gathered there on August 7 signed a declaration that became known as the "Sirnagalih Declaration".[60] It said in part, "[Because] freedom of speech, access to information, and freedom of association [are] the basic rights of all citizens…we reject all kinds of interference, intimidation, censorship and media bans which deny freedom of speech and open access to information."[61] There were fifty-eight signatories, including Goenawan Mohamad, Fikri Jufri, Aristides Katoppo, Arief Budiman, Toriq Hadad, and Bambang Harymurti.

Government condemnation of AJI was harsh. In March, 1995, PWI Secretary General Parni Hadi announced that signing the Sirnagalih Declaration was grounds for expulsion from PWI. Eighteen signatories, including many from *Tempo*, were expelled.[62] Even worse, PWI urged that all members of AJI not be permitted

---

[60] It was Andreas Harsono who proposed that the signatories call it the Sirnagalih declaration. As he explained, "It is a Sundanese word. *Sirna* means fading away, *Galih* means your physical body. It's like your body, your physical emotions have faded away and you are living beyond life." Andreas says that he also proposed the name of the Alliance of Independent Journalists, as "*aji*" means mantra. Interview with Andreas Harsono, July 16, 1998.

[61] A full statement of the Sirnagalih Declaration can be found at www.indopubs.com.

[62] When I asked Bambang Harymurti how he was able to become executive editor of *Media Indonesia* if he had signed the Sirnagalih Declaration, he explained that although he signed the first draft of the statement, he had to leave early to attend his nephew's birthday celebration. They then changed the draft and asked people to sign it again. "So my name's there but my signature is not, and that created ambiguity. The PWI could not fire me because there was no signature, and yet my name was there." This ambiguity was, however, enough to prevent Harmoko from

to work in any kind of press business.[63] It was at this point that Surya Paloh made the rather surprising announcement that he would "open the door" to anyone who had joined AJI. "Of course he didn't advertise," Bambang said, "but he said you can tell everyone, any AJI who does not have a job, you can tell them to come to me and I will give them a job." But that was a problem, Bambang added, since "most AJI people didn't want to work for him because he has this link to the president."[64]

While AJI was challenging the morality of the PWI's claim to "represent" all Indonesian journalists, on September 7, 1994, Goenawan Mohamad and forty-three ex-*Tempo* journalists were challenging the legality of Harmoko's withdrawal of their SIUPP by filing suit against the Department of Information in Jakarta State Administrative Court. They claimed that the ministerial decree permitting the Department of Information to withdraw *Tempo*'s permit to publish violated the Basic Press Law.[65] It was the first time in Indonesian history that any banned publication had challenged such an act by suing the Department of Information.

Goenawan Mohamad has always said that the idea of taking the Department of Information to court was Bambang Harymurti's.[66] Although *Tempo*'s senior editors admitted privately that they had little hope of winning, they believed it was important to demonstrate that they had pursued every possible legal channel. This was also the reason why one day prior to the filing of the lawsuit, a separate group of ex-*Tempo* journalists applied to the Department of Information for a license to publish a new magazine to be called *Opini*. As team leader Bambang Bujono later explained,

---

accepting his name as chief editor of *Media Indonesia*. Interview with Bambang Harymurti, March 28, 1998.

[63] Alumni Majalah *Tempo, Mengapa Kami Menggugat*, p. 7.
[64] Interview with Bambang Harymurti, October 11, 1998.
[65] See "Goenawan Mohammad Gugat Menteri Penerangan ke PTUN", *Kompas*, September 8, 1994.
[66] Interview with Goenawan Mohamad, February 9, 1998.

in order to get a license, the group needed letters of support from both the PWI and SPS, the Newspaper Publishers' Association. "We got the permission from the SPS," Bambang Bujono said, "but we didn't get permission from PWI. Of course we didn't get permission from the government either, but we knew at the beginning that this would happen. What we wanted was to prove that the government didn't want us."[67]

Testimony in the trial began on February 2, 1995, and ended on March 9.[68] The key issue in the lawsuit was that the withdrawal of *Tempo*'s SIUPP amounted to a *defacto* banning, thereby violating the Basic Press Law that stated explicitly that bannings were not permitted. A secondary issue was that the Department of Information had not followed its own regulations: the Press Council had not approved of the decision to withdraw the licenses of the three banned publications.

On May 3, 1995, to the astonishment of most observers, the Jakarta State Administrative Court decided in favor of Goenawan Mohamad and the former *Tempo* employees. Benjamin Mangkoedilaga, the head of a panel of three judges, ruled that the Department of Information's decision to revoke *Tempo*'s SIUPP contradicted the Press Law, and he ordered Harmoko to reissue the license. The decision was greeted with jubilation, as *Tempo*'s friends joined with other pro-reform elements in congratulating the three judges on their independence and the victory of the rule of law. Theoretically, at least, *Tempo* was free to publish again.[69]

The Department of Information quickly appealed the decision. Although Benjamin Mangkoedilaga's ruling was upheld

---

[67] Interview with Bambang Bujono, February 23, 1998.

[68] For a complete account of the lawsuit, including statements from many of the individuals involved as well as transcripts of what was said in court, see Alumni Majalah Tempo, *Mengapa Kami Menggugat*.

[69] For details, see the cover story in *Forum Keadilan*, May 25, 1995. At the time, *Forum Keadilan* was partially owned by Grafiti Pers.

Goenawan Mohamad after the reading of the Supreme Court decision, 1996. [*Tempo*]

by the State Administrative High Court, on June 13, 1996, the Supreme Court overturned the earlier decision. In a ruling that surprised no one, the Supreme Court decreed that the Department of Information's withdrawal of *Tempo*'s Permit to Publish had been lawful. The banning of *Tempo* would stand. Even the otherwise cautious Indonesian press pointed out that in this instance political factors had obviously trumped legal ones.

According to *The Jakarta Post*'s account, the reading of the Supreme Court verdict attracted a crowd of about one thousand people.[70] Stepping outside the courtroom, Goenawan Mohamad was immediately thronged by journalists. Wearing a white shirt, black armband, and *peci* (a fez-like hat), Goenawan Mohamad raised his arms and declared, "For me, the struggle for freedom of the press by legal means ends here. Now the struggle must take another form."[71]

In truth, the struggle by other means had already begun.

---

[70]   "'*Tempo*' ban declared lawful", *The Jakarta Post*, June 14, 1996.

[71]   "*Bagi saya, perjuangan ke arah kebebasan pers menurut hukum sudah selesai sampai di sini. Kini tinggal perjuangan lain.*" Quoted in "Enak Dibaca dan Berakhir di Kasasi", *Umat*, July 8, 1996.

Early in October 2004, Goenawan Mohamad had approached Andreas Harsono with the idea of establishing a *lembaga perjuangan*, or an institution to engage in political struggle. At the time, Andreas was working at *The Jakarta Post*. The son of a Chinese-Indonesian businessman from Jember, East Java, Andreas was a serious young man with a degree in electrical engineering and a passion for integrity in journalism. Although Andreas had been working as a journalist for longer than the probationary period required to join the PWI, for political reasons he had managed not to join. In October, *The Jakarta Post* appointed Andreas to a team assigned to cover the APEC conference, but the PWI secretariat rejected Andreas' application. As Andreas explained, "After the establishment of the Alliance of Independent Journalists, PWI increased the pressure and asked editors to make sure that every journalist in their organization joined PWI."[72] Shortly thereafter he was fired by *The Jakarta Post*. The next day Goenawan asked Andreas to join him in establishing ISAI.

Andreas remembers that Goenawan told him of his concern that the Alliance of Independent Journalists was "too fired up", that "it would lose its energy." Like the *pemuda* or youth organizations of the revolutionary period, AJI was full of fire, but lacked discipline. According to Andreas, Goenawan Mohamad said "we need another place to channel money and spread the struggle."[73]

Goenawan recalls that he had decided to ask Andreas to join him after seeing his dedication in establishing the Alliance of Independent Journalists. "I was really moved by AJI," Goenawan said. "One day I went to their office, in the *kampung*, and they were frying these nuts, and I said what are you doing? 'To celebrate Lebaran [the end of Ramadhan].' They didn't have money. Their office was so tiny. But their commitment!"[74]

---

[72]   Interview with Andreas Harsono, July 16, 1998.
[73]   Interview with Andreas Harsono, July 5, 1999.
[74]   Interview with Goenawan Mohamad, July 11, 2002.

Goenawan Mohamad knew that he needed good organizers as well as good fighters. His plan for ISAI was bold and unprecedented. The goal was to build an institution dedicated to *perjuangan* [struggle], but one that would also endure. The student movement of the 1960s had taught Goenawan that real change took both organization and hard-headed planning. "We believed that things would change with the New Order," he said. "But we were naive to expect that kind of thing would happen under a military type regime." In April, 1998 – one month before Soeharto resigned – Goenawan told me "as long as you are not in power you don't change things. That's why my idea of democratic change in this country is not dependent on what the students have been doing. It will depend on how organized the opposition is. And that's why I'm helping it."[75]

In December, 1994, Goenawan called a meeting at the restaurant Koi in the Blok M area of South Jakarta. He invited journalists and intellectuals Fikri Jufri, Aristides Katoppo, Mochtar Pabottingi, M. Dahana, and Andreas Harsono, and explained that he wanted to set up a foundation. When Aristides suggested that they include people from outside Jakarta, the others agreed, and they invited Ashadi Siregar of Yogyakarta and Sunjaya of Radio Mara Bandung to join them. Dahana declined to participate. After the first meeting, Andreas and Toriq Hadad were asked to prepare the plans for the foundation. The legal document creating ISAI was signed in January 1995.[76]

The biggest funder of ISAI was the U.S. Agency for International Development (USAID). Goenawan Mohamad says it was Arief Budiman who first introduced him to Mark Johnson, who was at that time the USAID Program Officer for non-governmental organizations at the American Embassy. "Mark Johnson is very daring," Goenawan said. "I didn't know him before."[77]

---

[75] Interview with Goenawan Mohamad, April 17, 1998.
[76] Email correspondence with Andreas Harsono, July 9, 2002.
[77] Interview with Goenawan Mohamad, October 10, 1998.

Today Mark Johnson is retired from USAID. A former Peace Corps worker, Johnson is a tall man with iron-grey hair and a relaxed demeanor that supports his ISAI friends' characterization of him as a "former hippie". He fondly remembers "cutting his teeth" on pioneer projects in South Africa that emphasized the "advocacy side" of developing civil society.

Johnson describes his first meeting with Goenawan Mohamad as being a bit surreal. Someone had arranged for them to meet at the "Big Boy" restaurant near *Tempo*'s former office on Jl. Rasuna Said. "There was even the boy with the big burger out front," Johnson chuckled. "I didn't know Goenawan and he didn't know me. I got the feeling that he was uncomfortable. He was under a lot of stress, strain."

From the perspective of the American government, the most difficult aspect of funding "indigenous NGOs" is identifying organizations that have the history, accounting procedures, and organizational structure necessary to meet American standards of accountability. According to Johnson, once it became apparent that ISAI's biggest problem would be meeting USAID's financial requirements, "Goenawan put in some of his own money, and they ran a number of transactions. They used all the books and accounting of *Tempo*," he said. The man who kept the books at ISAI was Zulkifly Lubis, one of the founders of *Tempo* and also a member of ISAI's board of directors. Goenawan describes Zulkifly as both an "activist" and "someone who could fight."[78]

From Johnson's perspective, the ISAI people proved to be excellent administrators. "I've done these kinds of grants all over the world," Mark Johnson said, "but ISAI was the "fastest and most capable one in terms of getting themselves organized

[78] Interview with Goenawan Mohamad, July 11, 2002. ISAI's board consisted of six members from *Tempo* and five non-*Tempo*. The six from *Tempo* were Goenawan Mohamad, Fikri Jufri, Yusril Djalinius, Zulkifly Lubis, Toriq Hadad, and Bina Bektiati. The five non-*Tempo* were Aristides Katoppo, Ashadi Siregar, Sunjaya, Mochtar Pabottingi, and Andreas Harsono.

financially and programmatically. I think we really did put the whole thing together in two months. They came from nowhere both programmatically and financially."[79]

In March of 1995, at about the same time that Goenawan and his lieutenants were meeting regularly with Mark Johnson, the government launched a systematic attack on AJI. The PWI formally expelled the eighteen of its members who had signed the Sirnagalih Declaration. The Department of Information banned AJI's newsletter *Independen* for publishing without a license, and the police raided AJI's Halal Bihalal ceremony at the Hotel Wisata International in Central Jakarta. Three people were arrested. Two of the detainees were former *Tempo* journalists Ahmad Taufik and Eko Maryadi. The third, Danang Kukuh Wardoyo, was an office boy at AJI's office. Ahmad Taufik and Eko Maryadi were each sentenced to three years in prison; Danang was sentenced to eighteen months.[80]

There were several connections between the clampdown on AJI and the establishment of ISAI. The most obvious was, as Goenawan Mohamad explained, the "lessons" they learned on how to operate underground publications. "It was the first time in history that we had such a well-organized underground media," he said. "I can claim that we did very well, because I knew that people in the intelligence community wanted to infiltrate, and they never did."[81] Equally significant was the fact that much of Jakarta – including the police – believed that it was AJI that was somehow responsible for the underground news services that began

[79] Interview with Mark Johnson, August 15, 2002. Johnson remembers the size of the grant as being probably $100,000 to $200,000 for two or three years, although this was "co-mingled" with money from other USAID-supported American NGO's such as The Asia Foundation.

[80] During 1995 and 1996 a total of four AJI members were jailed for publishing an unlicenced newspaper and defaming Soeharto. Andreas Harsono, "Indonesian Press, Freer Now, Still Struggles with Economic Crisis", *American Reporter*, July 8, 1998. See also Alumni Majalah *Tempo, Mengapa Kami Menggugat*, p. 12.

[81] Interview with Goenawan Mohamad, October 10, 1998.

to flourish after 1995. According to Goenawan, no one – with the possible exception of Kopassus – suspected that it all originated from the small, "arty" community and media think tank at No. 68H Jl. Utan Kayu. Even the other *Tempo* journalists, the group based at Tebet, didn't know. They may have "heard", but they didn't know. "We kept them safe," Goenawan said. "They were part of the resistance, but they were not guerillas."[82]

Irawan Saptono is in his early thirties now. A heavyset man with dark curly hair, he has a ready laugh. When I met him in 2002, he was the business manager of *Pantau* magazine, an innovative media watch magazine edited by Andreas Harsono. Just a few years earlier, he had been one of the directors of "Blok M", an underground unit headquartered at ISAI. He had helped to coordinate an internet news service serving thousands of readers, as well as numerous journalists and activists working in a secret network. His daily work involved false names, safe houses, and reports encrypted for distribution on the internet. On some occasions it also involved helping kidnaped or "disappeared" political activists.

"The government was never suspicious of this place because people who worked here never joined demonstrations, never joined anti-government discussions," Irawan explained. "So it couldn't be traced. All the people we recruited were all clean. They couldn't join activities like PRD [People's Democratic Party]."[83] Three key members of the group – Irawan Saptono, Stanley Yoseph Adi, and Andreas Harsono – had known one another since they were students together at Satya Wacana Christian University in Salatiga, West Java. At Salatiga they had been influenced by activist professors Arief Budiman, Ariel Heryanto, and George Aditjondro. Andreas said that this was perhaps one reason they could organize themselves so quickly. "It was like playing a soccer game," he said. "Without even

---

82   Interview with Goenawan Mohamad, July 11, 2002.
83   Interview with Irawan Saptono, July 10, 2002.

wasting a glance you can kick the ball to your friends."[84]

One of the people whom Goenawan had selected for his "institution of struggle" was *Tempo*'s former Jakarta bureau chief Toriq Hadad. Toriq was an accomplished journalist and, according to Goenawan Mohamad, "a very good organizer". Before the banning, Toriq had been responsible for a staff of twenty-one reporters in *Tempo*'s Jakarta Bureau.

Today, Toriq Hadad is assistant chief editor of *Tempo*. A handsome man with strong features and a thick black moustache, Toriq has a no-nonsense demeanor that belies his kind-heartedness and sense of humor. Committed to good values in journalism, he is one of the leading instructors in *Tempo*'s in-house training programs.

Toriq never wanted to be an activist. "It's not my world," he says. But in 1994, he felt he had no other choice. Toriq remembers that even before the December meeting at the restaurant Koi, Goenawan had spoken with him about his plan to build an institution that would continue *Tempo*'s role in journalism education – a place to learn to become a reporter, a writer, and also about design. All of this had been lost because of the banning. Toriq remembered that when he and Mark Johnson worked through the many drafts of the proposal that would go to USAID, each version included background on the banning of *Tempo* – how the banning had created a blockage in the flow of information, and how this new institution would help to re-open the channel. "Instant books, efforts to monitor corruption, campus discussions, trainings, anti-envelopes – all of these things were *Tempo*'s values," Toriq said, "and we would make them more widespread."

"First we dreamed of making an institution," Toriq said. "Second we thought of how to oppose the New Order. That was clear. When we began our discussions towards ISAI, it all began with Goenawan Mohamad. Even the name ISAI. It was all Goenawan Mohamad's idea."[85]

84   Interview with Andreas Harsono, July 16, 1998.
85   Interview with Toriq Hadad, July 11, 2002.

The name, of course, was Institut Studi Arus Informasi. In English it would be "Institute for the Study of the Free Flow of Information". Goenawan Mohamad recalls that Barbara Harvey, the popular deputy chief of mission at the U.S. Embassy, once asked him if the "S" stood for "study" or "supply". To this day he isn't sure whether or not she was joking.[86]

In the beginning, Toriq said, everything was open, on the surface. ISAI ran training programs, etc. "But then a stronger push was needed. So we began Project Blok M. Believe it or not, I only know the term Blok M. I never knew its location."[87]

Blok M is the name of an area in South Jakarta. It is crowded and popular, a jumble of sidewalk warungs and street vendors alongside of trendy restaurants, a noisy bus terminal, and an expensive shopping center. As Andreas Harsono explained, "we chose that name simply because it is a good camouflage. You can say, 'I want to go to Blok M,' and people will not feel curious. A lot of people go there. It was used as a code name for the underground unit – which was not located in the real Blok M area."[88]

"Blok M" produced six different underground internet news services. The first was a general news service called Pipa, and it began in early 1996. A second news service, called Bursa provided news about the economy and business. The two were shut down after a few months because there were concerns that the server wasn't secure enough. As Irawan said, "when reports were sent, it could be seen who had sent them." Moreover, the people who were on the mailing list were known to the authorities.

With the assistance of The Asia Foundation, ISAI was able to get a different, more secure server that utilized the most advanced encryption system available. Blok M began to provide several new

[86]   Email correspondence from Goenawan Mohamad, August 5, 2002.
[87]   Interview with Toriq Hadad, July 11, 2002.
[88]   Email correspondence from Andreas Harsono, August 5, 2002.

internet services, the most well-known being SiaR. SiaR (which means "broadcast") provided general news, but there were six other news services as well – including one consisting entirely of political jokes.[89]

Blok M's server was located in a safe house. Only a handful of people knew where it was. People who wished to obtain the news could join apakabar@clark.net, a mailing list managed by American scholar John MacDougall. Apakabar's stories were archived at Murdoch University in Australia, and in Germany as well. Many organizations used news originating from Blok M to create mailing lists of their own, but as Irawan said, the source of the news couldn't be traced.

The secrecy was extraordinary. By all accounts, Goenawan himself was the "mastermind", and designed much of the security system. Stanley, the head of Blok M and a former journalist from the magazine *Jakarta-Jakarta*, designed the system of cells. Goenawan did not know the location of Blok M, nor did Andreas Harsono. They also used false names. As Toriq said, "We used to change our names every month. If you called ISAI, my name wasn't Toriq. This month, my name begins with T. Next month, it begins with O. Who was the most confused? The phone operators!" He laughs. "Goenawan used to forget his names. I sometimes did too."[90]

There were six people working at Blok M in Jakarta, as well as staff in Dili, Papua, and Aceh. Blok M also had a network of journalists in the field. As Irawan said, "We searched for journalists in the region. Journalists from papers like *Kompas*. If they had stories that couldn't pass the censors, they would send them here. But they didn't know to whom those reports were going."

---

[89]   The others were Istiqlal (opinion), Matebeam (news from East Timor), Mamberano (news from Papua), and Meunasah (news from Aceh). TNI Watch dealt with the military, and Goro-goro contained political jokes. The jokes were later published in book form. Goenawan Mohamad says that he wrote about 60% of them.

[90]   Interview with Toriq Hadad, July 11, 2002.

Toriq Hadad describes what they were doing as advocacy journalism. "We hoped we could push people," he said. "We still did check and recheck, although not as tight as normal media. We would interview someone and then send it out. It was then printed – and on a scale that was pretty big."[91]

Irawan estimates that the internet news service had about three thousand regular readers. In the mid-1990s, the internet was still new in Indonesia, and users were rare. Of far more concern to the authorities – and therefore far more dangerous – were the print publications that also originated from ISAI. One was called *X-Pos*, and it had a circulation of fifty thousand. Another was called *Bergerak!* [Move!], and although it was produced for the PRD [People's Democratic Party] activists, it was actually published by ISAI. Irawan chuckled and explained, "later, the print version was claimed by PRD. It was on the left. It was done by us, but people thought it was done by PRD. And they claimed it!"[92]

When I asked Irawan if people suspected that Goenawan Mohamad was behind this, he shook his head no. "They thought AJI was behind it," he said.

Did USAID know the extent of ISAI's underground activities? According to Mark Johnson, he didn't really want to know. "Money is fungible," he said. "You see they would take the advances and use it, and they would submit receipts for these advances. And while they had the advanced money, that was what was being used." Johnson pointed out that ISAI also used Goenawan's own money, as well as that of other donors. "So part of it was cash flow," he said. "If we're on the run tomorrow and we're going to do this, and the only money in the pot is AID money, we'll use it for two weeks, but then we'll replenish it with somebody else's money, and then we won't claim it against AID."

In other words, Mark Johnson's biggest concern was ensuring that nobody would present to him a receipt that suggested the

91   Interview with Toriq Hadad, July 11, 2002.
92   Interview with Irawan Saptono, July 10, 2002.

U.S. government was funding an underground news service like SiaR. "But if we pay for a computer," he said, and that particular computer ends up on the back of a truck going to a safe house somewhere in South Jakarta, "well, we don't sign off on the details."[93]

The influence of ISAI is difficult to measure. To this day, most people have no idea that Komunitas Utan Kayu was the source of either the underground newspaper *X-Pos* or the clandestine internet news service SiaR. The activities of *Tempo Interaktif*, the internet version of the banned magazine which was also edited by Toriq Hadad were well-known, but as Irawan Saptono said, "*Tempo Interaktif* was totally different."

"It was above ground," he said. "They had bylines, and they had to practice self-censorship. They were more brave than the general media, though. The government knew who worked for *Tempo Interaktif.* They got away with it because it was the internet and because it was new. There weren't any other people at *Tempo Interaktif* who knew about Blok M. If Toriq found stories that couldn't be included in *TI*, he would send them to Blok M."[94]

Goenawan Mohamad adds that the "above ground" activities were a pretext, a subterfuge, and a means of confusing the police. According to Goenawan, it was useful to have the authorities believe that *Tempo* had "gone underground" and was being produced at Utan Kayu. In reality, *Tempo Interaktif* was done at the Grafiti Pers building on Jl. Proklamasi. It was SiaR that was produced out of the Utan Kayu complex in East Jakarta.

Goenawan believes that "courage, like fear, is infectious." For that reason it was important to produce *Tempo Interaktif*, just as it was important to support the lawsuit at the State Administrative High Court. "It's very symbolic," he explained, "just to say that we will never succumb."[95]

---

93   Interview with Mark Johnson, August 15, 2002.
94   Interview with Irawan Saptono, July 10, 2002.
95   Interview with Goenawan Mohamad, July 11, 2002.

It was these kinds of symbolic victories that motivated the middle class, the people who had read *Tempo*. Arief Budiman and Olle Törnquist have argued convincingly that the majority of the supporters of the anti-banning movement in 1994 came from the urban middle class. What united them was their need for independent information and their sense that by banning *Tempo*, *Detik*, and *Editor*, the New Order government had arbitrarily and unfairly closed off these channels in a manner that was at once anti-democratic and authoritarian.[96]

It was the sacrifices of *Tempo*'s middle class defenders that transformed Goenawan Mohamad into "the most dangerous man in Indonesia." As editor-in-chief of *Tempo* magazine, Goenawan had been somewhat removed from the students and intellectuals and pro-democracy activists who had been trying to bring about change in Indonesia. "A good editor can have no friends," Goenawan often said.

Arief Budiman remembers that Goenawan was so deeply moved by the willingness of the students and other demonstrators to defend him that he attended the trial of every single person who had been arrested in *Tempo*'s name. "Every single court!" Arief said. "He came every day, and was so tired. He would postpone his visit to some other places just because he wanted to be there."

"I was with him," Arief said, "and he would say 'I have to go to the court now, the court of that guy who was defending *Tempo*.'"

"'Goen, you cannot go every time,' I said."

"'No, no, I feel obliged,' he said. 'I want to say thank-you, again and again.'"

---

[96] Arief Budiman and Olle Törnquist, *Aktor Demokrasi*, pp. 152-158. Middle class Indonesians protested the banning of *Tempo* in a variety of ways. For example, Chodidah Rahardjo, a senior cultural specialist at the American Embassy, and her husband Eko Budi Rahardjo had been regular subscribers of *Tempo* since they were students in the 1970s. Chodidah (or Toto) told me that after *Tempo* was banned she and her husband refused to purchase *Gatra*. "The birth of *Gatra* was not based on free, fair and sincere competition. It was based on dirty competition which was against my belief," she wrote. "This was not right and it was not in line with my conscience." Email correspondence, July 31, 2002.

epilogue

Jakarta, June 21, 2004

The Central Jakarta District Courthouse looks its age. On Jl. Gadjah Mada in Jakarta's old city, the white cement building dates back to Dutch colonial times, but has no particular charm. It is just old.

On the second floor, off a wide veranda marking a shady exterior court, are a series of drab courtrooms. Each is furnished with a dozen or so simple wooden benches. In the front of each room, behind a low gated fence, are two sets of plain tables, each covered with green felt. The tables on the left are reserved for the prosecutors, those on the right for the defense attorneys. A lone bench for the defendants sits in the center of the fenced-off area. Its serial number, stenciled in large white letters, is visible from the back of the room. A team of three judges sits on a raised platform in the front. The wood-paneled room is unadorned, except for a 2004 calendar hung on the wall behind the prosecutors. The state seal of the Republic of Indonesia hangs over the chairs reserved for the judges, which are the only padded seats in the room. There is nothing in the Jakarta Central District Court building to suggest that Indonesia has entered a new era of Democratic reform.

Bambang Harymurti [center], Ahmad Taufik [left], and T. Iskandar Ali, Jakarta Central District Court, June 2004 [*Tempo*/Santirta M.]

The criminal trial of Bambang Harymurti, Ahmad Taufik, and T. Iskandar Ali Thamrin began in December 2003, and is convened every Monday morning at 10 AM. The three *Tempo* journalists have been accused by Tomy Winata – a millionaire businessman with close ties to the police, as well as to Indonesia's political and military elite – of libel, defamation of character, and publishing an article that could provoke disorder. If found guilty, the three could be sentenced to up to ten years in jail.

The news story in question seemed straight-forward enough. Late in February 2003, a fire at Jakarta's massive Tanah Abang textile market burned out of control for five days. *Tempo*'s edition of March 3-9 included a follow-up story that described a proposal to renovate the market complex. According to an anonymous *Tempo* source, the proposal had been submitted to the city-owned management company P.T. Pasar Jaya several months prior to the fire, and named Tomy Winata's Artha Graha Group as the project's financial backer. As a sentence near the end of the story asked, "won't the fire, whether intentional or not, make the implementation of the plan a lot easier?"[1]

---

[1]   "Ada Tomy di 'Tenabang'?", *Tempo*, March 3, 2004.

On June 21, 2004, prosecutors completed their cross-examination of the three defendants. Bambang Harymurti was called first, followed by Taufik and Iskandar. Most of the key aspects of the case were recapitulated in the day's proceedings. Iskandar, who edited the piece called "Ada Tomy di 'Tenabang'?" (Was Tomy at Tanah Abang?) is asked several times to explain his insertion of the term *pemulung besar*, or "scavenger extraordinaire", to describe Tomy Winata. An older man, Iskandar's broad back and shoulders show the strain of the past few months. He doggedly sticks to his answer that his use of the term "scavenger" was not intended to insult. *Tempo*'s story began with the image of a forty-seven-year old woman gathering scraps of cloth from the debris of the fire. Iskandar's description of Tomy Winata as a "scavenger extraordinaire" was metaphorical, he said. He inserted it merely to repeat the image of the opening line.

Ahmad Taufik is likewise asked several times to explain how he came to see the proposal for a multi-million dollar renovation of the market that would be funded by Tomy Winata. Taufik is nattily dressed in a black *peci*, long blue shirt, batik pants and sandals; Bambang Harymurti's wife, Marga Alisjahbana, says that

Tomy Winata, Jakarta, 1997 [*Tempo*/Rully Kesuma]

Supporters of Tomy Winata, *Tempo*'s office in Jl. Proklamasi,
March 8, 2003 [*Tempo*/Rendra]

Taufik has "a theatrical streak". Taufik says he first learned of the proposal from an architect friend, but that he had also seen the proposal himself. Taufik agreed to keep secret the names of both of his sources. This, he points out, is allowable under the 1999 Press Law as well as the code of ethics of the Indonesian Journalists' Association.

On the Saturday after the *Tempo* article appeared, Taufik was attacked by a mob of thugs who said they represented Tomy Winata.[2] It happened right in front of *Tempo*'s office – and also in front of the police, who stood by and watched. In court, Taufik's posture is erect. His words are polite, but not unduly deferential. Later he tells me that he is not afraid. Taufik has already been to prison once, during the Soeharto regime. After *Tempo* was banned in 1994, he was arrested for his role in publishing the Alliance of Independent Journalists' newspaper, *Independen*.

When Bambang Harymurti takes the witness stand, he tells the judge that, as *Tempo*'s chief editor, it is he who must bear the

---

[2]   Ahmad Taufik, "Kronologi Penyerbuan Tomy Winata ke *Tempo*", unpublished manuscript. For a published English-language account based on this manuscript, see *The Jakarta Post*, March 13, 2003.

ultimate responsibility for the article. He accepts this responsibility not only as his duty and obligation, but also in accordance with the Press Law – a law which, in this particular case, is not being applied. The law that is being used in the case against Bambang, Taufik, and Iskandar is part of the Criminal Code dating back to Dutch times.[3]

Speaking clearly and with conviction, Bambang explains that after the February fire, there were rumors circulating among the traders in Tanah Abang that Tomy Winata was involved with the plans to renovate the market. After *Tempo* decided to do a follow-up story, a reporter was assigned to contact Tomy by phone. Tomy said that *Tempo*'s reporter was the sixth journalist to have approached him with questions about the proposal, and he vehemently denied that he had been involved. The Jakarta Governor's office also denied that Tomy Winata had submitted such a proposal.

Bambang says that by the time he saw the Tanah Abang story, it was clear that there were two contradictory sets of facts. "Either the *Tempo* reporter was right, or Tomy was right," he says. "It was just like what happens in court. When there are two opposing sides, both must be given an equal chance to present their views."

One of the judges nods. It is the one seated on the left, the one whom *Tempo* people hope may be somewhat sympathetic.

But more importantly, Bambang adds, *Tempo*'s story on Tomy Winata and the fire was an example of running news. "An unconfirmed rumor is more dangerous than an explanation," Bambang says. "Either the reporter was wrong, or Tomy was wrong." Or perhaps there was a third possibility. Perhaps Tomy Winata's name had been included in the proposal without his permission.

---

[3]   The three are being charged with Articles 310 and 311 of the Criminal Code on defamation, and under Article 14 for provoking disorder. The maximum sentence for the libel charges is four years in prison; for provoking disorder the maximum sentence is ten years. On July 19 and 26, 2004, prosecutors demanded two-year jail terms for all three defendants – effective immediately upon sentencing.

Bambang suggests that this, in fact, was what he had personally believed to be the truth – that is until Tomy's thugs attacked *Tempo* on the Saturday after the story was published. What did they want? The name of the informant. If Taufik would just give them the name, they had said, there would be no more trouble. If they didn't get the source's name, they would burn *Tempo* to the ground.

At 1 PM, there are no more questions, and the panel of judges agrees to a three-week recess before the prosecutors wind up their case. Although no one in the courtroom has mentioned it, June 21, 2004 is the tenth anniversary of the banning of *Tempo*. This particular case is not the only suit that Tomy has brought against *Tempo*, but is rather one of four in which he is demanding damages totaling 400 billion rupiah – or four times the value of the company. Tomy Winata's goal appears to be to "ban" *Tempo* by bankrupting it.

For Trimoelja D. Soerjadi, one of the attorneys who is working *pro bono* to defend *Tempo* against Tomy Winata, and who represented the magazine in its 1996 lawsuit against the Department of Information, the situation is more perilous now than it was eight years ago. Before, he said, the banning was illegal. But now the trial is supposedly going according to law.

When *Tempo* journalists prepared to return to publication in 1998, for the first time in many years they were free to create a magazine in any manner they chose without fearing government censorship. The planning meetings that took place in June 1998 reflected a strong sense that the reform era demanded a new kind of magazine. They created new rubrics, and decided that *Tempo* would have a fresh focus on opinion and investigation – two departments that would have been unimaginable four years earlier. As Malela Mahargasarie explained, the new "face" of *Tempo* would be more analytical and more focused on politics and the economy, which he described as the two biggest crises facing the Indonesian people in the wake of Soeharto's fall.[4]

---

[4]   Interview with Malela Mahargasarie, July 1, 1998.

Indeed, one of the most significant developments in *Tempo* since its return to publication in 1998 has been its new orientation towards an explicit depiction and analysis of the political process. Stories now openly present conflict between political elites, and no longer use the elliptical language of the previous era. These general impressions – obvious to anyone who picks up the magazine – were borne out by the results of my content analysis of the National section, which I continued up until March, 2000 [see Figure 1].[5] The total percentage of National stories about government activity dropped significantly after *Tempo*'s return to publication (from 56.01% to 41.25%), and the content of these stories likewise underwent a discernable shift. Whereas before the banning only 3.2% of the National stories were about conflict among political elites, my post-banning sample included more than twice that percentage. Many of the stories were either about military activity, or the role of the military in the reform era. Of the stories that had a non-government focus, the largest single category (15%) was political party activity.

The stories I examined also suggest that the "whos" of the National section have changed. Political party leaders were more than twice as likely to appear as main actors than they were before the banning, whereas the ministers, cabinet-level officials, and former public officials who dominated coverage in the New Order dropped from 19.2% to 8.7% of the total – less than half of what it was before. An emerging civil society was likewise evident in the increased presence of leaders of national committees, foundations, and professional groups. Only two of the stories that I examined from the post-banning period had victims as the main actors.

Today, the announcements, bannings, and national ceremonies that were typical of the Soeharto-centered "theater-state" have

---

[5]   Because I completed the analysis in the spring of 2000, my coders and I were only able to analyze a sample of ninety-two National stories.

disappeared.[6] During the New Order, *Tempo* portrayed the nation of Indonesia as engaged in an ongoing moral drama in which the power of the state was pitted against ordinary people and their champions.[7] Despite the ever-present threat of government censorship, writers for the National section used a variety of rhetorical devices to defend the weak and present the suffering of "victims" in ways that subtly undermined the authority of the regime. Today, political party leaders and democratically elected public officials take a larger role, and are routinely shown to be engaged in open political struggle. As Bambang Harymurti once said, in the past it was often difficult to decide on the contents of the National section when there was officially "no news." In this era of unprecedented press freedom, *Tempo* – like other Indonesia media – is now free to report on the politics as well as the process of governance.

Yet *Tempo*'s new emphasis on conflict is disconcerting for readers who came of age in a political culture that favored harmony over clear expressions of disagreement, and perhaps one way of interpreting the case of Tomy Winata versus *Tempo* is as an example of the difficulty of nurturing public understanding of freedom of expression in a society that is still suffering the consequences of thirty-two years of authoritarian rule. This problem was acknowledged by a group of prominent pro-democracy activists who signed a petition in support of *Tempo* on September 1, 2004. Warning that the use of the Criminal Code in defamation cases threatened a basic pillar of democracy, they also noted that whereas during the Soeharto era the greatest threat to freedom of the press had come from the regime, today "it is coming from a different source: the public."[8]

Although President Abdurrahman Wahid dismantled the Department of Information in 1999, thus continuing the process of freeing the press begun by President B.J. Habibie, many

[6]   See Clifford Geertz, *Negara: the Theatre State in Nineteenth Century Bali*.
[7]   Significantly, the banning of *Tempo* itself took place outside the moral drama – in the political process that officially didn't exist.
[8]   "Activists Say Free Press in Peril", *The Jakarta Post*, September 2, 2004.

problems remain.[9]   There are still grave challenges to press freedom – sometimes coming from criminal elements, and sometimes from frivolous law suits that can have serious consequences in a legal system that is notoriously corrupt. Control of press outlets by conglomerates close to those who hold political office demonstrates how crony capitalism can undermine freedom of expression. Journalists have been accused of being irresponsible, of being "out of control" [*kebablasan*] and of not following their own code of ethics.[10] Despite the passage of a landmark Press Law in 1999 that contains mechanisms like the "right of reply" and mediation by the Press Council as a means of settling disputes, under President Megawati Soekarnoputri, the government has chosen instead to use the Criminal Code to prosecute cases of defamation.[11] In one of these cases, prosecutors successfully sued the newspaper *Rakyat Merdeka* for insulting the president, and the paper's editor received a six-month suspended sentence.

Since I first met Bambang Harymurti in 1997, he has been a tireless champion of the idea that journalists themselves must play a major role in advancing the cause of press freedom. Bambang believes that journalists can achieve this goal by regulating themselves through their own professional codes of conduct, and through independent organizations like the Press Council. Like many reform-minded journalists, Bambang believes in the importance of civic education. Paradoxically, media coverage of his own criminal trial has proven to be an important means of underscoring the vital role of a free press in a democracy.[12]

9   Philip Kitley, "After the Bans: Modelling Indonesian Communications for the Future", in Grayson Lloyd and Shannon Smith, eds., *Indonesia Today: Challenges of History* (Singapore: Institute of Southeast Asian Studies, 2001).

10   Kukuh Sanyoto, "Indonesian Television", in Russell Heng, ed., *Media Fortunes, Changing Times*, (Singapore: Institute for Southeast Asian Studies, 2002).

11   See "Indonesia", in Committee to Protect Journalists, Attacks on the Press, 2004, http://www.cpj.org/attacks04/asia04/indonesia.html.

12   Bambang's defense statement, for example, was widely quoted in the Indonesian press. Bambang Harymurti, *Wartawan Menggugat*, Nota Pembelaan (Pleidooi), Perkara No. 1426/Pid.B/2003/PNJKT.PST.

Presidential candidate Susilo Bambang Yudhoyono [left] and Bambang Harymurti [right], *Tempo*'s office in Jl. Proklamasi, August 2004 [*Tempo*/Mohamad Irfanto]

On September 16, 2004, Bambang Harymurti was sentenced to one year in prison, while Ahmad Taufik and T. Iskandar Ali Thamrin were acquitted of the charges against them.[13] The sentencing provoked a firestorm of criticism in the Indonesian media as well as in the international press, and *Tempo* vowed to carry on the fight. It is the hope of many *Tempo* journalists, including Bambang Harymurti, that the criminal defamation case will not only be overturned on appeal, but that the decision will also become a landmark in the history of press freedom, a *"New York Times Co. v. Sullivan"* for Indonesia. Just as the 1964 U.S. Supreme Court decision strengthened freedom of expression in the United States by introducing the thresholds of "actual malice" and "reckless disregard of the truth"as necessary for awarding punitive damages in libel suits, Bambang hopes that his case will result in an end to Indonesian journalists' fear that they will be sentenced to prison because of something they have written.

---

[13]   Bambang's sentence was suspended, allowing him to stay out of prison during the appeal process. In the case of Taufik and Iskandar, the court ruled that "the responsibility lies in the hands of the chief editor." Interestingly, in this instance, the court based its decision on the Press Law. "'*Tempo*' editor gets a Year", *The Jakarta Post*, September 17, 2004.

As Goenawan Mohamad said in 1998, Soeharto may have left too soon, forced to resign before the basic infrastructure of democracy was in place. The years since his fall have witnessed a series of struggles to create these institutions, and like much of the Indonesian press, *Tempo* has been at the vanguard of these efforts. Even those who criticize the "excesses" of the press must acknowledge that the information now available to the Indonesian public has made it possible to bring about reforms – like the first direct election of a president in 2004 – that would never before have been imaginable. Corruptors can no longer hide from the scrutiny of the press, and what were once "open secrets" are now public knowledge, investigated and proven in the pages of newspapers and magazines like *Tempo*.[14]

Since its founding, *Tempo* has stood for freedom of expression. The views of *Tempo* founder Goenawan Mohamad have remained consistent since the early 1960s, when he signed the Cultural Manifesto and proclaimed the absolute necessity of creative freedom. Although the slow ossification of the New Order forced *Tempo* to make certain political compromises in order to survive, the editors of the magazine nevertheless managed, week after week, to present a version of events that subtly but unmistakably challenged the government's view.

Melani Budianta once observed that one of the most stubborn obstacles to democracy in Indonesia has been the difficulty of creating non-government institutions that can outlast their founders. That Goenawan Mohamad was able to step down as chief editor of *Tempo* and pass the magazine on to Bambang Harymurti and a new generation of leadership is testimony to his skill as an institution builder. Like Goenawan Mohamad, Bambang Harymurti believes that the duty and role of journalists is to supply

---

[14] For an example of the media's ability to provide proof of what were formerly "open secrets", see *Tempo*'s investigative piece "Harmoko", which proved that the former minister of information and his family owned shares in dozens of press publications. *Tempo*, January 13, 2003.

credible information to the public. Comparing journalists to the lamps that light up a room, he once warned that if journalists allow themselves to be extinguished by intimidation from evil forces, those same forces will only "steal more in the darkness."[15]

A few weeks after President Soeharto was forced to resign in 1998, the poet and writer Eka Budianta told me that for many Indonesians, the end of the New Order was like coming out of a dark room into the brightness. People were blinded, bewildered, and unsure of their footing. It is difficult to find your way in the dark, but perhaps even more so to find your way in the sudden brightness of day. The case of Tomy Winata suggests that once again *Tempo* has a significant role to play in securing freedom of expression in Indonesia. Until press freedom is institutionalized and safeguarded by law, the struggle to reform the system will remain incomplete. This continues to be the challenge for *Tempo*, to create a forum for the discussion and debate that is essential to true democracy, and by so doing to lead Indonesia into the brightness.

---

[15] "*Tempo* Editor Bambang, 'We Shall Continue the Fight'," *The Jakarta Post*, September 17, 2004.

acknowledgments

I could not have written this book without the help of Bambang Harymurti and Goenawan Mohamad.

Bambang's enthusiasm, his patience with my seemingly endless questions, and his willingness to introduce me to anyone I needed to meet, were essential to the completion of this book. His support, as well as his clear signals that I was to have complete access to anything that interested me at *Tempo,* gave me unparalleled entree to the magazine. His unflagging optimism and willingness to face down the powers of darkness continue to inspire and humble me.

I owe my greatest debt to Goenawan Mohamad. His graciousness and willingness to open his life, letters, and work to the scrutiny of a foreign scholar touch every page of this book. I only hope that I have been able to do justice to what Bambang Bujono once referred to as "Mr. Goenawan's greatest poem".

S. Malela Mahargasarie took time out of his demanding schedule to design the cover of this book. Malela's friendship, unwavering support, and explanation of the symbolic language of *Tempo*'s cover art influenced me in ways that may not be immediately evident from the text. I would like to thank *Tempo* for giving me permission to use the photographs, and Priatna for his kindness and generosity in sharing with me both his knowledge of the photo archives and his amazing retrieval system.

Nearly every *Tempo* journalist I know added something to this manuscript, and although I have tried to credit individuals in the footnotes, such thanks can't begin to express the extent of my gratitude to all of those who offered friendship and help. I am especially grateful to Yusi Avianto Pareanom for reading parts of this book at its early stages, and to Karaniya Dharmasaputra for his careful reading and critique of the entire manuscript. Joel Kuipers encouraged me at all times during the research and writing, and offered a number of key insights.

Atmakusumah provided me with wise counsel as my sponsor and friend, and with a broader historical context to *Tempo*'s story. ISAI gave me office space and other invaluable kinds of friendship and support; Andreas Harsono and Yayasan Pantau gave me opportunities to teach and inspired me with their enthusiasm for improving the quality of journalism in Indonesia. Aristides Katoppo was my *malaikat penjaga* or guardian angel, blessing me not only with his insights, but also with his uncanny ability to turn up at the moments when I most needed help or encouragement.

I am grateful to Equinox Publishing, copy editor Laura Noszlopy, and especially publisher Mark Hanusz, whose professionalism, good cheer, and willingness to listen made him a dream editor and friend.

Melani and Eka Budianta, Chodidah (Toto) and Eko Budi Rahardjo, and Manneke Budiman and their families provided friendship and sustenance in Indonesia. Jerry Macdonald, Jim Goodyear and Indira Kotval, and Elizabeth Bowen helped me get through difficult days both here and abroad, and any successes I have had are in large part due to them.

The Department of State, the American-Indonesian Education Foundation (Aminef), the Council for the International Exchange of Scholars, the Ford Foundation, the School of Media and Public Affairs at the George Washington University, and the Public Affairs Section of the U.S. Embassy in Jakarta provided me with travel grants and opportunities for teaching that made this research possible. Nelly Paliama of Aminef gave me invaluable advice and assistance in applying for visas and research permits from LIPI, the Indonesian Research Institute.

I would especially like to thank my mother, Ellen M. Steele, for her gift that allowed me to complete my content analysis in 2000. It is impossible to express the gratitude I feel both to her and to my late father, Robert E. Steele, for their confidence in this project and in me.

At Idul Fitri, the holiday marking the end of the holy month of Ramadhan, Indonesian Muslims ask forgiveness of one another for their actions during the past year, and on this Eid I would like to extend my deepest apologies to my friends for any unintentional harm I may have caused in the writing of this book. It was a labor of love, but in love as in all things, it is possible to make grievous errors. Any such errors are my responsibility alone.

Janet Steele
November 14, 2004
Washington, DC

TABLE 1

"what" from
march 27, 1971 to june 4, 1994

CATEGORY	COUNT%	TOTAL
GOVERNMENT	629	56.01%
Ideology, Politics Structure	293	26.10%
Pancasila	5	0.45%
Laws	29	2.58%
Changes in government officials	46	4.10%
Conflict	36	3.21%
Issues of justice	20	1.78%
Bannings	40	3.56%
National ceremonies	15	1.34%
Holding elections	18	1.60%
Military policy issues	19	1.69%
Other announcements	44	3.92%
Other	21	1.87%
Military, International Relations	189	16.83%
Military, police operations	29	2.58%
Military public relations	25	2.23%
International Relations	135	12.02%
Economy	65	5.79%
Money and banking	8	0.71%
Industry and trade	21	1.87%
Infrastructure	25	2.23%
Human resource development	11	0.98%

Public Welfare	**58**	**5.16%**
Transmigration, population	12	1.07%
Health	5	0.45%
Education	10	0.89%
Art, culture, tourism	7	0.62%
Religion	6	0.53%
Women	1	0.09%
Other public welfare issues	17	1.51%
Other	24	2.14%
Political Party Activity	**65**	**5.79%**
Routine Parliamentary action	**17**	**1.51%**
NON-GOVERNMENT	**412**	**36.68%**
Activity of organizations	**81**	**7.21%**
NGO activity	3	0.27%
Press	7	0.62%
Professional organizations	2	0.18%
Business	7	0.62%
Independence/regional autonomy movements	6	0.53%
Customary law	4	0.36%
Religion	27	2.40%
Political prisoner activity	7	0.62%
"Organizations without shape"	5	0.45%
Other	13	1.16%
Conflict	**129**	**11.48%**
Opposition/protest	69	6.14%
Demonstrations	23	2.05%
Strikes	9	0.80%
Riots	11	0.98%
Issues of SARA	10	0.89%
Offensive acts	7	0.62%

Crime	96	8.55%
General crime	33	2.94%
Corruption, misuse of authority	26	2.32%
Subversion	28	2.49%
Scandalous crime	9	0.80%
General news	**106**	**9.44%**
Accidents	15	1.34%
Natural disasters	16	1.42%
Society news	21	1.87%
Social conditions	25	2.23%
Other	29	2.58%
TOTAL WHAT	**1123**	**100.00%**

Table 2

"where" from
march 27, 1971 to june 4, 1994

PROVINCE	COUNT	%TOTAL
Jakarta	530	47.03%
West Java	53	4.70%
Central Java	45	3.99%
Yogyakarta	31	2.75%
Throughout Java	17	1.51%
East Java	54	4.79%
Bali	16	1.42%
Aceh	18	1.60%
North Sumatra	42	3.73%
West Sumatra	11	0.98%
Jambi	0	0.00%
Riau	19	1.69%
Bengkulu	2	0.18%
South Sumatra	2	0.18%
Lampung	16	1.42%
West Kalimantan	4	0.35%
East Kalimantan	5	0.44%
Central Kalimantan	2	0.18%
South Kalimantan	2	0.18%
West Nusa Tenggara	5	0.44%
East Nusa Tenggara	7	0.62%
East Timor	19	1.69%
North Sulewesi	5	0.44%
South East Sulawesi	2	0.18%

Central Sulawesi	1	0.09%
South Sulawesi	6	0.53%
Maluku	4	0.35%
Irian Jaya	17	1.51%
Throughout Indonesia	61	5.41%
Overseas	59	5.24%
Unclear	72	6.39%
TOTAL WHERE	**1127**	**100.00%**

Table 3

"who" from
march 27, 1971 to june 4, 1994

CATEGORY	MAIN ACTOR	%TOTAL
KNOWNS	911	76.68%
President	68	5.72%
DPR-MPR	33	2.78%
Ministers, cabinet-level officials, former public officials	228	19.19%
Regional public officials (governors, bupati, etc.)	80	6.73%
Military leaders	107	9.01%
Political party leaders	83	6.99%
Leaders of NGOs	5	0.42%
Journalists	12	1.01%
Leaders of labor organizations	7	0.59%
National committees, foundations, professional groups	38	3.20%
Regional autonomy/independence leaders	11	0.93%
Religious leaders	53	4.46%
Business leaders	25	2.10%
Ambassadors, leaders of international organizations	63	5.30%
Other "knowns"	98	8.25%

UNKNOWNS	**228**	**19.19%**
Demonstrators, strikers, rioters	33	2.78%
Victims	62	5.22%
Suspects, criminals	61	5.13%
Other ordinary people	72	6.06%
Anonymous	2	0.17%
No "who"	47	3.96%
TOTAL WHO	**1188**	**100.00%**

TABLE 4

percentage of type
of product by year

	1971	1972	1973	1974	1975	1976	1977	1978	1979	1980	1981
English text	18.5	17.6	21.4	5.6	6.3	17.6	15.8	15.4	20	17.5	3.3
Products aimed at businesses	3.7	5.9	7.1	16.7	12.5	11.8	15.8	0	0	17.5	13.3
Fashion and accessories	0	5.9	0	0	6.3	11.8	5.3	7.7	5	5	0
Financial services	7.4	5.9	7.1	5.6	6.3	5.9	0	7.7	0	0	3.3
Food and beverage	0	0	0	11.1	6.3	5.9	5.3	0	10	2.5	0
Home furnishings	0	0	0	5.6	0	0	10.5	0	5	5	0
Jewelry, watches, glasses	0	5.9	0	5.6	6.3	5.9	5.3	7.7	25	5	3.3
Travel/leisure	37	29.4	14.3	5.6	12.5	11.8	5.3	7.7	15	2.5	3.3
Real estate	0	0	0	0	6.3	0	5.3	0	0	2.5	0
Courses and seminars	0	0	0	0	0	0	0	0	0	2.5	6.7
Automotive	3.7	5.9	0	5.6	0	0	0	0	0	5	3.3
Media and books	22.2	23.5	7.1	11.1	6.3	11.8	10.5	38.5	0	7.5	6.7
Tobacco and cigarettes	0	0	7.1	0	6.3	5.9	26.3	7.7	10	10	1
Toiletries and beauty care	3.7	0	7.1	5.6	6.3	5.9	0	0	15	5	6.
Drugs and vitamins	22.2	11.8	42.9	22.2	18.8	23.5	10.5	15.4	15	17.5	26
Electronic goods	0	5.9	0	0	0	0	0	0	0	12.5	17
Other	0	0	0	5.6	12.5	5.9	5.3	7.7	0	2.5	(

1982	1983	1984	1985	1986	1987	1988	1989	1990	1991	1992	1993	1994	1998	1999
13.6	9.5	9.1	10	3	6.4	12.9	11.6	31.7	22.5	37	31	24	32.4	27.8
13.6	19	20.5	20	12.1	8.5	14.5	11.6	15.9	15	22.2	7	16	16.2	16.7
3.4	4.8	6.8	0	3	0	1.6	2.9	2.4	1.3	2.5	1.4	0	5.4	5.6
1.7	0	2.3	2.5	6.1	0	1.6	7.2	14.6	6.3	3.7	2.8	8	8.1	5.6
5.1	0	0	0	0	6.4	0	1.4	0	1.3	1.2	4.2	2	2.7	0
1.7	4.8	0	17.5	0	0	4.8	1.4	0	0	2.5	5.6	2	0	0
3.4	4.8	4.5	5	6.1	4.3	8.1	8.7	7.3	3.8	3.7	8.5	4	2.7	0
8.5	0	2.3	5	9.1	6.4	8.1	4.3	8.5	8.8	12.3	5.6	4	5.4	2.8
1.7	0	2.3	0	3	0	0	2.9	0	3.8	11.1	7	0	0	0
5.1	9.5	4.5	7.5	3	4.3	9.7	8.7	6.1	13.8	14.8	18.3	22	5.4	8.3
8.5	4.8	6.8	2.5	9.1	12.8	4.8	4.3	6.1	1.3	2.5	9.9	4	0	0
1.7	19	6.8	10	21.2	14.9	4.8	8.7	13.4	17.5	9.9	12.7	22	8.1	27.8
3.4	4.8	6.8	5	6.1	8.4	9.7	4.3	4.9	3.8	2.5	2.8	4	10.8	11.1
8.5	9.5	2.3	5	9.1	2.1	0	7.2	6.1	6.3	1.2	4.2	2.0	8.1	5.6
16.9	19	31.8	17.5	3	23.4	22.6	18.8.	6.1	8.8	1.2	1.4	0	5.4	2.8
3.6	0	2.3	2.5	6.1	4.3	4.8	5.8	2.4	3.8	6.2	4.2	2	8.1	2.8
3.4	0	2.3	2.5	6.1	6.4	6.5	4.3	7.3	7.5	6.2	4.2	12	16.2	13.9

the advertisements

June 12, 1982

May 24, 1980

Biarkan si dia memandang bentuk tubuh Anda, menembus melalui kemeja Anda.

Mengapa tidak – jika bentuk tubuh Anda cukup mengagumkan.

Bila kemeja biasa tidak bisa, Brigade, koleksi baru kemeja Arrow model Perancis menonjolkan dengan cara halus bentuk tubuh Anda yang patut dikagumi si dia.

Pinggang ramping, coup-naad yang dijahit di tempat yang paling tepat, tangan kemeja potongan pas, jahitan lengan yang lebih tinggi dan ujung tangan dengan dua kancing yang dapat disesuaikan dengan pergelangan tangan Anda menjadikan model ini berbeda dari kemeja lainnya.

Bergaya dalam Revolusi dari Perancis – Brigade · buatan Arrow, koleksi model Perancis.

Brigade
from the French Collection of
►Arrow►

June 14, 1975

October 25, 1975

May 17, 1980

September 13, 1975

June 12, 1982

June 12, 1982

June 12, 1982

March 13, 1976

Figure 1

comparison of "what" before and after the banning

"What" – March 1971 to June 1994

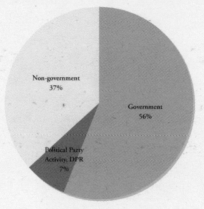

"What" – October 1998 to March 2000

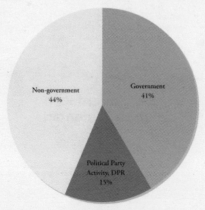

works cited

Alumni Majalah Tempo. *Buku Putih Tempo: Pembredelan Itu*. Jakarta: Yayasan Alumni Tempo, 1994.

Alumni Majalah Tempo. *Mengapa Kami Menggugat*. Jakarta: Yayasan Alumni Tempo, 1995.

Anderson, Benedict R. O'G. *Java in a Time of Revolution: Occupation and Resistance, 1944-1946*. Ithaca: Cornell University Press, 1972.

Anderson, Benedict R. O'G. *Language and power, Exploring Political Cultures in Indonesia*. Ithaca: Cornell University Press, 1990.

Anderson, Benedict R. O'G. Mythology and the Tolerance of the Javanese. Ithaca: Cornell University Modern Indonesia Project, Southeast Asia Program, 1996.

Bellwood, Peter. "Hierarchy, Founder Ideology, and Austronesian Expansion." In *Origins, Ancestry, and Alliance*, edited by James J. Fox and Clifford Sather, 18-40. Canberra, Australian National University, 1966.

Boorstin, Daniel. *The Americans: The Democratic Experience*. New York: Vintage Books, 1974.

Bourchier, David. "Crime, Law and State Authority in Indonesia." In *State and Civil Society in Indonesia*, edited by Arief Budiman, 177-212. Monash Papers on Southeast Asia no. 22. Clayton, Victoria: Monash University, 1990.

Bresnan, John. *Managing Indonesia: The Modern Political Economy*. New York: Columbia University Press, 1993.

Budianta, Melani. "Discourse of Cultural Identity in Indonesia during the 1997-1998 Monetary Crisis." *Inter-Asia Cultural Studies* I (2000): 109-128.

Budiman, Arief. "The Student Movement in Indonesia: A Study of the Relationship between Culture and Structure." *Asian Survey* 18, (June, 1978): 609-625.

Budiman, Arief and Olle Törnquist. *Aktor Demokrasi: Catatan Tentang Gerakan Perlawanan di Indonesia.* Jakarta: Institut Studi Arus Informasi, 2001.

Carey, James C. *Communication as Culture: Essays on Media and Society.* Boston: Unwin Hyman, 1988.

Carey, James C. "Why and How: The Dark Continent of American Journalism." In *Reading the News,* edited by Robert Manhoff and Michael Schudson,146-196. New York: Pantheon Books, 1986.

Cribb, Robert, ed. *The Indonesian Killings, 1965-1966: Studies from Java and Bali.* Monash Papers on Southeast Asia no. 21. Clayton, Victoria: Monash University, 1990.

Crouch, Harold. *The Army and Politics in Indonesia.* Revised edition. Ithaca: Cornell University Press, 1993.

Darnton, Robert. "Writing News and Telling Stories." Daedalus, 104 (1975): 174-194.

Dhakidae, Daniel. "The State, The Rise of Capital, and the Fall of Political Journalism." Ph.D. diss., Cornell University, May 1991.

Dick, Howard. "Further Reflections on the Middle Class." In *The Politics of Middle Class Indonesia,* edited by Richard Tanter and Kenneth Young, 63-70. Clayton, Victoria: Monash University, Centre of Southeast Asian Studies, 1990.

Djalil, Mucharor. "Ladang Bisnis Seorang Arsitek." *Infobank* 218 (November, 1997): 32-35.

Feith, Herbert, and Castles, Lance, eds. *Indonesian Political Thinking 1945-1965.* Ithaca: Cornell University Press, 1970.

Foulcher, Keith. *Social Commitment in Literature and the Arts: The Indonesian 'Institute of People's Culture' 1950-1965.* Clayton, Victoria: Monash University, 1986.

Gans, Herbert. *Deciding What's News: A Study of CBS Evening News, NBC Nightly News, Newsweek, and Time.* New York: Pantheon, 1979.

Geertz, Clifford. *Negara: The Theatre State in Nineteenth-Century Bali.* Princeton: Princeton University Press, 1980.

Geertz, Clifford. *The Religion of Java.* Illinois: The Free Press of Glencoe, 1960.

Geertz, Clifford. *Available Light: Anthropological Reflections on Philosophical Topics.* Princeton: Princeton University Press, 2000.

Gitlin, Todd. *The Whole World is Watching: Mass Media and the Making and the Unmaking of the New Left*. Berkeley: University of California Press, 1980.

"Gong! Tempo, Majalah & Mithos." *Jakarta-Jakarta* 58 (July 24-August 6, 1987): 1.

Hachten, William A. *The Third World News Prism: Changing Media, Clashing Ideologies*. Ames: Iowa State University Press, 1987.

Harsono, Andreas. "Indonesian Press, Freer Now, Still Struggles with Economic Crisis, *American Reporter,* July 8, 1998.

Harymurti, Bambang. *Wartawan Menggugat*. Nota Pembelaan (Pleidooi), Perkara No. 1426/Pid.B/2003/PNJKT.PST.

Hefner, Robert W. *Civil Islam: Muslims and Democratization in Indonesia*. Princeton: Princeton University Press, 2000.

Hefner Robert W, ed. *Market Cultures: Society and Morality in the New Asian Capitalisms*. Boulder, Co.: Westview Press, 1988.

Heryanto, Ariel. "Public Intellectuals, Media and Democratization: Cultural Politics of the Middle Classes in Indonesia." In *Challenging Authority*, edited by Ariel Heryanto and Sumit K. Mandal, 24-59. London and New York: RoutledgeCurzon, 2003.

Heryanto, Ariel and Stanley Yoseph Adi. "Industrialized Media in Democratizing Indonesia." In *Media Fortunes, Changing Times*, edited by Russell H. K. Heng, 47-82. Singapore: Institute of Southeast Asian Studies, 2002.

Heryanto, Ariel. *Language of Development and Development of Language: The Case of Indonesia*. Pacific Linguistics, Series D-86, Canberra: Australian National University, 1995.

Hill, David. "Mochtar Lubis: Author, Editor, Political Actor," Ph.D. diss, Australian National University, 1988.

Hill, David T. *The Press in New Order Indonesia*. Jakarta: Pustaka Sinar Harapan, 1994.

Hill, David T. "'The Two Leading Institutions': Taman Ismail Marzuki and Horison." In *Culture and Society in New Order Indonesia,* edited by Virginia Matheson Hooker, 245-261. Kuala Lumpur: Oxford University Press, 1993.

Jones, Adams. *Beyond the Barricades: Nicaragua and the Struggle for the Sandinista Press, 1979-1998*. Athens: Ohio University Press, 2002.

Jones, Sidney. *Al-Qaeda in Southeast Asia: The Case of the "Ngruki Network" in Indonesia*. Jakarta/Brussels: International Crisis Group, August 8, 2002.

Kahin, George McT. *Nationalism and Revolution in Indonesia*. Ithaca: Cornell University Press, 1952,

"Kasak-Kasuk Sebelum Bobol." *Jakarta-Jakarta* 58 (July 24-August 6, 1987): 3-13..

Kitley, Philip. "After the Bans: Modeling Indonesian Communications for the Future." In *Indonesia Today: Challenges of History*, edited by Grayson Lloyd and Shannon Smith, 256-269. Singapore: Institute of Southeast Asian Studies, 2001.

Kovach, Bill, and Rosenstiel, Tom. *The Elements of Journalism: What Newspeople Should Know and the Public Should Expect.* New York: Three Rivers Press, 2001.

Lasch, Christopher. *The Agony of the American Left.* New York: Vintage Books, 1969.

Lee, Martin A., and Solomon, Norman. *Unreliable Sources: A Guide to Detecting Bias in the News Media.* New York: Carol Publishing Group, 1990.

Lerner, Daniel. "The Passing of Traditional Societies." In *From Modernization to Globalization: Perspectives on Development and Social Change,* edited by J. T. Roberts and A. Hite, 119-133. Malden: Blackwell Publications, 2000.

Lev, Daniel S. And McVey, Ruth, eds. *Making Indonesia: Essays on Modern Indonesia in Honor of George McT. Kahin.* Ithaca: Cornell Southeast Asia Program Publications, 1996.

Lev, Daniel S. "Notes on the Middle Class and Change in Indonesia." In *The Politics of Middle Class Indonesia,* edited by Richard Tanter and Kenneth Young, 44-52. Clayton, Victoria: Monash University, Centre of Southeast Asian Studies, 1990.

Lewis, Bernard. *The Political Language of Islam.* Chicago and London: The University of Chicago Press, 1988.

Lichter, Robert S., Rothman, Stanley, and Lichter, Linda S. *The Media Elite: America's New Powerbrokers.* New York: Adler and Adler, 1986.

Liddle, William R. *Leadership and Culture in Indonesian Politics.* Sydney: Allen and Unwin, 1996.

Lubis, Mochtar. "Kata Pengantar", in *Bang Ali Demi Jakarta 1966-1977,* edited by K. H. Ramadhan, 9-14. Jakarta: Pustaka Sinar Harapan, 1995.

MacDougall, John James. "The Technocratic Model of Modernization: The Case of Indonesia's New Order." *Asian Survey* 16 (Dec. 1976): 1166-1183.

Mackie, Jamie. "Changing Patterns of Chinese Big Business." In *Southeast Asian Capitalists,* edited by Ruth McVey, 161-190. Ithaca: Cornell Southeast Asia Program Publications, 1992.

Magenda, Burhan D. "Gerakan Mahasiswa dan Hubungannya dengan Sistem Politik: Suatu Tinjauan." In *Seri Prisma I: Analisa Kekuatan Politik di*

Indonesia, 129-173. Jakarta: Lembaga Penelitian, Pendidikan dan Penerangan Ekonomi dan Social, 1985.

Makarim, Nono. "The Indonesian Press: And Editor's Perspective." In *Political Power and Communications in Indonesia*, edited by Karl P. Jackson and Lucien W. Pye, 259-281. Berkeley: University of California Press, 1978.

Manzella, Joseph C. "Negotiating the News: Indonesian Press Culture and Power During the Political Crisis of 1997-8." *Journalism* 1 (2000): 305-328.

Marchand, Roland. *Advertising the American Dream: Making Way for Modernity, 1920-1940*. Berkeley: University of California Press, 1985.

McCargo, Duncan, "Killing the Messenger, The 1994 Press Bannings and the Demist of Indonesia's New Order." *Press/Politics* I (Winter, 1999): 29-45.

McVey, Ruth. "The Materialization of the Southeast Asian Entrepreneur." In *Southeast Asian Capitalists,* edited by Ruth McVey, 7-33. Ithaca: Cornell Southeast Asia Program Publications, 1992.

Mohamad, Goenawan. *Kesusastraan dan Kekuasaan*. Jakarta: P. T. Pustaka Firdaus, 1993.

Mohamad, Goenawan. *Sidelines: Thought Pieces from Tempo Magazine*, translated by Jennifer Lindsay. Jakarta: Lontar, 1994.

Nashel, Jonathan. "The Road to Vietnam: Modernization Theory in Fact and Fiction." In *Cold War Constructions: The Political Culture of United States Imperialism, 1945-1966*, edited by Christian G. Appy, 132-154. Amherst: University of Massachusetts Press, 2000.

Nitisastro, Widjojo. "Kata Pengantar", in *Simposium Kebangkitan Semangat '66: Mendjeladjah Tracée Baru*. Universitas Indonesia: Djakarta, 1966.

Peterson, Theodore. "The Social Responsibility Theory of the Press." In *Four Theories of the Press*, edited by Fred S. Siebert, 73-103. Urbana: University of Illinois Press, 1963.

Pontoh, Coen Husain. "Konflik Tak Kunjung Padam." *Pantau* (August 2001): 44-61.

Ramadhan, K. H. *Bang Ali: Demi Jakarta 1966-1977*. Jakarta: Pustaka Sinar Harapan, 1995.

Ransom, David. "Ford Country: Building an Elite for Indonesia." In *The Trojan Horse: A Radical Look at Foreign Aid*, revised edition, edited by in Steve Weissman, 93-116. Palo Alto, CA: Ramparts Press, 1975.

Reeve, David. "The Corporatist State: The Case of Golkar." In *State and Civil Society in Indonesia*, edited by Arief Budiman, 151-176. Monash Papers on Southeast Asia no. 22, Clayton, Victoria: Monash University, 1990.

Riggs, Fred W. *Thailand: The Modernization of a Bureaucratic Polity*. Honolulu: East-West Centre Press, 1966.

Roberts, J. Timmons, and Hite, Amy, eds. *From Modernization to Globalization: Perspectives on Development and Social Change*. Oxford: Blackwell Publishers, 2000.

Robison, Richard. *Indonesia: The Rise of Capital*. North Sydney, Australia: Allen and Unwin, 1986.

Robison, Richard. "Industrialization and the Development of Capital." In *Southeast Asian Capitalists*, edited by Ruth McVey, 65-88. Ithaca: Cornell Southeast Asia Program Publications, 1992.

Robison, Richard. "The Middle Class and the Bourgeoisie in Indonesia." In *The New Rich in Asia: Mobile Phones, McDonalds and Middle-class Revolution*, edited by Richard Robison and David S. G. Goodman, 79-101. London and New York: Routledge, 1996.

Romano, Angela. *Politics and the Press in Indonesia: Understanding an Evolving Political Culture*. London: RoutledgeCurzon, 2003.

Romano, Carlin, "The Grisley Truth About Bare Facts." In *Reading the News,* edited by Robert Manhoff and Michael Schudson, 38-78. New York: Pantheon Books, 1986.

Rostow, W. W. *The Stages of Economic Growth*, second edition. London: Cambridge University Press, 1971.

Sanyoto, Kukuh. "Indonesian Television." In *Media Fortunes, Changing Times*, edited by Russell H. K. Heng, 83-105. Singapore: Institute of Southeast Asian Studies, 2002.

Saunders, Frances Stoner. *The Cultural Cold War: The CIA and the World of Arts and Letters*. New York: New Press, 2000.

Schudson, Michael. *Advertising, the Uneasy Persuasion: Its Dubious Impact on American Society*. New York: Basic Books, 1984.

Schudson, Michael. *Discovering the News: A Social History of American Newspapers*. New York: Basic Books, 1978.

Schwarz, Adam. *A Nation in Waiting: Indonesia in the 1990s*. Boulder: Westview Press, 1994.

Sen, Krishna and Hill, David T. *Media Culture and Politics in Indonesia*. New York: Oxford University Press, 2000.

Siegel, James. *A New Criminal Type in Jakarta: Counter-Revolution Today*. Durham: Duke University Press, 1988.

Sigel, Leon. "Sources Make the News." In *Reading the News,* edited by Robert Manhoff and Michael Schudson, 9-37. New York: Pantheon Books, 1986.

Simposium Kebangkitan Semangat '66: Mendjeladjah Tracée Baru. Djakarta: Universitas Indonesia, 1966.

Steele, Janet E. "Don't Ask, Don't Tell, Don't Explain: Unofficial Sources and Television Coverage of the Dispute over Gays in the Military." *Political Communication* 14 (January-March, 1997): 83-95.

Steele, Janet E. "Experts and the Operational Bias of Television News: The Case of the Persian Gulf War." *Journalism and Mass Communication Quarterly* 72 (Winter 1995): 799-812.

Steele, Janet E. *The Sun Shines for All: Journalism and Ideology in the Life of Charles A. Dana*. Syracuse: Syracuse University Press, 1992.

Surjomihardjo, Abdurrachman ed. *Beberapa Segi Perkembangan Sejarah Pers di Indonesia*, 2nd printing. Jakarta: Kompas, 2002.

Tanter, Richard and Young, Kenneth, eds. *The Politics of Middle Class Indonesia*. Monash University: Centre of Southeast Asian Studies, 1990.

Toer, Pramoedya Ananta. *The Mute's Soliloquy: A Memoir*, translated by William Samuels. Jakarta: Lontar Foundation, 1999.

Teeuw, A. *Modern Indonesian Literature*, vol. II. The Hague: Martinus Nijhoff, 1979.

Tuchman, Gaye. "Objectivity as Strategic Ritual: An Examination of Newsmen's Notions of Objectivity." *American Journal of Sociology* 77 (January 1972): 660-679.

van Langenberg, Michael. "The New Order State: Language, Ideology, Hegemony." In State and Civil Society in Indonesia, edited by Arief Budiman, 121-149. Monash Papers on Southeast Asia no. 22. Clayton, Victoria: Monash University, 1990.

Wolfe, Tom, and Johnson, E.W., eds. *The New Journalism*. New York: Harper and Row, 1973.

Zulkifli, Arif. *PDI di Mata Golongan Menengah Indonesia*. Jakarta: Pustaka Utama Grafiti, 1966.

index

also from
EQUINOX PUBLISHING